SMALL ISLAND, LARGE OCEAN

Small Island, Large Ocean

MAURITIUS AND THE INDIAN OCEAN WORLD

BURKHARD SCHNEPEL

MANOHAR
2023

First published 2023

ISBN 978-93-94262-47-8

Published by
Ajay Kumar Jain *for*
Manohar Publishers & Distributors
4753/23 Ansari Road, Daryaganj
New Delhi 110 002

Typeset by
Kohli Print
Delhi 110 051

Printed at
Replika Press Pvt. Ltd.

For
Conny

Contents

List of Illustrations

Figures

Maps

Acknowledgements

This collection of essays is the result of more than two decades of research on the Indian Ocean world in general and on Mauritius in particular. As far as Mauritius is concerned, research in the field and in archives was undertaken jointly with my wife Cornelia, and we published together on tourism and Séga in Mauritius. All in all, research in and on Mauritius would not have been possible without Conny's substantial support, close collaboration, and enduring encouragement. Therefore, I dedicate this book to her with great affection and respect, even though this symbolic act is hardly adequate to express the amount of gratitude she properly deserves.

This book is the result of fieldwork and research in and on Mauritius, and the larger Indian Ocean world, that started in 2002 when I was co-founding the Institute of Social Anthropology at the Martin Luther University at Halle-Wittenberg. I am very much obliged to the University and its authorities for having provided me with a sound and well-equipped institutional base as a professor supporting me to start my studies of the Indian Ocean world soon after arriving in Halle, having previously done research on Africa and India. During term breaks and sabbaticals, more than a dozen research trips to Mauritius usually lasting one month each were made between 2003 and 2018, expenses for which were covered initially by the Martin Luther University and the Fritz Thyssen Foundation. In later years, research and field trips were made possible through a generous Fellowship Programme on 'Connectivity in Motion' in the Indian Ocean world, which I enjoyed from 2012 to 2020 thanks to the Max Planck Society, Munich, and the Max Planck Institute for Social Anthropology. My sincere gratitude goes to the authorities of both Martin Luther University and the Max Planck Institute of Social Anthropology in Halle. From among the colleagues who supported and inspired me in various ways, special mention should be made of Chris Hann and his team, who also aided me in organizing four international conferences and workshops on Indian Ocean themes at the Max Planck Institute.

Among the international scholars who visited Halle for these events, with whom I co-edited three volumes arising out of the conference presentations, I wish to express my collegial appreciation and gratitude to Edward A. Alpers, Tansen Sen and Julia Verne. I am also grateful to the VolkswagenStiftung for enabling me, in close collaboration with Tansen Sen, to stage three international Summer Schools on Indian Ocean themes, two in Halle and one in Shanghai. At the University institute, the bi-weekly sessions of my Indian Ocean Research colloquium, which ran for roughly two decades with constantly changing membership, were intellectually as beneficial to me as I hope they were to the various members of this group who were working on their theses. To all of them I owe great debt. During our stays in Mauritius, Conny and I encountered a lot of friendly and helpful people from all strata and sections of society, who thankfully were always willing to talk to and share their knowledge with us. Special mention should be made of Vinesh Y. Hookoomsing and Vijaya Teelock, without whose support, especially in the first phase of fieldwork, things might not have proceeded as well as they eventually did.

A lot of the painstaking work to make this book publishable in terms of style-sheet requirements and other formal and technical matters was undertaken by Antje Seeger. I am as much obliged to her as I am to Manohar, especially Ramesh Jain, who did not hesitate to agree to publish this volume, my fourth publication with Manohar as author or editor. Readers of previous publications of mine will know that, for more than three decades now, my writings in English have been greatly improved by the work of Robert Parkin as language editor. This holds true for the present volume as well, and again I wish to acknowledge his support with great gratitude.

Editorial note: While overall the present publication is a collection of essays that could be read and understood individually, serious efforts have been made, including by writing new chapters and bridging paragraphs, allowing it to be read lineally from beginning to end as a coherent book with a stringent line of argument, a steadily growing amount of empirical data and gradually developing theoretical propositions. The various chapters also move forward in the history of Mauritius from the beginnings towards the present and possible future of this island.

Halle
May 2022

BURKHARD SCHNEPEL

CHAPTER 1

Small Island, Large Ocean: An Introduction

'SMALL PLACES, LARGE ISSUES'

This book is about a small island, namely Mauritius in the south-western Indian Ocean. It is also about the Indian Ocean world – its peoples, histories and cultures. Ultimately, it represents an endeavour to cast light on the life of an island through what is known not only from the island itself, but also through what is known about the Indian Ocean world as a whole. And it is also about this ocean by focussing on an island which, in many senses and dimensions, is not only a model of, but in some respects a model for[1] wider developments and features of relevance to the Indian Ocean world as a whole.

The issues tackled and the perspectives applied in this book are mainly historical, social anthropological, geographical and ethnohistorical. Social anthropologists especially will be aware of the fact that the title of this book – *Small Island, Large Ocean* – involves both an allusion to and modification of the title of one of the most influential introductions to Social Anthropology, namely Thomas Hylland Eriksen's *Small Places, Large Issues.*[2] This title captures poignantly what anthropologists do (and do best, I think), namely discuss and throw light on large issues such as globalization, migration, or systems of exchange, to name just a few, not although they study small places, but exactly because they do so. In this vein, this study proposes to contribute something to the large Indian Ocean world not despite its focus on a small place, or rather island, but precisely because it applies such a 'zooming-in' perspective. Furthermore, even though the title makes a 'large ocean' out of Eriksen's 'large issues', the various chapters in this book address not only a large ocean in its entirety, but also a variety of larger issues of significance to it: islandness (Chapter 2), maritime violence (Chapter 3), seaborne pandemic diseases (Chapter 4), diasporic identities (Chapter 5), maritime hubs (Chapter 6), tourism (Chapter 7), and cultural performances and identity construction (Chapter 8). All these chapters can be read individually,[3] but when read in the order of succession proposed here, they also make up and develop an argument that joins them into a coherent book with a stringent line of argumentation.

However, before we plunge into the task of contributing to the study of a small island and a large ocean (as well as the larger issues that arise from using such a dialectical perspective), in this Introduction I will provide some basic background information on first, the island itself (Section 2), and secondly the ocean in question (Section 3), before I conclude with some remarks on 'Indian Ocean Studies' more generally (Section 4) and the question of how to study an ocean, particularly this one (Section 5).

THE ISLAND

While from the geopolitical and social anthropological perspectives the small island of Mauritius can tell us a lot about the Indian Ocean world writ large, this is not the case in a purely historical sense. Looking at Mauritian history does not lead us very far back in time. Apart from the occasional Arab and Portuguese sailors who landed on its shores in medieval and early modern times, seeking shelter from a storm and/or wishing to replenish their water and food supplies, the island did not become a site of human habitation until the early seventeenth century. Its human and political history can be said to have started only in 1598, when one of the ships in an early Dutch merchant flotilla, heading east towards Java on a southern route through the so-called 'Roaring Forties' (an allusion to its approximate latitude), was blown off course by heavy storms and landed on the island more or less by chance. Given the already well-established symbolic act of land-grabbing, Captain Warwick officially took possession of the island for the Dutch by naming it after Prince Maurice of Nassau and fastening an emblem of this Dutch aristocratic house

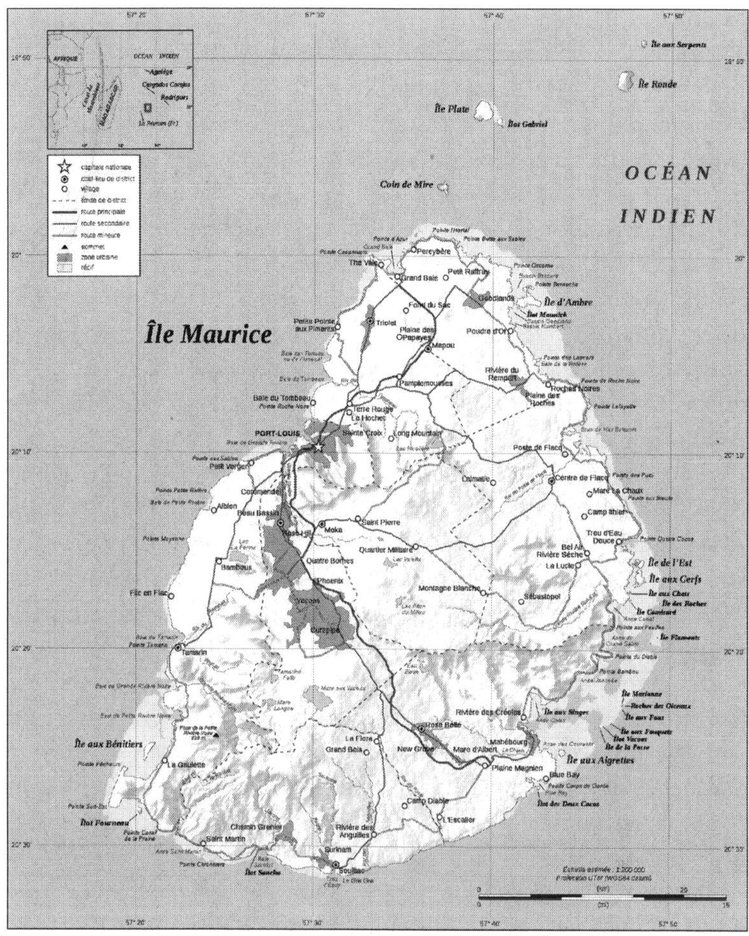

Map 1.1: Map of Mauritius Island

near where his ship had landed, namely in the southeast of the island.[4]

However, subsequent Dutch attempts to colonialize the island and introduce a permanent settlement there from 1610 onwards were beset with disaster and were ultimately unsuccessful. In 1706, the last settlers, having suffered bad harvests, disastrous cyclones and an ever-increasing population of rats, abandoned the island and left it uninhabited again – apart from a few slaves who had fled the garrison to go into the forests. In 1715, the French *Compagnie des Indes*, already well established on the neighbouring Mascarene island of Île Bourbon since 1642, symbolically took possession of Mauritius by installing a large wooden cross decorated with the *fleurs-de-lys* emblem of the French royal house in the northwest of the island and renaming it the Île de France. The first groups of settlers from Île Bourbon arrived soon afterwards, but serious settlement on this new French colonial possession did not start before 1722, when Governor Nyon arrived from France with 210 soldiers, 80 settlers and 30 slaves. After initial difficulties recalling the failure of the earlier Dutch settlers, a more stable island colony was finally established, especially during the reign of the energetic Bertrand François Mahé de Labourdonnais, who governed the island from 1739 to 1746.[5]

When, in July 1810, British troops first conquered the neighbouring Mascarene island formerly called Île Bourbon, since renamed Réunion, without any resistance, the fate of the Île de France was doomed as well. After a first sea battle off the southeast of the island near Mahébourg, which the British lost in August of that year (actually the only sea battle Napoleon's navy ever won against '*Perfide Albion*'), a few months later, in December 1810, the British finally invaded the island from the north, taking it against only minor resistance and with few losses of their own.[6] The British restored the name 'Mauritius' and henceforth governed it for more than a century and a half. In 1968, the island finally gained independence, with Mauritius becoming a presidential republic headed. Today, Mauritius, approximately 2,000 square kilometres in size, hosts around 1.3 million inhabitants of diverse ethnic, religious, linguistic and regional backgrounds, discussed in detail in Chapter 5.[7] Globally, Mauritius has become a major tourist attraction – usually advertized under the label of 'Paradise Island' – in which capacity it is visited by roughly a million tourists a year (Chapter 7). Apart from the sun, sand and sea, these visitors also cherish the island's cultural heritage, among it a dance called Séga, originally a cultural performance helping slaves ameliorate their fate, but now presented by the descendants of these slaves in hotels in versions suitable for tourists (see Chapter 8).[8]

Clearly, then, Mauritius, in all its social, cultural, political and economic aspects, was a colonial creation, being intricately linked with European seaborne imperialism. Colonialism and imperialism are forces that by their very innate nature continuously strive for an expansion of their spheres of dominance and their exploitation of natural and human resources. In the context of this overall ambition, Mauritius, a deep-water island almost in the middle of nowhere, was initially what could be called a 'frontier society'. This term has been used by various authors to draw attention to more fluid and shifting processes and structures, which, they argue, might be lost or misinterpreted when using terms such as 'boundary' or 'border', which connote instead well-established and clearly circumscribed territories. A key example of such a moving and permeable 'frontier' can be found in America's eighteenth- and nineteenth-century history, with its steady expansion westwards of the habitat and sphere of domination of white immigrants. The data and insights drawn from this specific historical and geopolitical example were then transferred by scholars to other regions as well, among them Siberia and Latin America, all representing vast land masses.[9]

One of the more intriguing aspects of the study of 'frontiers' and 'frontier societies' has been the steady influx of pioneers and settlers into regions the latter regarded as 'wild' and 'uncivilized', but which in most cases were not uninhabited at all and hosted societies and cultures in their own right. Therefore, one very important, if not the most significant dimension that studies of 'frontiers' and 'frontier societies' have addressed and thrown light on are the encounters of these pioneers and settlers with the original inhabitants whom they met in such 'contact zones'. Typically, in the beginning these encounters often took the form of peaceful barter and other economic, socio-cultural and political exchanges, which proved vital for the survival of the newcomers as well as advantageous to the existing occupants. However, more often than not these encounters tended to become exploitative and violent, ending in the subordination or expulsion, if not extinction, of indigenous populations.

Even though the focus of this book is on a small, deep-water island in the middle of a vast ocean, and not on a large terrestrial region such as typically features in 'frontier studies', Mauritius, at least in its early phase of colonization, can fruitfully be viewed as a 'frontier society'. By discussing in particular Mauritius as a hub society in

Chapter 6, it will be shown that the islands of the Indian Ocean constituted significant frontiers and springboards for the various seaborne empires of relevance to its waters (Portuguese, Dutch, French, British and, at present, American and Chinese) when striving to extend and control their spheres of power across the sea and into the terrestrial hinterlands. Islands, both coastal and deep-water ones, occupied salient strategic positions not only for trade, but also for the colonial project as such, especially if they were situated along the more frequented sea lanes or could act as suitable bridgeheads into the mainland. Mauritius undoubtedly occupied such an advantageous position, lying as it did roughly 2,000 kilometres from the East African coast and 800 kilometres east of northern Madagascar on a monsoon-friendly sailing route between the Cape of Good Hope and India.

To make adequate analytical use of the term of 'frontier' in the Mauritian case, however, it is necessary to be aware of significant differences in the terrestrial paradigm. The maritime dimension of this island, and of islands in general, urges one to qualify and alter the model. Any reconfiguration of the empirical and methodological basis of this model for use in ocean studies first of all requires one to dissociate oneself mentally from the plains, steppes, marches, bushlands and forests of the prototypical frontiers on land. Mobility-wise, we also have to re-imagine the means and agents of expansion. The movement forward to ever-new frontiers is no longer on wagons or horseback, but across the sea and on ships with the special regimes, micro-sociologies and trajectories that maritime mobilities entail. When anchoring off a new coast or on the shores of a hitherto unknown island, some passengers were dropped off to start a new life as settlers or colonial administrators with a view to building a 'brave new world', while the vessel with its seamen and other passengers sailed on, searching for ever new horizons and 'last frontiers'. These maritime agents were not just sent by their respective monarchs or by various commercial companies, like the Dutch *Vereenigde Oost Indische Compagnie* or the English East India Company. There were a number of other significant pioneers in maritime discovery and avant-garde agents in the exploitation of new regions and resources. Pirates and whalers, in particular, played important roles on sea that are comparable to the deeds of trappers, gold-seekers, fur-hunters or 'cowboys' on land, as will be shown in Chapter 3, which deals with pirates in the southwestern Indian Ocean in the late seventeenth to mid-eighteenth centuries.

As far as the first settler communities along the coasts and on the islands are concerned, their lives, while basically littoral and maritime in kind, were nonetheless comparable to the lives of settlers on terrestrial frontiers and in contact zones. They bartered with aboriginal peoples and reached basic understandings with them that were vital for their survival. Sooner or later, however, violence came to dominate in the place of reciprocity and mutuality. Deplorable developments of this kind were not just common – even, unfortunately, the rule – in arid contact zones, but in maritime frontier societies as well. This observation, however, leads us to another significant difference from the 'Wild West' model when it comes to understanding Mauritius as a frontier society. This fertile island, blessed with plentiful fresh water, a fertile soil and an abundance of flora and fauna thriving in a mild tropical climate, was probably one of the last inhabitable regions of the world that had been left uninhabited by humankind thus far. In brief, the Mauritian 'contact zone' lacked any humans with whom to make contact. However, in Mauritius there was a first contact of another kind, namely an ecological one. The first settlers encountered an ecological system that had yet not experienced a human presence and (mis-)use. This encounter ultimately resulted in the large-scale destruction of endemic plants and animals, while at the same time, both deliberately and inadvertently, new animal species such as rats, pigs, monkeys, goats, fleas and deer, or new plants such as fir trees and sugarcane, which were alien to the island and often detrimental to its existing life, were introduced.[10] Along with these invasive species, moreover, came pathogens which resulted in a dark history of seaborne diseases breaking out among the island population, discussed especially in Chapter 4.

The first encounter with an 'ecological frontier' was, of course, with the sea itself, but even when this natural barrier had been mastered and a coast or island had come into view, to enter it could prove difficult. As far as Mauritius is concerned, most of the island is surrounded some miles out by coral reefs that not only shelter it from heavy waves (and today's tourist beaches from sharks), but also hamper ships seeking to anchor in its bays. Only two major passages, one in the southeast near Mahébourg, the other in the northwest near Port Louis, really allow the larger ships to approach the island in relative safety. Once the pioneer sailors set foot on land, moreover, they found the coasts and interior of this hitherto virgin island to be almost impenetrable due to the growth of thick shrub, bushes and tropical forests. However, among this abundant vegetation was also the much-desired hardwood, especially fine ebony trees, a profitable commercial enterprise, despite the difficulty of cutting it with the tools of that time. Nonetheless the 'ebony frontier' was steadily pushed deeper into the interior the further the wood-cutting operations progressed. Soon there was hardly any ebony left at all, and the disappearance of most of the island's forests soon resulted in a significant, unwelcome change of climate and rainfall.[11]

Under the French, the northwest bay in which the first French ships anchored grew into a port with crucial facilities, which itself developed into a port city, named Port Louis, that became a capital city with administrative and political functions, as well as with economic activities that were not directly connected to the sea. Politico-militarily, what used to be a 'camp' in the beginning developed into a colonial headquarters, especially after the French decided to make Port Louis their *chef-lieu* in the southwestern region of the Indian Ocean world from the 1730s onwards. The French, or rather their African and Asian slaves, constructed some relatively decent stone houses for the Company's leading officers and personnel, and barracks for the soldiers. They also built wooden huts for the hard-working French settlers of lower standing (or *petits blancs*) and, segregated in other parts of the town, for the slaves. Other important buildings soon followed, such as the first hospital, a fort and cannons facing the sea to watch and deter any preying British ships, a church, a school and various government buildings. In the hinterland, if this term can be applied at all to an island, more and more land was cleared for agriculture and plantations. Numerous larger and smaller estates, with manor houses for the estate owners and huts for the unfree labourers, started to dot the insular landscape all around. Roads and bridges were built, both along the coasts and into the interior, gradually connecting the various settlements, estates and towns with each other across the island.

In this way, during roughly 100 years of French rule, large parts of the island were domesticated, with the 'inner frontier' steadily being pushed further inland and up the hills of this volcanic island.[12] While the 'first encounter' of Mauritian settlers was therefore with nature, not an indigenous population, the settlers also discovered, to their anxiety, not to say fear, that they were not alone. Hidden deep inside the forests and more inaccessible regions of the island, small communities of runaway slaves, so-called *marrons*, had established a free, albeit fugitive and burdensome existence as early as the Dutch period. These maroon communities steadily increased during French rule, when significant percentages of slaves each year continued to abscond and take this highly desired but risky step into some sort of liberty. These ever-increasing communities of maroons meant that, despite the absence of true indigenous populations, there was a 'contact zone' after all, namely one in which settlers and maroon communities, small and dispersed though the latter were, encountered each other. For fear of being detected, these communities had been forced into the least inhabitable and remotest locations on the island. Especially the area around Morne Brabant in the southern part of the island developed into a favourite refuge for runaway slaves. For the settlers, these maroon communities constituted not only an imagined, but also a real threat, for escaped slaves often felt they had no other option but to raid estates at night, stealing food and killing settlers, in their struggle to survive. At the same time, maroons were constantly in fear that slave-hunting parties would discover their merely temporary retreats and kill them. Even when abolition was in the air in the early 1830s, the fear of being caught by slave-hunters was so great that when maroons living on the steep Morne Brabant saw policemen coming closer in order to tell them, so the legend has it, that slavery had been abolished and that they could return free and unharmed, jumped off the mountain to their certain deaths in order to avoid what they mistakenly thought was their being captured and then murdered or enslaved again.[13]

Furthermore, while Mauritius did not experience a classic frontier situation involving encounters between pioneers or settlers and an indigenous population, it nevertheless had yet another 'contact zone' of a special kind. Ships arriving on the island disembarked people hailing from different regions of the world and from a great variety of socio-cultural, linguistic and religious backgrounds. These people had unequal statuses and were meant to fulfil different functions, from the governor of the Company and the well-to-do estate owner down to the soldier and *petit blanc*, and further down to the Chinese shop-keeper and the slave or indentured worker on an estate. All of these people had their own pasts and heritages, their own world views and religions, as well as their own ideas and habits of how to live a good and righteous life, of how to govern themselves and be governed, of how to worship and whom to pray to. But they had unequal, some-times even no powers and opportunities to make their own ideas, wishes, conceptions and beliefs survive and perhaps impress them on others. The present-day consequences of these multiple origins – and

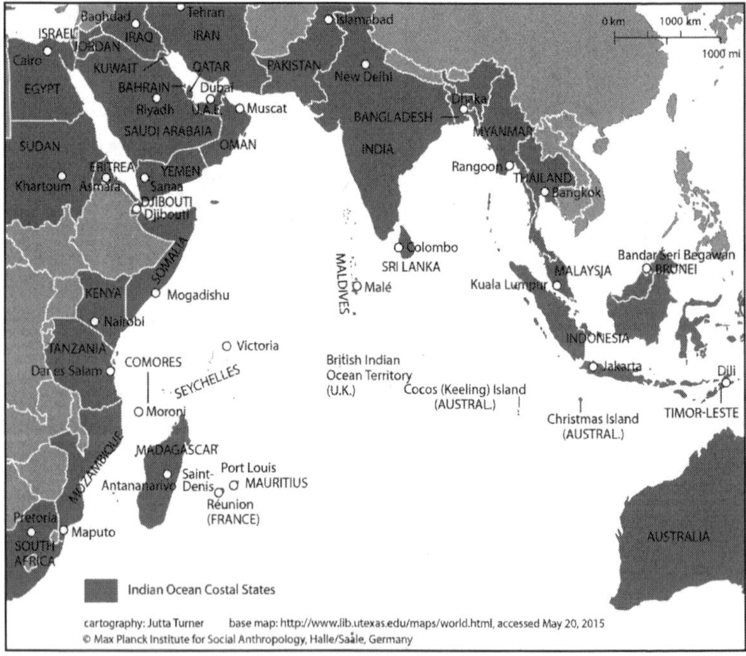

Map 1.2: The Polities of the Contemporary Indian Ocean World

of the *métissage*, but also segregation, that developed on the island consequently – will be discussed in Chapter 5, when addressing the question of whether Mauritian society today is best conceived as a 'Little India', or as a postcolonial 'Creole' society.

THE INDIAN OCEAN WORLD

The Indian Ocean, by one reckoning,[14] measures roughly 75 million square kilometres, thus constituting the third largest ocean of the world after the Pacific and the Atlantic, and covering approximately 20 per cent of the earth's maritime surface. Geographically speaking, it is framed by the coasts of East Africa in the west and the Indonesian Sunda Islands in the east. Its southernmost points are the Cape of Good Hope in South Africa and Fremantle in Western Australia, while its northernmost locations are Karachi in Pakistan and Calcutta in India. One could visualize the Indian Ocean as the letter 'M' with the Indian subcontinent and its approximately 7,600 kilometres of shoreline as the triangle in the middle. This subcontinent also divides the Indian Ocean into a western and an eastern half. Among its subsidiary seas, included in its 70 million square kilometre area, are the Red Sea, the Persian or Arabian Gulf, the Arabian Sea, the Gulf of Oman, the Bay of Bengal and the Andaman Sea, historically all with identities of their own.

As far as its littorals are concerned, these consist of the coasts of the Arabian Peninsula, East and Southeast Africa (from Somalia in the north through Kenya, Tanzania and Mozambique to South Africa in the south), South Asia (Pakistan, India, Bangladesh and Sri Lanka) and Southeast Asia (Myanmar, Thailand and Malaysia, as well as Indonesia, from where the Indian Ocean spills over into the South China Sea and the Pacific). These coasts are, geologically speaking, quite diverse. Some offer sheltered bays, others face the open undulating sea; some are green and fertile, others are arid and barren; and some smoothly blend into the hinterland, while others are cut off from the further mainland by mountains or deserts. In general, and ignoring more subtle variations, the coasts of South and Southeast Asia are green and fertile, suitable for agriculture and cattle-raising, while the coasts of West Asia and East Africa are less adaptable to agriculture and pastoral ways of living or not suitable for human habitation at all. While the coasts of the Indian Ocean thus differ from each other geologically, they all host 'littoral societies' which may, following Pearson (2006), have more in common with each other, no matter where they are, than with their respective hinterlands.[15]

Apart from the coasts, with their innumerable bays and harbours, among the most important structural affordances and contingencies that have determined movement across the Indian Ocean are the myriad of Indian Ocean islands, which are often overlooked in Indian Ocean Studies (in terms of their existential mode *as islands*); many of these have constituted important intermediate stops and hubs for transmaritime movements and circulations across the Indian Ocean world, as will be discussed in Chapter 2 of this book. Other 'deep structure'[16] factors are the various choke points and capes which sailors had to pass through (or, respectively, circumnavigate) in order to enter the Indian Ocean world. From Europe, sailing into the Indian Ocean was only possible (and then only after 1497) by circumnavigating the Cape of Good Hope, a maritime venture, which, as the name of this Cape indicates, led to numerous shipwrecks, costing substantial amounts of lives and cargoes on account of the heavy winter storms, malicious swells and dangerous currents that dominate the sea there. From the northwest, mariners could enter the Indian Ocean proper through the Red Sea, though in doing so they had to master dangerous reefs and coral banks as well as unpredictable winds. Furthermore, before the completion of the Suez Canal in 1869, there was still a stretch of land to be crossed on foot and with pack animals before Red Sea travellers and their cargoes could continue their journeys into the Mediterranean or vice versa. In the south of the Red Sea, one had to pass the narrow strait of the Bab el Mandeb (tellingly, the 'Gate of Tears') lying between Yemen and Eritrea before passing the 'Horn of Africa' and arriving in the Arabian Sea and ultimately the Indian Ocean proper. An alternative route – historically often shifting in popularity with the Red Sea – is through the Persian or Arabian Gulf, which, in its southernmost part, can only be entered or left through the narrow Strait of Hormuz just 21 nautical miles across. On its eastern fringes, the Indian Ocean can be approached or departed through the Strait of Malacca, which at one point is merely eight nautical miles wide. It has therefore constituted a veritable bottleneck not only historically, but also at the present day, with roughly 50,000 ships passing the strait yearly from China and other East Asian countries to the Indian Ocean world and Europe, or in the other direction. Further south, ships, especially the very largest, find an alternative to the Strait of Malacca in the Sunda and Lombok Straits that lead out of the Indian Ocean past Sulawesi to the Philippines, Japan and the East China Sea or welcome ships from there. Other narrow straits of some nautical importance are the Palk Strait between India and Sri Lanka and the Mozambique Channel.

Situated along all these narrow passages and choke points, one can find some of the most important port cities and entrepots of the Indian Ocean world. At the southeastern end of the Strait of Malacca is Singapore, which replaced eighteenth-century Georgetown on Penang and the even older Malacca on the same strait from around the mid-nineteenth century onwards as the major port in the region and which today hosts one of the largest container terminals in the world. On Sulawesi (formerly Celebes) is the historically important hub of Makassar. Maritime routes through both the Red Sea and the Gulf found a convenient trading post and harbour in Aden at the southernmost tip of Yemen, being of importance, on and off, from the earliest times onwards. Mozambique Island (under Portuguese rule) and the Ceylonese (now Sri Lankan) capital of Colombo on the Palk Strait are further examples of important ports at these choke points, whereas Cape Town welcomed and revictualled ships and their crews passing the Cape of Good Hope from the seventeenth century onwards. This pattern of establishing important port cities on straits, capes and other choke points can also be found further east in the South China Sea, such as Quanzhou on the Formosa Strait between Taiwan and the Chinese mainland, one of the largest port cities in the twelfth and thirteenth centuries.

By comparison with the other oceans of the world, the Indian Ocean can thus be considered closed, though its maritime frontiers towards the east, especially into the South China Sea, have historically proved to be more porous than those into the Atlantic Ocean or the Mediterranean. By far the most important factor in the navigation of the

Indian Ocean in the age of sail was the regular pattern of the trade winds that dominated the macro-region and acquired some fame under the originally Arabic word 'monsoon' (*mausam*). These winds change direction twice a year, blowing from the northeast in the winter months (November till March) and from the southwest in summer (May-September), the latter change bringing lots of rain on land with it and thus ensuring the food supplies of millions and millions of people. Notwithstanding all its regional variations and seasonal aberrations, it is the existence of these rather regular and steady winds (or, rather, the *deciphering* of the monsoonal 'code' already in the centuries immediately before the Common Era) which made regular sea passages and constant trade connections across the Indian Ocean both possible and manageable in the age of sail.[17] Before the arrival of steamboats in the Indian Ocean from around the mid-nineteenth century onwards, it was impossible to travel across the Ocean as a whole, for example, from the Red Sea to Malaya or from South China to East Africa, in one go. It was always necessary to stop somewhere in between for several weeks and even months at a time. Going from the Persian Gulf to Guangzhou/Canton in China (close to today's Hong Kong) and back could thus take a total of four years, if not more. Once regular trade exchanges across the Indian Ocean had risen to a certain level of frequency, reliability and volume, this troublesome and costly necessity for in-between stops led to the establishment of so-called 'emporia' or hubs. In these hubs, ships coming from one direction off-loaded their cargoes, half-way, as it were, and took on board cargoes brought by other ships doing likewise from the opposite direction, each trying to catch early winds home. Convenient places for such emporia included the Coromandel and Kerala coasts in South India, and sites in Ceylon, Sumatra and Java.

STUDYING THE INDIAN OCEAN

Various authors have debated whether the Indian Ocean can really be viewed and understood as one and united, or rather, following the views of medieval Arab and Chinese seafarers, as a loose conglomeration of different seas. As far as the contemporary period is concerned, just a look at the political map above shows 32 nation states on the ocean's rim with quite diverse systems and regimes of governance. However, a political map of this sort can only be of limited value. Coastal people, to follow Pearson, 'knew little of political borders' (2006: 365), while the Indian Ocean world has always been, as Bremner puts it, 'a fluid space where many transnational systems, practices and imaginaries intersect and overlap' (2013: 1). Without, then, ignoring the undoubtedly great diversity of the Indian Ocean world in its geographical, regional, linguistic, cultural, economic, religious, social and, last but not least, (geo-)political aspects, it can well be argued that the Indian Ocean world represents some kind of unity. Identifying what this 'kind' may be, one is quickly led to view it in respect of the transmaritime movements and exchanges that have been taking place across the Indian Ocean for millennia. Thus, McPherson, in his history of the Indian Ocean, states: 'The essential unity of the Indian Ocean world was determined by the rhythms of long-distance maritime trade. . . . It was this trade which enabled people and ideas to cross the Indian Ocean, leading to the spread of three great world religions – Hinduism, Buddhism and Islam – and the growth of cosmopolitan civilizations in Asia and Africa which drew their inspiration from a great range of cultures along the shores of the Ocean' (1993: 3). For McPherson, then, the Indian Ocean is 'a highway linking a great variety of peoples, cultures and economies' (ibid.: 5). Similarly, Pearson, significantly adding cultural elements to McPherson's predominantly economic view, points out that '. . . it is people, not water, that created unity and a recognizable Indian Ocean that historians can study' (2003: 27). The unity of the Indian Ocean therefore only becomes evident, and its study in its entirety only makes sense, if we put transmaritime movements and exchanges at the forefront of attention and analysis.[18]

As far as this dimension of mobility is concerned, the Indian Ocean or parts of it have been traversed in all directions for millennia now by vessels transporting human beings and commercial goods of many diverse kinds. Together with their more commercial cargoes, these ships and their passengers also circulated flora, fauna, ideas, ideologies, religions, rituals, sociocultural practices, cultural performances, art genres, political systems, technologies, languages, knowledge, money, and unfortunately also waste and diseases across the Ocean. All of these movements, and the maritime exchanges that have accompanied them, have been thoroughly studied by historians, geographers, anthropologists, archaeologists and scholars of other disciplines, casting light on the various means and modes of circulating these 'things' across the sea.[19] Moreover, they have also provided insights into the various translations in meaning, function and value that these things experience before, during and after their journeys. And they have studied the places where these movements started, made intermediate stops or ended, as well as the actors who were instrumental in this. All these studies can be and have been subsumed under the title of 'Indian Ocean Studies', not only when they address the Indian Ocean as a whole,[20] but also when they deal with just one geographical area, historical period or social group of the Ocean, provided they integrate the existence and effects of movements and exchanges across the ocean into their studies and analyses.[21]

In order to grasp the rather fleeting and multidirectional movements and exchanges across the Indian Ocean world, and in order to study the places and actors that incited them, I have suggested elsewhere the concept of 'connectivity in motion'.[22] In studies guided by this concept, islands and port cities are not understood as essentialized and *a priori* foundations of the networks and movements of which they are parts, but rather in terms of their relational effects, that is, as emerging products that constantly define, redefine, shape, make and unmake one another. Port cities and islands may no doubt achieve some stability and agency of their own and thus become important actors in the interplay of a vast number of other human and non-human actors. All of these more stable elements, however, are the outcome of the dynamic, ever-changing and precarious relations between heterogeneous (human and non-human) elements and actors.[23] Studying connectivity in motion in the sense proposed here is therefore more concerned with activities and processes of *networking* than with networks; it is about shifting relations *between* elements as much as it is about changes *of* and *within* already existing elements. Also, it is about the constitution of new actants as well as the disappearance of old ones in ever-changing, constantly extending or shrinking networks. In other words, if the currently rather popular term 'connectivity' is meant to reach beyond the discussion of networks, this is best realized by emphasizing the addition of 'in motion' to it. The words 'in motion', both temporal and spatial in kind, are decisive here, as they clearly indicate that work within the field of 'Indian Ocean Studies' needs to position itself as contributing to the field of what has come to be called 'Mobility Studies'. 'Mobility Studies', in brief, arose as a response to the way in which the social sciences have long been static, ignoring 'the importance of the systematic movements of people for work and family life, for leisure and pleasure, and for politics and protest' (Sheller and Urry 2006: 208).[24]

This also raises the question of why one should speak of the Indian Ocean *world* rather than just 'the Indian Ocean' on its own. The reason is that investigating transmaritime links and movements framed by the geographical Indian Ocean also urges us to follow the things and people that move out of the Indian Ocean, for example, to China and Japan in the east or to Europe or America in the west. Investigating maritime connections and links, therefore, cannot be limited to the Indian Ocean as a clearly geographically defined maritime zone. Rather, the Indian Ocean *world* sometimes extends as far as Lisbon or Amsterdam in the west or Zaiton (Quanzhou) and Nagasaki in the east.

CONCLUDING REMARKS

For any study that puts mobility and the exchanges of material and immaterial or human and non-human cargoes first, it is of course vital to look more closely at the very places and their inhabitants that are instrumental in circulating these things. These special places and their agents – paradigmatically port cities and islands such as Mauritius – can be called 'hubs', that is, they can be regarded as agentive knots in networks of transportation systems. As 'the effective centre of an activity, region, or network' (*Oxford Dictionary Online*), hubs are significant points of convergence, entanglement and divergence in the global streams of human beings, animals, finances, ideas and other matters, as well as being instrumental in the networks that these streams create. However, hubs are to be understood as more than simple knots or nodes in networks and in the processes of networking. Hubs are also charged with an extraordinary energy that affects their own inner lives, exhibiting a certain dynamic vitality with regard to more than just putting things and beings in motion or making them circulate and flow. Hubs are also, and quite significantly so, agentive when it comes to translating the meanings, functions, usages, forms and values, both material and ideational, of all things and beings that pass through them or ultimately stay with them. More often than not, these changes add value to the things, part of which remains in the hub and thus makes it profit from being a centre of circulation.

However, this is also the place to dampen somewhat any tendency to indulge in over-exalted celebrations of mobility, circulation and flow of the sort that have entered the humanities, social sciences and historical sciences during the last couple of decades. Already in a publication which may well count as one of the triggers of mobility studies, Clifford (1997) rightly pointed out that, in studying 'traveling cultures', one always has to deal with not mobility alone, but the dialectics of travelling *and* dwelling.[25] In other words, there are always people who do not move and who have to (or are allowed to) remain where they are. In fact, it may even be essential for those who move that some people do not and cannot move. Furthermore, as Ferguson has argued, 'the "global" does not "flow" thereby connecting and watering contiguous space; it hops instead, efficiently connecting the enclaved points in the network while excluding (with equal efficiency) the spaces that lie between the points' (2006: 47). Overemphasizing mobility, circulation and flow may therefore entail the danger of ignoring those places and times where and when people, things and ideas did not and do not move, where and when there were and are encumbrances and stagnation. Furthermore, and equally importantly, such a view will fail to identify the crucial points in space and time where things start to flow again and, more often than not, with Ferguson, even hop or jump. What is required in this context is therefore a clear identification of the 'jumping off point', the *punctum saliens*, of a movement in both history and space.

So far, then, I have outlined some of the themes, approaches and perspectives through which Oceanic studies, especially Indian Ocean studies, can be pursued.[26] When it boils down to actually conducting such studies, however, there is of course no way round doing down-to-earth (or down-to-water) empirical studies both in the field and in the archives or libraries. Against the background of acknowledging that the Indian Ocean world is a heavily interconnected macro-region with a long history, scholars from within the field of Indian Ocean studies also conduct empirical studies in and on small places and about shorter periods. This endeavour refers back to my statements at the beginning of this chapter: studying 'small places' (and short time spans) contributes salient insights to 'large issues' (and a large ocean with a long history of mobility across it) not although these studies zoom in, as it were, but exactly because they do so. Separately from the question of how significant Mauritius is in the real world of politics and the economy, or of how significant its historical role has actually been, the *intellectual* worth of this island – our 'small place' – for an understanding of large issues, and a large ocean, has the potential to be great.

NOTES

1. Here I follow Clifford Geertz's distinction: see Geertz (1973), also McPherson (2009).
2. See Eriksen (1995).
3. Some of these chapters have appeared on their own in earlier versions, as will be indicated where this applies.
4. On the early Dutch period of the island's history, see Chan Low (2001) and Moree (1998).
5. On Labourdonnais and the history of the island during his reign, see Vaughan (2005: 35–48) and Storey (1997: 14–20).
6. For a detailed account of the taking of the Île de France by British ships and forces, see Graham (1967: 46–52).
7. For comprehensive histories of Mauritius through all periods of its settlement, see Selvon (2001) and Teelock (2001).
8. However, one part of this multifaceted cultural performance genre, the 'Traditional Mauritian Sega', was awarded with the title of 'Intangible Cultural Heritage of Humanity' in 2014.
9. The intellectual history of the study of 'frontiers' and 'frontier societies' is discussed by Osterhammel (2011: 464–531).

10. The ecological consequences of land-grabbing and settlement in frontier societies were, of course, also important in those contact zones where there were human counterparts. See Osterhammel (2011: 474–5).
11. This was noticed painfully by colonial administrators and settlers from at least the late eighteenth century onwards. See Grove (1995: 126–84).
12. Today roughly 70 per cent of the Mauritian land area is used for sugar cultivation.
13. This legend has been taken up in literature, among others, by le Clezio (1985), and, in music, by the group Cassiya in their song 'Le Morne'.
14. Determining the size of the Indian Ocean depends in large part on whether or not one includes the subsidiary seas into the count and where exactly one draws the line with the Antarctic Ocean or Southern Ocean, the latter having been acknowledged since 2010 as a separate ocean.
15. For more detailed accounts of Indian Ocean coasts with their settlements and ports, see Barendse (2002) on the Arabian Sea in the seventeenth century, Reid (1988) on the Malayan archipelago in the age of mercantilism (*c.* 1450–1680) or Graham (1967) for the Indian Ocean from 1800 to 1850, hence the period in which it was becoming a 'British Lake'.
16. I am here referring to Pearson (2003), who entitles the first chapter of his book on the Indian Ocean as 'Deep Structure', following Braudel (1972) in this terminology.
17. On the monsoon's effects on Indian Ocean shipping, see, among others, Alpers (2014: 7–9), Beaujard (2019: 9–13), Gupta (2012), Hall (1998), and Sheriff (1987: 10–11).
18. The issue of the unity in diversity of the Indian Ocean world has been discussed, among others, by Barendse (2002: 68–70) and Chaudhuri (1985: 1–6).
19. On 'things', see Hodder (2011), Schnepel (2022), Schnepel and Verne (eds. 2022).
20. See, for examples, the monographs of Abulafia (2021: chap. 2), Alpers (2014), Beaujard (2019), McPherson (1993), Pearson (2003), and Toussaint (1973). Among the numerous thematically arranged volumes on the Indian Ocean world, see Gupta and Pearson (eds. 1987), Moorthy and Jamal (eds. 2010), Schnepel and Alpers (eds. 2018), Schnepel and Sen (eds. 2019), and Sheriff and Ho (eds. 2014).
21. For examples, see Bose (2010) and Ho (2006).
22. This was the title and guiding theme of my Max Planck Fellowship Programme, which ran from 2012 to 2018 at the Max Planck Institute of Social Anthropology in Halle, Germany. See also Schnepel (2018).

23. 'Actants' in Actor Network Theory parlance.
24. See also Urry (2007).
25. See also Friedman (2002).
26. For some other works which deal with methodological and theoretical issues regarding Indian Ocean Studies, see Bremner (2014), Bouchard and Crumplin (2010), Hofmeyer (2007), and Vink (2007).

REFERENCES

Abulafia, D. 2019. *The Boundless Sea: A Human History of Oceans.* London: Allen Lane.

Alpers, E.A. 2014. *The Indian Ocean in World History.* Oxford: Oxford University Press.

Barendse, R.J. 2002. *The Arabian Seas: The Indian Ocean World of the Seventeenth Century.* London: Routledge.

Beaujard, P. 2019. *The Worlds of the Indian Ocean: A Global History.* Cambridge: Cambridge University Press.

Bose, S. 2006. *A Hundred Horizons: The Indian Ocean in the Age of Global Empire.* Cambridge MA: Harvard University Press.

Bouchard, C., and W. Crumplin. 2010. 'Neglected no Longer: The Indian Ocean at the Forefront of World Geopolitics and Global Geostrategy'. *Journal of the Indian Ocean Region* 6: 26–51.

Braudel, F. 1972. *The Mediterranean and the Mediterranean World in the Age of Philip II.* London: HarperCollins.

Bremner, L. 2014. 'Folded Ocean: The Spatial Transformation of the Indian Ocean World'. *Journal of the Indian Ocean Region* 10: 18–45.

Chan Low, J. 2001. *La VOC, T'Eyland Mauritius et Rodigues.* Mauritius: National Library.

Chaudhuri, K.N. 1985. *Trade and Civilisation in the Indian Ocean: An Economic History from the Rise of Islam to 1750.* Cambridge: Cambridge University Press.

Clifford, J. 1997. *Routes: Travel and Translation in the Late Twentieth Century.* Cambridge: Harvard University Press.

Eriksen, T.H. 1995. *Small Places, Large Issues: An Introduction to Social and Cultural Anthropology.* London: Pluto Press.

Ferguson, J. 2006. *Global Shadows: Africa in the Neoliberal World Order.* Durham NC: Duke University Press.

Friedman, J. 2002. 'From Roots to Routes: Tropes for Trippers'. *Anthropological Theory* 2: 21–36.

Geertz, C. 1973. *The Interpretation of Cultures: Selected Essays*. New York: Basic Books.

Graham, G. 1967. *Great Britain in the Indian Ocean: A Study of Maritime Enterprise, 1810–1850*. Oxford: Clarendon Press.

Grove, R.H. 1995. *Green Imperialism: Global Expansion, Tropical Island Edens and the Origins of Environmentalism, 1600–1860*. Cambridge: Cambridge University Press.

Gupta, P. 2012. 'Monsoon Fever'. *Social Dynamics* 38(3): 516–27.

Gupta, A.D., and M. Pearson (eds.). 1987. *India and the Indian Ocean, 1500–1800*. Calcutta: Oxford University Press.

Hall, K.R. 1998. *Empires of the Monsoon: A History of the Indian Ocean and Its Invaders*. London: HarperCollins.

Ho, E. 2006. *Graves of Tarim: Genealogy and Mobility Across the Indian Ocean*. Berkeley: University of California Press.

Hodder, I. 2011. 'Human-thing Entanglement: Towards an Integrated Archaeological Perspective'. *Journal of the Royal Anthropological Institute* 17: 154–77.

Hofmeyr, I. 2007. 'The Black Atlantic Meets the Indian Ocean: Forging New Paradigms of Transnationalism for the Global South. Literary and Cultural Perspectives'. *Social Dynamics* 33: 3–32.

Hookoomsing, V., R. Ludwig, and B. Schnepel (eds.). 2009. *Multiple Identities in Action: Mauritius and Some Antillean Parallelisms*. Berlin: Peter Lang.

Le Clezio, J.M. 1985. *Le Chercheur d'Or*. Paris: Gallimard.

McPherson, K. 1993. *The Indian Ocean: A History of People and the Sea*. New Delhi: Oxford University Press.

——, 2009. 'Mauritius: Mirror and Model of History'. In Hookoomsing, Ludwig, and Schnepel (eds.) 2009: 31–44.

Moorthy, S., and A. Jamal (eds.). 2010. *Indian Ocean Studies: Cultural, Social and Political Perspectives*. New York: Routledge.

Moree, P.J. 1998. *A Concise History of Dutch Mauritius, 1598–1710*. London: Kegan Paul.

Osterhammel, J. 2009. *Die Verwandlung der Welt: Eine Geschichte des 19. Jahrhunderts*. Munich: C.H. Beck.

Pearson, M.N. 2003. *The Indian Ocean*. London: Routledge.

——, 2006. 'Littoral Society: The Concept and the Problems'. *Journal of World History* 17: 353–73.

Reid, A. 1988. *Southeast Asia in the Age of Commerce, 1450–1680. Volume One: The Land Below the Winds*. New Haven: Yale University Press.

Schnepel, B. 2018. 'Introduction'. In Schnepel and Alpers (eds.) 2018: 3–31.

——, 2019. 'Travelling Pasts: An Introduction'. In Schnepel and Sen (eds.) 2019: 3–20.

——, 2022. 'Cargoes in the Indian Ocean World: A Thematic and Methodological Introduction'. In Schnepel and Verne (eds.) 2022: 1–29.

Schnepel, B., and E.A. Alpers (eds.). 2018. *Connectivity in Motion: Island Hubs in the Indian Ocean World.* New York: Palgrave.

Schnepel, B., and T. Sen (eds.). 2019. *Travelling Pasts: The Politics of Cultural Heritage in the Indian Ocean World.* Leiden: Brill.

Schnepel, B., and J. Verne (eds.). 2022. *Cargoes in Motion: Materiality and Connectivity across the Indian Ocean.* Athens: Ohio University Press.

Selvon, S. 2001. *A Comprehensive History of Mauritius.* Mauritius: Mauritius Printing Ltd.

Sheller, M., and J. Urry 2006. 'The New Mobilities Paradigm'. *Environment and Planning A: Economy and Space* 36: 207–26.

Sheriff, A. 1987. *Slaves, Spices & Ivory in Zanzibar: Integration of an East African Commercial Empire into the World Economy, 1770–1873.* London: James Currey.

Sheriff, A., and E. Ho (eds.). 2014. *The Indian Ocean: Oceanic Connections and the Creation of New Societies.* London: Hurst & Company.

Storey, K.W. 1997. *Science and Power in Colonial Mauritius.* Rochester: University of Rochester Press.

Teelock, V. 2001. *Mauritian History: From its Beginnings to Modern Times.* Moka, Mauritius: Mahatma Gandhi Institute.

Toussaint, A. 1966. *History of the Indian Ocean.* London: Routledge & Kegan Paul.

Urry, J. 2007. *Mobilities.* London: Polity Press.

Vaughan, M. 2005. *Creating the Creole Island: Slavery in Eighteenth-century Mauritius.* Durham NC: Duke University Press.

Vink, M.P.M. 2007. 'Indian Ocean Studies and the "New Thalassology"'. *Journal of Global History* 2: 41–62.

CHAPTER 2

'Islandness': The World of Indian Ocean Islands

THE 'ISLAND FACTOR'

'Island studies', which have experienced quite an upsurge in the last two to three decades,[1] have made us increasingly aware of the fact that islands are not only specific 'bio-topes', exhibiting very unique (and fragile) systems of flora and fauna. They are also quite specific 'geotopes', 'chronotopes' and 'sociotopes'. That is, in addition to their particular biological features, they are places with quite unique geographical, historical and social traits – as islands. These characteristics are not only worth studying in their own right, but also because looking at maritime mobility and connectivity from a decidedly nissological point of view has been found to open up a variety of new insights that get lost in a more mainland-based perspective. Furthermore, apart from these geographical, historical and social dimensions, islands have always played an important role in human imaginaries, producing numerous literary and other creative works of world renown.[2] These island *imaginaries* could be ignored here if it were not for the fact that they have often played significant roles in how island *realities* are designed and shaped (in as much as these imaginaries were, of course, shaped by island realities in their turn).[3]

While a consideration of some of these island imaginaries and their impact on island realities will be woven into the coming discussion, three basic and powerful manifestations of such imaginaries need to be addressed beforehand. First, prototypically, islands tend to be imagined as small. A small island can be circumambulated or circumnavigated, an activity through which the island is domesticated and turned from being a mere 'place' into a 'space'.[4] Furthermore, one of the most prominent imaginaries of islands concerns their isolation. Islands are then conceived of as *isolas*, to refer to their characteristic Italian name. The idea of isolation and insularity involves seeing a place, a person, or a group as being some distance apart, even secluded, from the rest of the world or humanity. Notions of distance also imply that there are barriers or voids of some kind, usually water, which need to be overcome if one wants to reach an island. Therefore, the isolation of islands is not just measured in kilometres or nautical miles, it also applies to those islands that are not too far from the mainland. For, even in these cases, the fact remains that islands are surrounded by a natural barrier on all sides.[5] Third, there is the imaginary of what could be called the 'finite geography' (Baldacchino 2007: 4) of islands. In this imaginary, which was very prevalent in colonial times, islands are considered and in practice treated as clearly demarcated and self-contained units – readily manageable, comprehensible, and controllable. As such, they can be better regulated (at least so it is thought) than places on land, not only in external dealings, but also internally. With their 'finite geographies', islands constitute spaces that are (considered) good for being governed.[6]

Against this background, it is astonishing to note how little attention islands have captured in the field of 'Indian Ocean Studies' until quite recently. No doubt there is an abundance of literature on Indian Ocean islands in all academic sub-fields discussing a wide variety of thematic foci,[7] and it is probably not just by chance that one of the earliest studies of the Indian Ocean world was written by an islander.[8] But even where the maritime dimension of these islands is acknowledged – and how could it not be? – islands are seldom studied and understood as islands. To be sure, the concept of the 'littoral' proposed by Michael Pearson[9] has guided many previous studies. And islands certainly are littoral societies, for in a sense, their territorial borders are nothing but littoral. However, their 'islandness' – i.e., their specific forms and qualities *qua* islands – has only too often been pushed aside and even ignored when it comes to describing, understanding or explaining what is going on.[10]

The significance and seminal role of islands in producing connectivity and mobility across the Indian Ocean was especially noted by

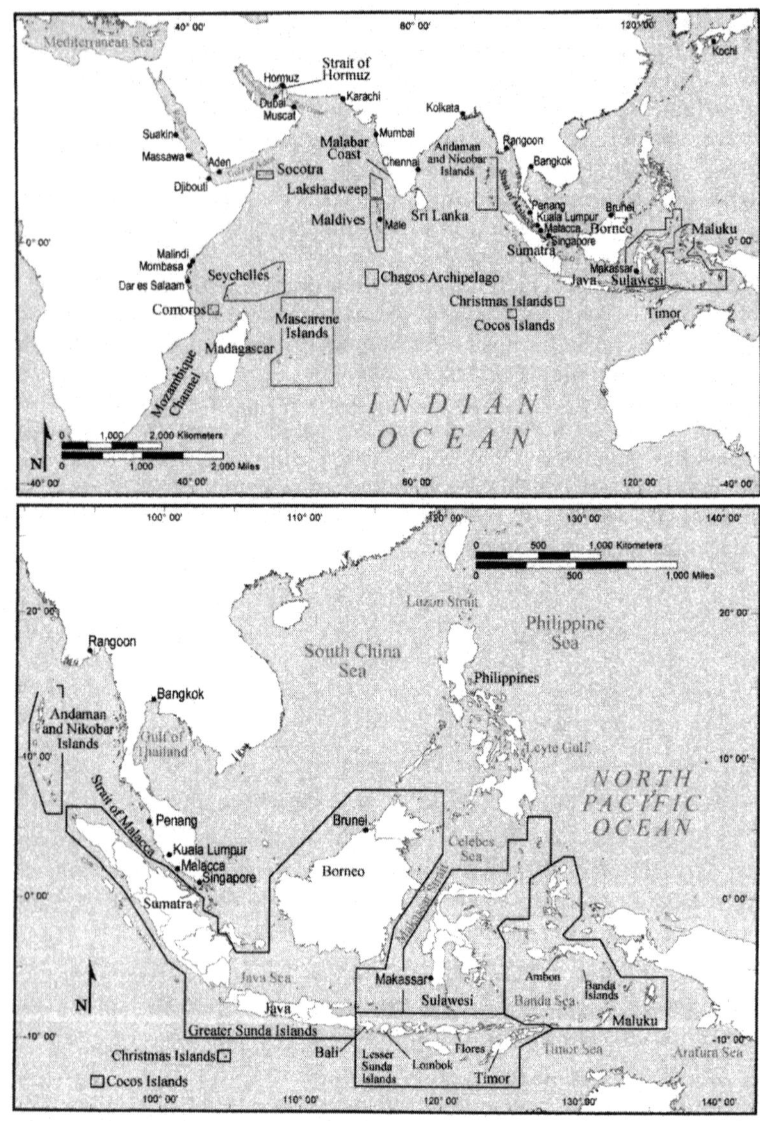

Maps 2.1-2.2: The World of Indian Ocean Islands

Edward A. Alpers when he made a decisive plea to consider what he called 'the island factor', criticizing a 'continental perspective . . . which only discusses islands in passing' (2009: 419). He further states that, 'although islands have certainly been recognized as an important factor in the Indian Ocean world by any number of scholars, no one has previously attempted to locate all the islands of the Indian Ocean in their relationship to the history of eastern Africa' (ibid., 40). This observation can surely be extended to the history of the Indian Ocean world at large, as well as to other academic disciplines than just history.[11] In the following we shall look at the 'island factor' in the Indian Ocean world by structuring our discussion in accordance with the themes that have been identified thus far: island geographies, island histories, and island societies. In a concluding section, we also discuss some of the potential functions and roles – or affordances – which islands of the Indian Ocean world have taken up over the millennia in a unique combination of island realities and imaginaries, especially their seemingly contradictory functions as 'hubs', 'prison islands', and 'paradise islands'.

ISLAND AS 'GEOTOPES'

All Indian Ocean islands are 'warm water' islands, as opposed to 'cold water' islands. Apart from that, there are a number of other ways for understanding and ordering the 'warm water' islands of the Indian Ocean world, with all the abundance and diversity they exhibit in geographical respects.

To start with the most obvious criterion, one could distinguish between islands on the basis of three types of geological origins and present-day formations. A vast number of Indian Ocean islands have come into existence and been built up, often over millennia, by the growth of corals. Well-known examples are the Seychelles and the Maldives. Other islands, like Réunion or the northern Moluccas, have emerged more rapidly from volcanic eruptions. Finally, some islands are granite-based islands that split off from continental landmasses, such as the prehistoric 'supercontinent' of Gondwana. To this group belong Madagascar and Sri Lanka, as well as some smaller islands, for example, Socotra in the Gulf of Aden and parts of the Seychelles.[12] Size would be another criterion. In fact, most islands in the Indian Ocean (as indeed in other oceans) are small, so classifying them by size only becomes necessary in cases where islands are large. An example is a large Indian Ocean island like Madagascar, which, with an area of just under 600,000 square kilometres, is the third largest island in the world.[13] Then, there are Sri Lanka in South Asia and the 'Greater Sunda Islands' of Sumatra, Java, Borneo, and Sulawesi in Indonesia. All the other islands are simply islands, suggesting the (discriminating?) criterion of 'small' be eliminated. Smallness may, however, count in other ways than size alone. As has been mentioned, island identities and island imaginaries typically envisage small islands, while on large islands quite a substantial number of people can lead and understand their lives without themselves possessing a sense of islandness.[14]

Using a different criterion, any empirical overview of the Indian Ocean world of islands could distinguish between those islands that are near to the mainland and those that lie further off in the sea, that is, 'deep-sea' or what Alpers (2019) calls 'distant-water' islands.[15] Among the coastal or offshore island category are the islands that stretch along the East African Swahili coast, from Somalia in the north to the mouth of the Zambezi River in the south. These islands and their port cities, such as Pate, Lamu, Mombasa, Pemba, Zanzibar, Mafia, Kilwa, or Mozambique, are often so close to the mainland that on most maps they are not easily discernible as being islands at all.[16] One also finds numerous islands situated along the western shore of the Red Sea, for example, the Dahlak archipelago off Eritrea. Some of these islets functioned and still function as the seats of regionally important port cities, with Suakin in the Sudan and Massawa in Eritrea representing two prime examples.[17] Further east, and still belonging to this group of offshore islands, there are the seven islands on which the present megacity of Mumbai (Bombay) was built, while further south on the west Indian coast we also find the old insular port city of Kochi (Cochin). Then there are the innumerable small islands stretching inshore along the Southeast Asian coasts of Myanmar, Thailand, Malaysia, and Sumatra. Some of these islands achieved commercial significance, such as the roughly 800 islands of the Mergui Archipelago in Myanmar, with its abundance of high-quality pearls and pearl shells.[18] Others, like the islands of Phuket and Kho Yao along the Thai coast, have become touristic hot spots, while yet others, like Penang in Malaysia, with its World Heritage City of George Town, formerly acquired some economic importance and but now are significant mainly on historical grounds.[19]

Comparable to these coastal islands and still within the category of offshore islands are those 'delta islands' which lie in the mouths of rivers, such as Sofala at the entrance to the Buzi River or Banjarmasin in the combined mouths of the rivers Barito and Martapura in South Kalimantan, Indonesia. Other fluvial islands may lie quite far up the river. Then there are those offshore islands located in gulfs or bays, such as the island of Kharg in the Persian Gulf or Diu at the entrance to the Gulf of Khambat in northwest India. Finally, in this context of offshore islands, we have what could be called 'choke-point islands', as represented most prominently by Hormuz in the Persian Gulf or Singapore at the southeastern tip of the Straits of Malacca. The category of offshore islands also includes those islands that lie close to the mainlands of larger islands. For example, *la grandeîle* of Madagascar has many small islands immediately off its coasts, such as Nosy Boraha (Île Sainte Marie) to the northeast and Nosy Be to the northwest.

Before we come to look at the other side of this categorization of islands, namely those islands that lie quite a distance from the mainland or are even 'in the middle of nowhere', let us add for convenience's sake another characteristic of the Indian Ocean world of islands: islands seldom come alone, more often than not consisting of multi-island archipelagoes. This fact raises a number of additional questions: how are the islands that form an archipelago related to each other? Is there a relative equality among them, or are their relationships hierarchical? Is there a division of labour between them? Is the 'significant other' that is needed for the self-identification of a given island population a place on the mainland or the mainland as such, or is it another island, perhaps visible from its shores and within reach? Take, for example, Lamu, which is not just, as might have been suggested above, a single island but also the name of an archipelago consisting of three islands with strong competition between their respective trading centres, especially Pate and Lamu. Also, of great practical and ideational significance was and is the extent and affordability of shipping services *between* the islands of a single archipelago, which, more often than not, may lie at considerable distances from one another.[20]

Let us now continue our overview of the island world of the Indian Ocean and look at the other, the 'deep-water' side. The most striking example here is the Malay Archipelago, with its roughly 25,000 islands. Approximately 18,000 of these, around 6,000 of which are inhabited, today belong to the Republic of Indonesia, with its more than a quarter of a billion inhabitants. Stretching roughly northwest to southeast (and now omitting the 'Greater Sunda islands' mentioned earlier), the 'Lesser Sunda Islands' include Bali, Lombok, Flores, and Timor. East of Sulawesi and west of New Guinea are the roughly one thousand Moluccas (Maluku Islands), with their approximately two million inhabitants, to mention here only the larger islands of Halmahera in the north and Ceram in the south of this archipelago, as well as the smaller islands of Ternate and Tidore in the northern Moluccas, and the Banda Islands in the south. It is quite stunning, at least at first glance, that it was these latter tiny volcanic islands, and not their larger neighbours, that achieved political and economic power over a wide range of other islands, including territorially much larger ones during the fifteenth and sixteenth centuries. John Villiers identifies three factors which allowed these islands to achieve local and even regional supremacy across the sea, namely 'production of exportable goods, entrepot trade, shipping and navigation' (1990: 83). Smallness also seems to have been an advantage in this respect of achieving influence and power, and this criterion could be added to these three factors on account of reasons to be addressed later.

In the Gulf of Bengal, we find two further groups of islands, namely the Andaman and Nicobar Islands, today under Indian rule. Even though these two archipelagoes in the so-called Andaman Sea are already mentioned in early Tang-Chinese sources, they never developed into or accommodated regularly frequented ports of call. For a long time in history, the indigenous inhabitants of these islands, Sentinelese people of Palaeolithic origins, have been well known for their unwillingness to enter into any kind of regular communication or trade with outsiders. Today, the two archipelagoes consist of almost 600 islands with roughly 400,000 predominantly Hindu inhabitants.

In the western half of the Indian Ocean, immediately south of the equator and roughly 1,500 kilometres east of the East African coast, lie the Seychelles, consisting of more than a hundred islands. The three 'Inner Islands' of Mahe, Prasline, and La Digue contain the great majority of the Seychellois population of just over 90,000. In terms of population and land area (around 450 square kilometres), the archipelago represents the smallest African state, though the Seychelles' maritime *Exclusive Economic Zone* of 1.3 million square kilometres is immense. Situated at about the same latitude but further east is the Chagos Archipelago, which for a long time was a dependency of Mauritius, some 1,000 kilometres to the south. Shortly before Mauritius was granted independence in 1968, the British, the colonial power in decline, in a move that is still controversial today, established the so-called 'British Indian Ocean Territory' (BIOT) out of these 65 coral islands and the waters surrounding them. Clearly Asian in character are two archipelagoes lying roughly 200 and 400 kilometres off the southwest coast of India and Sri Lanka respectively, namely Lakshadweep and, further south, the Maldives. The great majority of the populations of both of these archipelagoes is Muslim. With the arrival of Europeans on the scene, both archipelagoes temporarily came under first Portuguese, then Dutch, and finally British supremacy. Lakshadweep consists of 27 coral islands, only ten of which are inhabited by 65,000 persons, most of them Malayalam-speakers. The Republic of the Maldives consists of two chains of 26 atolls with almost 1,200 coral islands and islets, stretching in a north-south direction. The majority of these islands are not inhabited; numerous others just provide space for foreign-owned luxury hotels and their affluent guests. Roughly one-third of the almost 400,000 speakers of Dhivehi, an Indo-Aryan language, reside in the capital Malé, which counts as one of the most densely populated islands and port cities in the world.

In the southwestern part of the Indian Ocean there are two archipelagoes, namely the Comoros Islands and the Mascarenes. The four islands of the Comoros Archipelago, that is Grande Comore (Ngazidja), Mohéli (Mwali), Anjouan (Ndzuani), and (Maore), found themselves at the southernmost limit that sailors could reach and depart from when making use of the regular pattern of the monsoon winds in that region; consequently there is a strong Swahili influence in the Comoros Archipelago with a population of approximately 850,000 living on a total of 1,862 square kilometres.[21] The three main islands making up the Mascarenes, which lie respectively 700, 900 and 1,500 kilometres east of Madagascar, are Réunion (roughly 2,500 square kilometres, 835,000 inhabitants), Mauritius (approx. 2,000 square kilometres, 1.3 million inhabitants) and Rodrigues (110 square kilometres, 42,000 inhabitants). None of these islands had been settled by humans before Europeans arrived in the region from the seventeenth century onwards. These two archipelagoes, as well as the Seychelles, all came to be inhabited in large numbers by Africans. Notwithstanding the many historical particularities and contingencies that these islands in the southwestern part of the Indian Ocean have experienced, they all came under French colonial rule and influence, at least for some time. Therefore, a French legacy is still quite marked on these islands today, not only in language and culture, but also in important social, political, military, economic, and legal respects as well, while in religious matters the Comoro Islands, at least, have kept their long-standing Islamic character.[22]

One important geopolitical fact that has influenced island life in the Indian Ocean world to a great degree is the shifting whereabouts of the main trading routes. The coming into existence and the rise and fall of island societies have been greatly influenced by the question of whether certain islands were anywhere near these routes and then acquired roles as stop-overs and victualling stations, thus affording shelter from storms, providing refreshment, acting as military outposts for expansionist designs or conducting trade. There are some factors that make islands particularly well suited to becoming knots or hubs in maritime networks and in the ongoing exchanges of both material and ideational items. In order to become hubs for maritime transactions, islands need to have a natural harbour or at least a sheltered bay, while the winds and currents leading to and from them need to be navigable for most of the year. These factors of 'natural ecology', which were important not only in the age of sail but also, albeit to a lesser degree, for steamships as well, must be combined with favourable geostrategic and geopolitical positions. Islands can have all the qualifications that seafarers look for, yet they leave their potential for becoming hubs unfulfilled simply on account of their not being *en route.* If this is the case, and if in addition they have nothing to offer themselves, even islands with good harbours and the best nautical affordances may not be able to realize their potential as hubs and will thus be left behind, as was the case with the Andaman and Nicobar Islands.

A final geopolitical-dimension has to be considered. In this connection it helps to remind us of the threefold distinction which Pearson has made in connection with port cities. He distinguishes between, first, the *umland*, that is, 'the immediate surrounding area, directly connected to the city, frequently because it provides foodstuffs for the city' (1998: 67); secondly, the *foreland*, that is, 'the areas of the overseas world with which the port is linked through shipping, trade, and passenger traffic' (ibid.); and finally, the *hinterland*, which 'radiates out from the port city inland and so begins at the end of the umland' (ibid.). Pearson concludes by observing that, 'while all cities have umland and hinterlands only port cities also have forelands' (ibid.). Applied to small islands, or at least to those that have acquired the role of maritime hubs, one could thus say that, while they all have *forelands*, some have *umlands*, but only a few larger ones could be seen to have a *hinterland.* This leaves us to distinguish between small islands that have *umlands* and those that do not. Islands of the barren-no-*umland* type are usually compelled to import not only luxuries but also what is necessary for the day-to-day survival of their inhabitants. In some extreme cases, this includes even drinking water. However, there are also quite a number of islands, including small ones, which do not just have maritime products such as shells or seafood to offer, but even have an *umland* suitable for agriculture. These can sustain their populations without substantial help from the outside, an economic fact that has crucial implications for other domains, such as the political economy. Some of these islands (e.g., Zanzibar, Mauritius, Lakshadweep, Chagos, or the Banda Island), even have sustained plantations producing cloves, ginger, sugar, coffee, tea, rubber, palm-oil, spices or other products on a large scale for global export. Finally, and somewhat relativizing the statement that islands have no *hinterland*, one should add here the interesting cases where small coastal islands, such as Diu in northwestern India or several Swahili islands at the East African littoral, possessed or controlled quite significant portions of *hinterland* on the nearby mainland.[23]

ISLANDS AS 'CHRONOTOPES'

Now changing the perspective from geography to history, islands appear in a new light, as argued by Warrington and Milne when they write: '*Geography tends towards isolation*: it permits or favours autarchy, distinctiveness, stability and evolution propelled endogenously. *History*, on the other hand, *tends towards contact*: it permits or favours dependence (or interdependence), assimilation, change and evolution propelled exogenously' (2007: 383, their emphases). Stepping into historical analysis, then, one is quickly made to abandon the popular idea of islands as isolated and even 'without history'. By contrast, one is well advised to follow Sahlins here when he argues, in his *Islands of History*, that the '. . . histories of remote islands deserve a place alongside the self-contemplation of the European past – or the history of civilizations – for their own remarkable contributions to an historical understanding' (1985: 72). In the historiography of the Indian Ocean world in particular, studying the history of islands has led to scholars 'recentring the historiography away from imperial histories of oceanic expansion or national histories of resistance to one of oceanic exchange' (Falola, Parrot, and Sanchez 2019: 7).

If we restrict our concern with history to *human* history (ignoring, by and large, *natural* history), some islands obviously have a longer history than others. One prime example of this is Socotra, 500 miles east of Aden, at a crossroads between the Red Sea, the Arabian Peninsula, and the Swahili coast. Socotra, already mentioned in the so-called *Periplus of the Erythraean Sea*, written around 50 CE,[24] is known to have been used as a stopover by ships from ancient Egypt, Rome, Arabia, the Gulf, and India, as well as by the Portuguese and early modern pirates, as early as the beginning of the Common Era.[25] Another island with an even more ancient history is Tarout at the west bank of the Gulf (today in Saudi Arabia), which claims to have been inhabited by humans from 5000 BCE onwards and to have played a major role as part of the Dilmun kingdom (from the third millennium BCE onwards) in one of mankind's earliest maritime trade movements linking Mesopotamia and the Indus Valley.[26] To give two further examples, this time from the Malayan Archipelago, one could mention Java and Flores, where remains and signs (cave paintings) of some of the oldest known humans – the so-called *Homo erectus* or 'Java Man' and *Homo floresiensis* – were discovered, though little can be known about their maritime history. Other islands are relatively short-lived in terms of human history, like Mauritius.[27] Other islands with clearly *colonial* histories, to give a few examples, are Mozambique Island in southeast Africa and Diu in northwest India, which became important places for the Portuguese *Carreira da India* from the mid-sixteenth century onwards.[28] As for Penang and Singapore in Southeast Asia, these were late eighteenth- and early nineteenth-century British creations, even though the prior existence of small fishing communities on all these islands should not be ignored.[29]

Island histories were not only dependent on the existence of and historical changes to trading routes. Connected to the question of sea lanes or *routes* are the *spheres* of power that islands found themselves included in. This is what Warrington and Milne call the 'imperial connection' (2007: 385). They write: 'Consider what is possibly the most important element of an island's political economy, namely its geo-strategic profile, that is, whether it is central or peripheral in relation to the forces and powers at play in its neighbourhood' (ibid.: 384).[30] Were and are islands considered to belong to the domain of one or another imperial power (Asian or European)? If this was and is the case, how has this belonging manifested itself on a scale from subjugation to relative autonomy? Where, on a scale from centre to periphery, did the forced or voluntary submission of an island to a superordinate maritime power place it? Did the imperial or dominant power see the main function of an island as being a fortress, an entrepôt, a fief, or a colony to be settled and made into a plantation economy? Did the imperial power have an interest in the island's own resources and territory, or was it just important for reasons of maritime security, that is, to control the wider sea lanes and their traffic passing through them? Pursuing these questions will involve studying a variety of very distinctive individual histories for each island or archipelago in question.[31]

Furthermore, this special place of islands in colonial endeavours was oriented, as McCusker and Soares (2011: xi) argue, by a Western gaze that 'frequently imagined the island as an inferior, marginal or easily dominated space, as an obvious site for subjugation and organization by the colonizer. . . . Historically, the island was considered as an ideal locale, even laboratory, in which to materialize the colonial will' (ibid.). In such island laboratories, experiments took place that were far from being intended solely to enhance the knowledge of mankind. Rather, as Newitt points out: '. . . small islands are open to exploitation in a way that continental states are not. The very isolation that attracts the romantics provides havens for the scoundrels who can dump their waste, launder their illegal money, explode their bombs, or excavate for phosphates or sand out of sight, and therefore out of mind, of the rest of the world' (1992: 3).[32] Related to these views of islands as laboratories and finite geographies to be well exploited and governed is a further island imaginary, namely that islands are 'virgin soils'. 'In fact, a significant component of the contemporary intoxicating "lure" or "fascination" of islands', Baldacchino writes, 'has to do with the fact that islands suggest themselves as *terrae nullius*, empty spaces waiting, wanting to be possessed: potential laboratories for any conceivable and uninhibited human project, in thought or in action' (2007: 6). Some Indian Ocean islands were indeed uninhabited before uninhibited European colonization. Where this was not the case, islands were often conceived of and treated by sailors and settlers *as if they were* no-man's land – to be exploited and governed by them. An example here would be the Banda Islands, the indigenous population of which was too weak, at least in maritime power, to ward off Dutch traders and governors who came to rule over, abuse and kill them.[33] Another example of a Dutch colonial island is the man-made islet of Deshima from where the Dutch, after being expelled by the Nagasaki shogun, continued to conduct their difficult, but immensely profitable (Indian Ocean) trade with the Japanese. In other instances, the 'virginity' of islands, real or assumed, has turned them into places that are well suited to being turned into spaces of one's own design, free from external or already existing internal power structures. This is why islands have always attracted people not only with colonial designs, but also with utopian and heterotopian ones looking for alternative social, cultural, religious, and political ways of life, either in their literary works or as real-life enterprises, mostly condemned to failure.[34]

The various *colonial* pasts to which the islands of the Indian Ocean world were subjected have of course shaped and even determined their decolonization and their *post*colonial presents. These paths have led in many different directions, the variety of which is evident in the diversity of constitutional statuses that small islands have come to adopt after independence. Some have been integrated into or at least become associated with their former colonial powers: Réunion (French) and the Chagos Archipelago (as 'British Indian Ocean Territory') come to mind here.[35] Other islands, especially the offshore ones, have become integrated, with varying degrees of autonomy and different statuses, into mainland states, like Zanzibar into Tanzania, the Lakshadweep and the Andaman and Nicobar Islands as 'Union Territories' into India, or Penang as a Province into Malaysia. As a result of these processes, some archipelagoes lost their erstwhile geopolitical and, arguably, sociocultural cohesiveness, one prime example being the Islamic *Union des Comores*, with its 'breakaway' island of Mayotte (Maore), whose inhabitants opted to stay with France at independence. The east Indonesian island of Timor is an example of how such a split can even cut right through the middle of one small island alone, one part belonging to Indonesia and the eastern half being independent. Other islands and archipelagoes became independent, and not only the larger ones such as Madagascar or Sri Lanka, but also the archipelagoes of the Comoros (except Maore), the Mascarenes (as 'Republic of Mauritius', except Réunion), the Seychelles, and the Maldives, which today count officially as 'Small Island Developing States'.[36] By contrast, far from being small in its entirety, there is also Indonesia, the largest island state in the world.[37] Economically, some islands in the Indian Ocean are among the poorest in the world, while others have developed into relatively prosperous economies, such as the Seychelles, and some are even rich, most prominently Singapore, though overall prosperity of this sort does not mean the absence of considerable cleavages in wealth and education within the populations of these islands.

While studying the history of the Indian Ocean world of islands does mean studying colonial and postcolonial history, with all its discernible patterns and paths, it is also important to remain sensitive to the contingencies that can determine or change the fate of an island in any conceivable direction. In addition to unforeseeable and chance events of all kinds, studies of the Indian Ocean world may confound scholars who believe that the course of history is not just influenced by the deeds of (apparently) 'great men, so that one also needs to include the activities of subaltern groups in one's analysis. Somewhat against this premise, it is always striking to see how often the fates of island populations were in fact determined by the individual activities of those who might be labelled 'big men'. Small islands are strikingly often venues in which individual, usually male agency has had a better chance of making itself felt. Often these individuals or 'big men' founded or were representatives of dynastic families, or else represented an island's influential but tiny elite that affected the island's destiny both internally and with respect to external mainland and colonial forces, as is readily apparent in, among others, Maldivian politics.[38]

During the course of history, finally, some islands stopped being islands in the strict sense of the term, or in other words lost their 'islandness', their histories as islands coming to an end. Take, for examples, Tarout, Mombasa or Calicut, three islands today linked by multiple, heavily frequented causeways, pipelines and other material links to their respective mainland; others, like Singapore, are constantly filling up the swampy spaces between it and the mainland in order to acquire more land and thus extend their sovereign territory. Another historical example of such a 'de-islandization' is the seven swampy islands on which todays' mega-city of Bombay was built. Closer to the present, the closing of the channel separating Lamu from the Kenyan mainland by means of a dam constructed by Chinese 'belt-and-road' engineers is another example of how an island can lose its islandness.

ISLANDS AS 'SOCIOTOPES'

Before we look at island societies, or island 'sociotopes', in more concrete terms, it is necessary to remind ourselves that some of the key studies in shaping modern social and cultural anthropology were studies of islands. Examples include Bronislaw Malinowski's *Argonauts of the Western Pacific* (1922) on the Trobriand Islanders, Raymond Firth's *We, the Tikopia* (1936) or Margaret Mead's study of Samoa (2001 [1928]). As far as the Indian Ocean world is concerned, the Andaman Islands were seminal in functionalist theory-building through Radcliffe-Brown's voluminous study of Sentinelese life, first published in 1922. Even where early anthropologists, such as Evans-Pritchard, Fortes, Redfield, or Srinivas did not study islands but terrestrial societies, they treated 'their' tribes, village communities or subcastes *as if they were* islands and thus clearly bounded units – not only territorially, but also socially. In the words of Thomas Hylland Eriksen, '. . . a dominant paradigm in social anthropology still defines societies as islands – as virtually self-sustaining systems to be understood primarily in their own terms. . . , this idea should be abandoned since it was wrong from the beginning' (1993: 135).

If, then, small and 'primitive' societies on land are not islands, not even metaphorically, then we must recognize that not even islands (in this imagined sense of being isolated and closed) are islands. As a matter of fact, all human societies, whether on land or as islands in the middle of nowhere, are both open and closed, both connected and isolated. The movements between these two poles of social openness and closeness are full of contestation and tension, characterized by constraints and opportunities, and burdened by contradictions and ambiguities. Island life is no different in this regard, but the particular combination of *maritime* ecology, geography, and history does, of course, bring out a particular imprint in this respect. Small islands are 'sociotopes' that are special, not, as is often implicitly assumed, with regard to their being small, isolated and closed to outsiders, but with reference to the specific processes of social inclusion and exclusion that occur on them. Many islands in the Indian Ocean have in fact experienced a constant coming and going of people from all parts and directions of the maritime world. Some arrivals merely passed by or stayed for a little while only, but those who remained and settled brought and transplanted their own cultures, religions, languages, and ideals of governance or communal living with them. Therefore, the islands of the Indian Ocean world, instead of being places of homogeneity and uniformity, had a good chance – arguably a better chance than many mainland locations – to develop into places of cultural hybridity and openness to the world. Alpers underscores this assumption when he speaks of 'the extraordinary cross-fertilization of cultures, traditions, and languages that characterizes the islands of the Indian Ocean' (2009: 42), while Pearson likewise states that on islands 'one would expect to find . . . more concentrated mixings from various cultural influences' (1998: 38). Before subscribing to an '*éloge de créolité*'[39], however, one should be aware of the fact that those who arrived on an island were more often than not in unequal positions: from one and the same ship could disembark both high-caste brahmans and untouchables, both *petits blancs* and powerful governors, or, in the most extreme case of inequality, both white plantation owners and black slaves.

Island societies in the Indian Ocean world were subjected to various 'waves' of socio-cultural, religious, economic and political influences entering them from the outside, either from the mainland or from neighbouring islands and archipelagoes. There are, to begin with, the various phases of migration of Austronesian-speakers starting around 3000 BCE from Taiwan and South China and crossing the Philippines towards Borneo, Melanesia and the Sunda Islands in a sort of slow and intergenerational island hopping, bringing, among other things, the knowledge of rice cultivation and the entrepreneurial spirit of sea traders with them. These people, traversing the seas in outrigger canoes, populated the Southeast Asian islands by around 1000 BCE, mixing there with indigenous population strata and creating a new and distinctive Malayan culture. Some of them moved on to Madagascar from around 700 CE.[40] Later in history, many Sunda Islands were what used to be called 'Indianized', or better they 'Indianized' themselves, as these developments were less the results of colonization from India than the voluntary and syncretistic nostrification of some ideas and values from India, often brought by Chinese travellers making intermediate halts.[41] As a result, over a centuries-long process during roughly the first millennium of the common era, various rulers and subjects, especially from Java, Sumatra and the thalassocratic Srivijaya Empire, 'imported' Buddhist, Brahmanical and other Hindu ritual beliefs and practices, as well as the political and administrative ideals and practices that went along with these two historically much intertwined religions.[42] A similar wave of religion ('religion', again to be understood as a system of beliefs and practices which encompasses *all* dimensions of life, including the 'non-religious') occurred within the Swahili world of islands when littoral Bantu populations came under the sway of Muslim traders and preachers from the eighth century onwards.[43] Processes of 'Islamization' also occurred along the west coast of the Indian subcontinent at about the same time, while a 'Monsoon Islam' (Prange 2018) introduced by merchants also travelled to Lakshadweep and the Maldives, though later, from the twelfth century onwards. Furthermore, since the thirteenth century many parts of the Malay world of islands, with the notable exception of Bali, adopted the Muslim faith – so much so that Indonesia today is the nation with most Muslims in the world.[44] Western influences, including Christian proselytization, brought yet another change to the socio-cultural and religious life of islands in the Indian Ocean world. These external influences started with the (Catholic) Portuguese from the sixteenth century and were continued by the (Protestant) Dutch and the British East India Companies from the sixteenth and seventeenth centuries onwards respectively. Europeans also introduced new modes and technologies of production, especially plantation economies, initially based on slavery and later on indentured labour.[45] The establishment of plantation societies and economies on some of the Indian Ocean islands, which produced sugar, coffee, ginger, cloves, spices, or coconut and palm oil, led to yet another massive exchange and resettling of people of diverse regional, socio-cultural, linguistic and religious backgrounds on Indian Ocean islands, which has captured the attention of numerous scholars.[46]

While plantation islands, and Mauritius is a prime example of this category, lie at one pole of the continuum from open to closed, the Sentinelese people of the Andaman and Nicobar Islands certainly represent the other extreme, shooting arrows from the beach at intruders until quite recently. The Swahili group of islands, such as Mombasa or Pemba, could be located somewhere in the middle of this scale: there is, to be sure, a century-long coming and going, staying, and 'mixing' of people from Africa, Arabia, Persia and West

India which has turned these islands into cosmopolitan 'islands of history'. Nonetheless, Swahili society has established and advocated quite firm ideals and practices rooted in Islam, which, with all its established rules of conduct and religious dogmas, leads to some uniformity and hinders these islands from becoming 'Creole' or hybrid in a postmodern sense.

ISLAND AFFORDANCES

Islands are unique mixtures of biological, geographical, political, historical, social, cultural, religious, economic and, last but not least, imaginary factors – under maritime pretexts. The islandness resulting from these combinations has burdened islands with certain restrictions (for example, being remote and not being readily accessible), but also equipped them with a number of opportunities or affordances (some of them, ironically, resulting from just these restrictions) that have enabled them to play important roles and functions in the history of the Indian Ocean world.

Looking at some of these functions, arguably the most prominent and basic one is that islands act as hubs. It is striking to see that this role was not only taken up by deep-water islands offering welcome refreshment stops on long maritime journeys. Rather, one finds that many coastal or offshore islands were made into hubs as well, even if, when and where continental alternatives would have been possible. The narrow waterways between these islands and the mainland, which can be found most strikingly along the Swahili coast, seem to have provided not only nautical shelter for sailing dhows or other boats, but also to have protected them from raids by inland peoples. While islandness thus seems to be good for 'hubbing', one of the basic conditions for an island to become a hub is, to repeat, that it is situated *en route*. Those islands which have something to offer themselves, but which are not located along a major trading route, such as the Maldives with their cowrie shells or the Moluccas with their spices, usually only constitute destinations and starting points for intermediate, short- or middle-range routes that link up with longer ones. Thus, in the age of sail, cowrie shells were exported on local boats from the Maldives just to Ceylon, southwest India and Bengal, where they were transferred to vessels making transregional journeys.[47] Likewise, the traffic in nutmeg and cloves from the northern Moluccan Islands and the Banda Islands first went to Ambon or Makassar on Sulawesi, two insular 'centres out there', before reaching their final destinations as far away as Europe in the west or China in the east.[48] Other small islands, which had little or nothing to offer themselves, nevertheless managed to acquire important positions as ports of call and even entrepôts, just because they were lying close to an established trading route. One could mention here the Indonesian Riau Archipelago or the Bangka-Belitung Islands, which lie on major trading routes between West Kalimatan (Borneo) in the east and Singapore, Malaysia, and Sumatra in the west.[49]

However, if routes do change direction for various nautical, economic, or political reasons, or if new routes are discovered and become possible through technological innovation, then an island whose potential as a hub has so far lain dormant might come to the fore, while another one that has formerly acted as a hub might lose it. The former situation arose in the Maldives when Muslim traders, after Malakka's fall to the Portuguese in 1511, started to frequent this archipelago on their way to Arabia in their attempts to avoid Portuguese strongholds on the West Indian coast.[50] The latter situation developed when the almost simultaneous introduction of steamships and the opening of the Suez Canal in the second half of the nineteenth century left the Comoro and Mascarene Islands somewhat isolated. They lost their status as hubs (though not their potential as such), which they had assumed around three and a half centuries earlier, once European sailors had managed to round the Cape. One recent creation of a 'strategic hub' of a very special kind is Diego Garcia, the main island of the Chagos archipelago. In 1965 this archipelago was sold to the outgoing British colonial power by Mauritian politicians, a rather shabby deal which was probably backed up by promises to the colony that its path to independence would be speeded up. While feigning ecological interests, in the early 1970s the British leased these islands to the USA, who established a large military base there for both ships and airplanes. All Chagossians (some 500 or more), descendants of African and Indian workers on coconut plantations who had come to the islands three to four generations before, were forcefully evicted and simply dropped in Port Louis, where they have henceforth lived lives of misery and poverty.[51]

While the function of islands as hubs relies on their ability to connect and support maritime movement, yet other functions of islands are based on exactly the opposite affordance, namely on their (imagined and real) remoteness and isolation. In this context, numerous islands were and still are used as 'prison islands' or 'detention centres'. For example, the Seychelles were made into a place of confinement for political opponents under both Napoleonic and British rule, while the Andaman Islands were used by the British to detain political prisoners after the 'Great Mutiny' in India in 1857. Closer to the present day, Diego Garcia not only functions as military base from which Americans can monitor and attack countries in the 'Middle East' (for example, Iraq in 2003), it has also been used for detaining and interrogating captives in their 'War on Terror'. In the 'greater' Indian Ocean world, one could add the two (strictly speaking South Atlantic) 'prison islands' of Saint Helena and Robben Island, which kept two of the world's most prominent captives in custody, namely Napoleon Bonaparte and Nelson Mandela. Other islands in the Indian Ocean world – and again the Seychelles and the Chagos Archipelago come to mind here – were made into 'quarantine islands', that is, places of involuntary banishment for persons inflicted with leprosy or other infectious diseases, often leaving these unfortunates to care for themselves. Yet other islands did become Robinsonesque places of abandonment for shipwrecks or those who had been left behind by their vessels for various reasons.[52]

The affordances of islands as both hubs and remote places (that are difficult to get away from) combine in seemingly contradictory ways to bring about what is arguably the most salient and profitable function of islands these days: that of being 'paradise islands'. Islands and their beaches have become the objects of multibillion-dollar enterprises worldwide, forming the destinations of tourists from near and wide to consume and enjoy that specific island experience. Islands, especially warm-water islands, have exactly that what attracts tourists the most: sun, sand, and sea all-year around. One and the same island that was once a hell for some in another period of history might now be turned into a blessed 'Garden of Eden' for relaxation – hopefully with an exciting night life too. Like island hubs, these 'pleasure islands' or 'paradise islands' need to have the ability to let tourists come and go easily, usually these days by using airports and planes rather than ports and ships. Like 'prison islands' and 'quarantine islands', only more positive, they conjure up imaginaries of remoteness, solitude, timelessness and bounded security. They seem to be far away from the hustle and bustle of urban industrial life, being populated instead, or so the tourist agencies would have us believe, by smiling and exotic 'natives' who serve them or, when work is done, perform rhythmic music and erotic dances. 'Paradise islands' have thus become one of the most important assets in what is probably the world's largest industry today, generating substantial percentages of many islands' GDPs and foreign-exchange earnings, and providing numerous jobs to the locals. In fact, quite a number of islands and even island states (Maldives, Seychelles) are now so heavily dependent on tourism economically that any disturbance in the sector (an 'oil crisis', terrorism, bad weather, rising waters, pandemics, or an unforeseen shift in tourist tastes) can spell doom. In any case, even on the successful tourist islands, much of the profit generated through tourism does not really reach the island and the islanders, but rather enriches international travel agencies, hotel chains and airlines headquartered in Europe or America. What is paradise and pleasure for some is hard work, poverty and the loss of socio-cultural cohesion for others. Tourist islands, then, probably offer the most striking examples of the fact that islands are unique conflations of imaginaries and realities, and that they can come to accommodate and make use of quite ambivalent, if not straightforwardly contradictory qualities.[53]

To conclude, the Indian Ocean world is in important respects a world of islands. Maritime exchanges and expansion would not have been possible without the connecting and mediating roles of islands in linking regions, nations and even continents.[54] However, acknowledging the importance of islands as hubs for the *external* circulation of things (including humans) should not lead us to ignore the extraordinary dynamics and innovative agency that islands have exhibited *internal* matters, often transforming in value, meaning and function those travellers and cargoes that stopped on them for a while or stayed there for good.[55] Islands have also been important sites of scientific discoveries, as exemplified by Rumphius in Ambon or Poivre in Mauritius.[56] Islands also served as models of and models for the introduction of new regimes of labour and exploitation in the plantation economies of the eighteenth and nineteenth centuries, no matter whether they produced coffee in Réunion, sugar in Mauritius, cloves in Zanzibar, or palm oil in Lakshadweep. Most remarkable in this respect is probably the almost avant-gardist role some islands have played in 'the Creation of New Societies' (Sheriff and Ho, eds. 2014), with their cosmopolitan ways of living and their open states of mind. Islands, in short, are not only 'a must' to study on account of their factual importance in external and internal respects, they are also 'good to think', serving not just – then and now – as refreshment stops for seafarers, but also providing 'revictualling stations for ideas on the condition of nature, humankind or simply of ideas for their own sake' (Baldacchino 2007: 17).

NOTES

1. For a convenient overview of the field of 'Island Studies', see the thematically arranged articles in Baldacchino (ed. 2007). See also Edmond and Smith (eds. 2003), McCusker and Soares (eds. 2011), Skinner and Hills (2006), Pugh and Chandler (2021), as well as the *Island Studies Journal.*
2. For a glimpse at these works of fiction, see Baldacchino (2007: 12–14), also, the book-length study by Billig (2010).
3. The term 'imaginary' as used here is more collective in meaning than the alternative 'imagination' would be, but also more individual than 'collective representation'. 'The imaginary can thus be conceived', as Salazar puts it, 'as a mental, individual and social process that produces the reality that simultaneously produces it' (2010: 6).
4. See Ingold (2009).
5. On these points, see also Billig (2010: 20–1).
6. On 'island governance', see Warrington and Milne (2007).
7. As far as the Indian Ocean world of islands *as a whole* is concerned, see Guéborg (1999). Numerous studies deal with individual archipelagoes and islands of the Indian Ocean, for example, Chandra, Arunchalam, and Suryanarayan (eds. 1993); the last section in Gupta, Hofmeyr, and

Pearson (eds. 2010: 275–360); and more recently Sellström (2015); as well as Falola, Parrot, and Sanchez (eds. 2019: Part II).

8. Auguste Toussaint from Mauritius. See Toussaint (1966).
9. See Pearson (2006). Pearson himself acknowledges the importance of islands when he writes: 'Islands should be seen as the quintessential maritime locations' (2003: 258).
10. The term 'islandness' is used here instead of 'insularity', with its implicit negative connotations. See Baldacchino (2007: 15–16).
11. Alpers and I followed up this line of investigation with regard to the Indian Ocean world of islands at large and with an interdisciplinary objective. See Schnepel and Alpers (eds. 2018). See also Alpers (2019) and Schnepel (2018) of which the present chapter represents an updated and reconsidered version.
12. Types one and two are not as different as they might seem, because coral islands often started their lives on the tops of volcanoes that did not reach above the surface of the water. On islands' origins and ecologies, see Nunn (2007). On the various ways of defining and typologizing islands, see Royle (2007).
13. On the history of Madagascar, see, among others, Brown (2000).
14. On the 'importance of being small' with regard to islands, see Alpers (2018), Hintjens and Newitt (eds. 1992), Royle (2007: 42–3), Hannerz and Gingrich (eds. 2017), Gingrich (2018).
15. Alpers (2019) also suggests a tripartite grouping (of the Indian Ocean's African islands), adding the category of 'foreland islands' to the two that concern us here, while also subdividing coastal islands into inshore and offshore islands.
16. With regard to the Swahili world, see, among others, Barendse (2002: 20–34), Middleton (1992), Horton and Middleton (2000), Wynne-Jones and LaViolette (eds. 2018).
17. See Barendse (2002: 37–40).
18. See Machado, Mullins, and Christensen (eds. 2018).
19. See Pampus (2020).
20. This also raises the question of internal migration from an archipelago's peripheries to its centre, as Newitt (1992: 12–13) and other articles in Hintjens and Newitt (eds. 1992) have shown in particular.
21. Excluding Mayotte. On the Comoros, see Walker (2010, 2019).
22. See Houbert (1992). France also claims possession of some smaller islands, known as the Scattered Islands, lying in the Mozambique Channel and two small coral islets north of Madagascar, supporting its claims with military posts.

23. See Alpers (2019), Barendse (2002: 19–21, 68–70).
24. See Agatharchides and Huntingford (1980).
25. On Socotra, see Biedermann (2006) and Ray (2018). Today, it is officially part of the Republic of Yemen, though Huthi separatists seem to have captured it in June 2020.
26. See Beaujard (2019: especially 106–17).
27. In terms of a natural history, however, Mauritius is one of the oldest islands of the world, since it originated from volcanic eruptions some ten million years ago. On Mauritian (human) history, see, among others, Teelock (2001) and Vaughan (2005).
28. See Pearson (1998) and Alpers (2009: especially chap. 1).
29. On Penang, see Pampus (2020); on Singapore, see Heng and Aljunied (eds. 2011).
30. A distinction, inspired by 'World Systems Theory' à la Wallerstein (1974–89) or, with particular reference to the 'Worlds of the Indian Ocean', by Beaujard (2019) between 'cores', 'semi-peripheries', and 'peripheries' may help to bring some order to the dynamic and at times confusing overall picture, but it has the disadvantage that small islands always emerge as peripheries without fully acknowledging their pivotal role in Indian Ocean connectivity in motion.
31. For a more detailed discussion of these points, see Warrington and Milne (2007, especially 398–415).
32. The important imaginary and practical role of small islands for European colonization, as well as scientific endeavours, have been studied in exemplary fashion by Grove (1995) in his book *Green Imperialism.* See also Cook (2007).
33. See Boxer (1965: 107–9).
34. It is not by chance that Thomas Morus's *Utopia* (1516) is located on an island. On heterotopias, see Foucault (2005). On various attempts by European adventurers to establish utopian communities on islands in the southwestern Indian Ocean, see Schicho (2004). See also Falola, Parrott, and Sanchez (2019: 11–12).
35. The different ways in which France and Britain have dealt with their former small island colonies, not just in the Indian Ocean but in other oceans as well, are addressed in several articles in the volume edited by Hintjens and Newitt (eds. 1992). See also Baldacchino and Royle (2010).
36. This category was created, and acknowledged as special, at the UN Conference on Environment and Development in 1992.
37. While the larger islands of Sumatra, Java, and Sulawesi were integrated into and form the vital bases of Indonesia, Borneo was internally

divided between three states, namely Malaysia, Indonesia, and Brunei, with only the latter being based solely on the island. On Indonesia, see, among others, Taylor (2003).

38. See Wille (2018) on the Maldives.
39. See Bernabé, Chamoiseau, and Confiant (1993).
40. See Bellwood (1997), Schulze (2015: 13–18).
41. See the elaborations in Sen (2017).
42. The term 'Indianization' has to be treated cautiously, because, apart from trying to capture a historical process, it clearly is a product of modern-day Indian nationalist historiography and thus projects the traits, desires, and politics of that time and place on to the past. On the 'Greater India' paradigm, see also Bayly (2004). On India's influence on Southeast Asia during ancient times, see Kulke and Rothermund (1991 [1986]: 152–60), Ray (1994, 1999), Reade (ed. 1996), and Schulze (2015: 18–42).
43. See Horton and Middleton (2000).
44. On early modern Southeast Asian history, see Andaya and Andaya (2015), and Reid (1988, 1993).
45. On slavery in the Indian Ocean world, see, among many others, Clarence-Smith (1989), Campbell (ed. 2004, 2005), Allen (2015). On 'indentured labour', see Tinker (1974).
46. Hofmeyr has identified 'one broad theme of Indian Ocean studies' (2007: 9) that builds on 'the idea of the island as an epitome of Indian Ocean experiences of slavery and indenture' (ibid.). In this context she mentions scholars such as Carter and Torabully (2002), who have sought 'to understand the islands as Creole spaces, as the histories of people without reference to a nation: a kind of ultra-Caribbean model of European, African, and Asian traditions being violently brought together' (Hofmeyr 2007: 9).
47. See Heimann (1980), Knoll (2022).
48. See Benda-Beckmann (2018) and Nagel (2018).
49. See Reid (1988, 1993).
50. See Feldbauer (2004).
51. On Diego Garcia's 'military history', see Vine (2009); the plight of the Chagossians in Mauritius after their eviction and their struggle to return to their homeland is discussed by Johannessen (2014).
52. On this point, see also Royle (2007: 50).
53. On 'island tourism', see Gössling and Wall (2007).
54. This 'globality' of islands is especially emphasized by Falola, Parrot, and Sanchez (2019).

55. On the connective agency of cargoes in the Indian Ocean world, see Schnepel and Verne (eds. 2022).
56. For Rumphius, see Cook (2007: 329–38); for Poivre, see Grove (1995: 168–263). See also Storey (1997).

REFERENCES

Agatharchides and G.W.B. Huntingford. 1980. *The Periplus of the Erythraean Sea.* London: Hakluyt Society.

Allen, R. 2015. *European Slave Trading in the Indian Ocean, 1500–1850.* Athens: Ohio University Press.

Alpers, E.A. 2009. *East Africa and the Indian Ocean.* Princeton: Wiener Publications.

——, 2018. 'Islands Connect: People, Things, and Ideas among the Small Islands of the Western Indian Ocean'. In Schnepel and Alpers (eds.) 2018: 33–56.

——, 2019. 'Africa's Indian Ocean Islands, Near and Distant'. In Falola, Parrot, and Sanchez (eds.) 2019: 245–66.

Andaya, B.W., and L.Y. Andaya. 2015. *A History of Early Modern Southeast Asia, 1400–1830.* Cambridge: Cambridge University Press.

Baldacchino, G. 2007. 'Editorial: Introducing a World of Islands'. In Baldacchino (ed.) 2007: 1–32.

Baldacchino, G. (ed.). 2007. *A World of Islands.* Prince Edward Island: Institute of Island Studies.

Baldacchino, G., and S. Royle. 2010. 'Postcolonialism and Islands: Introduction'. *Space and Culture* 13(2): 140–2.

Barendse, R.J. 2002. *The Arabian Seas: The Indian Ocean World of the Seventeenth Century.* London: Routledge.

Bayly, S. 2004. 'Imagining "Greater India": French and Indian Visions of Colonialism in the Indic Mode'. *Modern Asian Studies* 38(3): 703–44.

Beaujard, P. 2019. *The Worlds of the Indian Ocean: A Global History,* 2 vols. Cambridge: Cambridge University Press.

Bellwood, P. 1997. *Prehistory of the Indo-Malaysian Archipelago.* Honolulu: University of Hawaii Press.

Bernabé, I., P. Chamoiseau, and R. Confiant. 1993. *Eloge de la Créolité.* Paris: Gallimard.

Biedermann, Z. 2006. *Soqotra: Geschichte einer christlichen Insel im Indischen Ozean vom Altertum bis zur frühen Neuzeit.* Wiesbaden: Harrassowitz Verlag.

Billig, V. 2010. *Inseln: Geschichte einer Faszination.* Berlin: Matthes & Seitz.

Boxer, C.R. 1965. *The Dutch Seaborne Empire, 1600–1800.* London: Hutchinson.

Brown, M. 2000. *A History of Madagascar.* Princeton: Marcus Wiener Publishers.

Campbell, G. (ed.). 2004. *The Structure of Slavery in Indian Ocean Africa and Asia.* London: Fran Cass.

——, 2005. *Abolition and its Aftermath in the Indian Ocean, Africa and Asia.* London: Routledge.

Carroll, B.W., and T. Carroll. 1999. 'The Consolidation of Democracy in Mauritius'. *Democratization* 6: 179–97.

Carter, M., and K. Torabully. 2002. *Coolitude: An Anthology of the Indian Labour Diaspora.* London: Anthem Press.

Chandra, S., B. Arunachalam, and V. Suryanarayan (eds.). 1993. *The Indian Ocean and its Islands: Strategic, Scientific and Historical Perspectives.* New Delhi: Sage.

Clarence-Smith, W.G. 1989. *The Economics of the Indian Ocean Slave Trade in the Nineteenth Century.* London: Frank Cass.

Cook, H.J. 2007. *Matters of Exchange: Commerce, Medicine, and Science in the Dutch Golden Age.* New Haven: Yale University Press.

Edmond, R., and V. Smith (eds.). 2003. *Islands in History and Representation.* London: Routledge.

Eriksen, T.H. 1993. 'In Which Sense Do Cultural Islands Exist?' *Social Anthropology* 1: 133–47.

Falola, T., R.J. Parrott, and D.P. Sanchez. 2019. 'Introduction: Arbiters and Witnesses of Change. Contextualizing Conversations on African Islands'. In Falola, Parrott, and Sanchez (eds.) 2019: 1–35.

Falola, T., R.J. Parrott, and D.P. Sanchez (eds.). 2019. *African Islands: Leading Edges of Empire and Globalization.* Rochester, NY: University of Rochester Press.

Feldbauer, P. 2004. 'Der Handel vor und nach der Kolonialexpansion Portugals'. In Rothermund and Weigelin-Schwiedrzik (eds.) 2004: 83–105.

Firth, R. 1936. *We, the Tikopia: A Sociological Study of Kinship in Primitive Polynesia.* London: George Allen and Unwin.

Foucault, M. 2005. *Die Heterotopien.* Frankfurt: Suhrkamp.

Gingrich, A. 2018. 'Small Island Hubs and Connectivity in the Indian Ocean World: Some Concepts and Hypotheses from Historical Anthropology'. In Schnepel and Alpers (eds.) 2018: 57–91.

Gössling, S., and G. Wall. 2007. 'Island Tourism'. In Baldacchino (ed.) 2007: 429–53.

Grove, R.H. 1995. *Green Imperialism: Colonial Expansion, Tropical Island Edens and the Origins of Environmentalism, 1600–1860.* Cambridge: Cambridge University Press.

Guébourg, J.-L. 1999. *Petites Iles et Archipels de l'Ocean Indien.* Paris: Karthala.

Gupta, P., I. Hofmeyr, and M. Pearson (eds.). 2010. *Eyes Across the Water. Navigating the Indian Ocean.* Pretoria: Unisa Press.

Hannerz, U., and A. Gingrich (eds.). 2017. *Small Countries: Structures and Sensibilities.* Philadelphia: University of Pennsylvania Press.

Heimann, J. 1980. 'Small Change and Ballast: Cowry Trade and Usage as an Example of Indian Ocean Economic History'. *South Asia* 3(1): 48–69.

Heng, D., and S.M.K. Aljunied (eds.) 2011. *Singapore in Global History.* Amsterdam: Amsterdam University Press.

Hintjens, H.M., and M.D.D. Newitt (eds.) 1992. *The Political Economy of Small Tropical Islands: The Importance of Being Small.* Exeter: University of Exeter Press.

Hofmeyr, I. 2007. 'The Black Atlantic Meets the Indian Ocean: Forging New Paradigms of Transnationalism for the Global South. Literary and Cultural Perspectives'. *Social Dynamics* 33: 3–32.

Horton, M.C., and J. Middleton. 2000. *The Swahili: The Social Landscape of a Mercantile Society.* Oxford: Blackwell.

Houbert, J. 1992. 'The Mascareignes, the Seychelles and the Chagos, Islands with a French Connection: Security in a Decolonised Indian Ocean'. In Hintjens and Newitt (eds.) 1992: 93–111.

Ingold, T. 2009. 'Against Space: Place, Movement, Knowledge'. In Kirby (ed.) 2009: 29–44.

Johannessen, S.F. 2014. *Sacralising the Contested: The Chagossian Diaspora and their First Pilgrimage to the Homeland.* Halle: Martin Luther University Halle-Wittenberg (PhD thesis).

Kathirithamby-Wells, J., and J. Villiers (eds.). 1990. *The Southeast Asian Port and Polity: Rise and Demise.* Singapore: Singapore University Press.

Kirby, P.W. (ed.) 2009. *Boundless Worlds: An Anthropological Approach to Movement.* Oxford: Berghahn Books.

Knoll, E.M. 2022. 'An Enduring Measure of Twelve Thousand Cowries: The Materialities and Life Histories of a Well-traveled Marine Product'. In Schnepel and Verne (eds.) 2022: 192–214.

Kulke, H., and D. Rothermund. 1991 [1986]. *A History of India.* Delhi: Rupa Paperback.

Machado, P., S. Mullins, and J. Christensen (eds.). 2020. *Pearls, People, and*

Power. Pearling and the Indian Ocean Worlds. Athens: Ohio University Press.

Malinowski, B. 1922. *Argonauts of the Western Pacific.* London: Routledge & Kegan Paul.

McCusker, M., and A. Soares. 2011. 'Introduction'. In McCusker and Soares (eds.) 2011: xi–xxviii. Amsterdam: Rodopi.

McCusker, M., and A. Soares (eds.). 2011. *Islanded Identities: Constructions of Postcolonial Cultural Insularity.* Amsterdam: Rodopi.

Mead, M. 2001 [1928]. *Coming of Age in Samoa: A Psychological Study of Primitive Youth for Western Civilisation.* New York: Harper Perennial.

Middleton, J. 1992. *The World of the Swahili: An African Mercantile Civilization.* New Haven: Yale University Press.

Nagel, J. 2018. 'Changing Connectivity in a World of Small Islands: The Role of Makassar (Sulawesi) as a Hub under Dutch Hegemony'. In Schnepel and Alpers (eds.) 2018: 397–420.

Newitt, M. 1992. 'Introduction'. In Hintjens and Newitt (eds.) 1992: 1–17.

Pampus, M. 2020. *Connected Heritages: The Inner-life of a Port City in the Indian Ocean World.* Halle: Martin Luther University Halle-Wittenberg (PhD thesis).

Pearson, M.N. 1998. *Port Cities and Intruders: The Swahili Coast, India, and Portugal in the Early Modern Era.* Baltimore: The Johns Hopkins University Press.

——, 2003. *The Indian Ocean.* London: Routledge.

——, 2006. 'Littoral Society: The Concept and the Problems'. *Journal of World History* 17: 353–73.

Prange, S.R. 2018. *Monsoon Islam: Trade and Faith on the Medieval Malabar Coast.* Cambridge: Cambridge University Press.

Pugh, J., and D. Chandler. 2021. *Anthropocene Islands. Entangled Worlds.* London: University of Westminster Press.

Radcliffe-Brown, A.R. 1922. *The Andaman Islanders.* Cambridge: Cambridge University Press.

Ray, H.P. 1994. *The Winds of Change: Buddhism and the Maritime Links of Early South Asia.* New Delhi: Oxford University Press.

——, 1999. *Archaeology of Seafaring: The Indian Ocean in the Ancient Period.* New Delhi: Pragati Publications.

——, 2018. 'From Salsette to Socotra: Islands across the Seas and Implications for Heritage'. In Schnepel and Alpers (eds.) 2018: 347–68.

Reade, J. (ed.). 1996. *The Indian Ocean in Antiquity.* London: Kegan Paul.

Reid, A. 1988. *Southeast Asia in the Age of Commerce, 1450–1680. Volume One: The Land Below the Winds.* New Haven: Yale University Press.

——, 1993. *Southeast Asia in the Age of Commerce, 1450–1680. Volume Two: Expansion and Crisis.* New Haven: Yale University Press.

Rothermund, D., and S. Weigelin-Schwiedrzik (eds.). 2004. *Der Indische Ozean: Das afro-asiatische Mittelmeer als Kultur- und Wirtschaftsraum.* Vienna: Promedia.

Royle, S.A. 2007. 'Definitions and Typologies'. In Baldacchino (ed.) 2007: 33–56.

Sahlins, M. 1985. *Islands of History.* Chicago: The University of Chicago Press.

Salazar, N.B. 2010. *Envisioning Eden: Mobilizing Imagineries in Tourism and Beyond.* Oxford: Berghahn.

Schicho, W. 2004. 'Die französische Kolonisierung der Inseln im Indischen Ozean. Der Mythos vom Glück und der leichten Liebe'. In Rothermund and Weigelin-Schwiedrzik (eds.) 2004: 227–46.

Schnepel, B. 2018. 'Introduction'. In Schnepel und Alpers (eds.) 2018: 3–31.

Schnepel, B., and E.A. Alpers (eds.). 2018. *Connectivity in Motion: Island Hubs in the Indian Ocean World.* New York: Palgrave.

Schnepel, B., and J. Verne (eds.). 2022. *Cargoes in Motion: Materiality and Connectivity across the Indian Ocean.* Athens: Ohio University Press.

Schulze, F. 2015. *Kleine Geschichte Indonesiens.* Munich: C.H. Beck.

Sellström, T. 2015. *Africa in the Indian Ocean: Islands in Ebb and Flow.* Leiden: Brill.

Sen, T. 2017. *India, China and the World. A Connected History.* London: Rowman and Littlefield.

Sheriff, A., and E. Ho (eds.). 2014. *The Indian Ocean: Oceanic Connections and the Creation of New Societies.* London: Hurst & Company.

Skinner, J., and M. Hills. 2006. *Managing Island Life: Social, Economic and Political Dimensions of Formality and Informality in 'Island' Communities.* Dundee: University of Abertay Press.

Storey, W.K. 1997. *Science and Power in Colonial Mauritius.* Rochester: University of Rochester Press.

Taylor, J.G. 2003. *Indonesia: Peoples and Histories.* New Haven: Yale University Press.

Teelock, V. 2001. *Mauritian History. From its Beginnings to Modern Times.* Moka: Mahatma Gandhi Institute.

Tinker, H. 1974. *A New System of Slavery: The Export of Indian Labour Overseas 1830–1920.* London: Published for the Institute of Race Relations by Oxford University Press.

Toussaint, A. 1966. *History of the Indian Ocean.* London: Routledge & Kegan Paul.

Vaughan, M. 2005. *Creating the Creole Island: Slavery in Eighteenth-century Mauritius.* Durham NC: Duke University Press.

Villiers, J. 1990. 'The Cash-Crop Economy and State Formation in the Spice Islands in the Fifteenth and Sixteenth Centuries'. In Kathirithamby-Wells and Villiers (eds.) 1990: 83–106.

Vine, D. 2009. *Island of Shame: The Secret History of the U.S. Military Base on Diego Garcia*: Princeton: Princeton University Press.

Wallerstein, I. 1974–1989. *The Modern World System*, 3 vols. New York: Academic Press.

Walker, I. 2010. *Becoming the Other, being Oneself: Constructing Identities in a Connected World.* Cambridge: Cambridge Scholars Publishing.

——, 2019. *Islands in a Cosmopolitan Sea: A History of the Comoros.* London: Hurst & Company.

Warrington, E., and D. Milne. 2007. 'Island Governance'. In Baldacchino (ed.) 2007: 379–427.

Wille, B. 2018. 'Big Men Politics and Insularity in the Maldivian World of Islands'. In Schnepel and Alpers (eds.) 2018: 289–317.

Wynne-Jones, S., and A. LaViolette (eds.). 2018. *The Swahili World.* New York: Routledge.

CHAPTER 3

'Not the Greatest Villains': Piracy in the Southwestern Indian Ocean (*c.* 1680-1750)[1]

INTRODUCTION

This chapter is about 'maritime violence' (Risso 2001), to begin by using a neutral concept. More specifically, it is about those manifestations of maritime violence which have been labelled, less neutrally, 'piracy' – that is, piracy in the old-fashioned sense of the term, namely to enter another vessel against the will of its crew and to rob it of its cargo and/or hold it ransom.[2] But inevitably this chapter also asks the question of who saw whom as a pirate, whereas other individuals resorting to a similar sort of maritime violence were not regarded as such. Hence, it is about the power to define and judge some forms of maritime violence as rightful and legitimate, others not. Finally, and most importantly, the present chapter examines the nature of the delicate, but more often than not intimate relationship and entanglement between pirates and piracy on the one hand, and those agents and activities on the sea and the coasts that were (considered) more legitimate on the other. I shall concentrate my investigation on European and American pirates operating in the southwestern Indian Ocean from around 1680 to 1750.

Piracy, both as a social practice and as an important trope in discourses of maritime power and marginality, is a global phenomenon that can be found on all oceans and seas during all historical periods. It exists in all places and at all times when and where maritime movements acquire a certain frequency and there is some value in the goods being transported.[3] Piracy as such is a multifaceted and dynamically shifting phenomenon and activity. It is not always nor even often possible to identify with ultimate clarity who is, was, and will be a pirate. Some individuals started their careers as ruthless and infamous pirates, only to find themselves, a little later, installed by King or Company as high-ranking captains or even governors tasked with fighting and stamping out piracy or attacking enemies. In numerous other cases, seamen were officially authorized and commissioned by their kings, governments, or trading companies to enter other ships forcibly and rob them, as long as these ships were of the right, that is, of enemy nationality or company affiliation. These men and their crews – one could almost call them a special kind of 'trading company'[4] – were then seen by those who commissioned them not as pirates but as privateers, corsairs, and even freedom fighters. However, the same persons who were considered legal and even glorified by one party were, from a different perspective – for example, if they transgressed their erstwhile commission and attacked the wrong boats – despised as and declared to be pirates and sea bandits, not only by other parties but also by their erstwhile patrons. At certain times and in certain places – either when economic fortunes had changed or if natural catastrophes had made life unbearable – the crews of whole ships and whole coastal or island communities could turn from being respected crews, merchants or fishing communities to being pirates, while their merchant or fishing vessels were turned into pirate boats and their villages or coasts into 'nests of piracy'.[5] Even whole nations or their companies – for example, the Dutch and their *Vereenigde Oostindische Compagnie* in the South China Sea during the seventeenth century – in a strange legal interpretation of what a *Mare Liberum* had to offer,[6] took to capturing and looting other vessels (in this instance, Spanish galleons or Chinese junks), killing or enslaving their passengers, and thus establishing, in their view, a legitimate sideline in trade and commercial ambitions.[7] 'The perception of piracy', as Alpers (2011: 18) aptly puts it, 'is essentially in the eye of the beholder'. Consequently, declaring a given seaman a 'pirate' or a certain manifestation of maritime violence to be 'piracy' is contested. As such it is relative to the situation and perspective of the person who defines or, better, has the power to define another person as a pirate.[8]

Alpers takes a step further in interpreting the matter, arguing that 'what outside observers call "piracy" is a consequence of exclusion from the international trade networks and access to the wealth produced by those who dominate them' (ibid.). He also suggests that 'piracy reflects the prevailing political economy and the relative placement of those who dominate any system and those who believe that they are either being marginalized by the existing relations of power or that they can break into it by force' (ibid.). Alpers concludes that piracy is 'an independent phenomenon that grows out of a process of exclusion from the dominant commercial exchange systems of the region' (ibid.: 33). This chapter, by extending and further qualifying this view, rather than simply contradicting it, aims to demonstrate that, at least at certain times and in certain places, piracy must be understood as more than just an expression and result of real and discursive exclusion. One has to question the bipolarity inherent in such statements and relativize the implied dichotomy between those who have power and are considered legal and those who lack power and are not recognized as legal. Rather, there were times and places in which the phenomenon of piracy was deeply integrated into established overseas systems of trade, credit, commerce and rule. Piracy in these specific spatiotemporal figurations, I shall argue, participated in and contributed to the emergence and stabilization of the power of those who dominated maritime trade and its hubs. In a nutshell, in some (significant) instances, piracy acted in support of those established networks across the sea, of those who built forts and factories and eventually established colonies. Piracy could be and often was 'translated' into an activity that became a useful aid in, and even an essential part of, the dominant maritime trade and the colonializing project to which this trade was geared.

In the last decade, historians and ethnohistorians have intensively searched colonial and national archives in London, Cape Town, Aix-en-Provence, Réunion, Mauritius, and elsewhere for more information on piracy in the southwestern Indian Ocean of around 1700. It is mainly on these painstaking studies by Alpers (2011), Bialuschewski (2005), Carter (2009), Ellis (2007), Hooper (2011), and others (to be mentioned in the footnotes) that the present endeavour to assess the pirates' functional role in connectivity across the Indian Ocean is based. My aim here is less to present a further contribution to this historiography than to use the available published data to discuss the theme of 'connectivity in motion' in the Indian Ocean world, and to do so from the margins, so to say.

EX-PIRATES OF THE CARIBBEAN, NEW PIRATES OF THE INDIAN OCEAN

The particular manifestation of the universal phenomenon of piracy addressed here refers to the southwestern part of the Indian Ocean during the late seventeenth and early to mid-eighteenth centuries. Piracy in this period and this part of the Indian Ocean, quite astonishingly at first glance, had its roots in the Atlantic and Caribbean. In these latter regions, pirates like Henry Morgan, Monbars 'the Exterminator', Edward Teach, and other men (and sometimes women) found easy prey in the Spanish, French, and English galleons that were traversing the Atlantic Ocean to and from their American colonies. While pirate ships also took part in and aided more 'regular' business ventures such as the slave trade from West Africa across the 'Black Atlantic' (Gilroy 1993), by and large they increasingly came to be regarded as a serious menace to the established trade and to the companies or nations that were conducting it. Hence, since from the turn of the century onwards, England, Spain, and France, as well as their Caribbean and North American dependencies, were making great efforts to stamp out unlicensed piracy in the West Indies and the wider Atlantic.[9] These efforts were enacted with such determination and led to so many losses on the pirates' side that they started to look for new 'pastures' in a move which Sellström characterizes as an 'extraordinary manifestation of the process of globalization' (2015: 12). Many of these adventurers, such as the Anglo-American pirates Henry Bowen, Henry Avery, William Kidd, and Thomas Tew, or the French pirates Oliver Misson and Oliver le Vasseur, chose the northern bays of Madagascar, especially the tiny island of Sainte Marie (Nosy Boraha), as well as the Mascarenes, the Comoros, and the Seychelles, as their main new bases. From there they started their raids on vessels of the Portuguese crown and of the Dutch, French, and English East India Companies. They also targeted the ships of the Indian Moghuls with pilgrims and riches plying between Surat and Jeddah, of which there were around two dozen a year and which yielded valuable booty.

All in all, the ex-pirates of the Caribbean and the new pirates of the western Indian Ocean found that the Indian Ocean had enough to offer to compensate them for their losses on the Atlantic trade route. By the end of the seventeenth century, the shipping lanes of the Indian Ocean were so well frequented with ships carrying such valuable cargoes that what some interpreters have seen as the pirates' 'flight' from the Caribbean could also be viewed as a turn to richer pastures that held out the promise of great 'prizes'.[10]

But let us look at the exemplary life histories of some of these pirates in greater detail.[11]

William Kidd

William Kidd started his career in the 1680s as a merchant and maritime trader. During the 'Nine-Year War' from 1688 to 1697, the English admiralty issued him with letters of marque as a privateer authorizing him to prey on French ships. In 1696, he was commissioned by Lord Bellamont, the then English Governor of New York and Massachusetts (and was supported financially by other high-ranking politicians and businessmen from the heart of the London establishment) to become a privateer. This time, however, he was given the explicit commission to hunt down not French merchant and navy vessels, but Anglo-American pirates like Henry Avery, who, in 1696, had attacked two large and richly laden Moghul ships in the Arabian Sea and thus jeopardized the East India Company's more regular business ventures in India.[12] However, the detailed instructions Kidd received were dubious, to say the least, because it turned out that one principal desire of these people of standing was not to stamp out piracy so much as to get for themselves some of the immense riches which the pirates of the Indian Ocean had acquired. Kidd, in the scheme of his bourgeois patrons, was to be a pirate against pirates.

On his way from New England into the Indian Ocean, however, Kidd not only changed the ocean of his activity, he also stepped over the line from privateer to pirate by attacking the Moghul pilgrim fleet himself, as well as ships which to his mind were French, but in fact were conducting Indian and English commerce. While roaming around the northwestern part of the Indian Ocean, at one point Kidd is reported to have stopped at the Laccadive Islands, where he and his men enslaved some male islanders to do menial and repair work on their ship, while torturing, raping, and killing other inhabitants of these islands. Yet again the Great Moghul not only complained bitterly to the English East India Company, but also had them compensate him for his losses. This, finally, stirred up the English East India Company and the politico-economic elite back in London, who saw their Indian assets dwindling, and they therefore decided to make a scapegoat of Kidd. When a general amnesty for pirates was issued in 1698, Kidd was omitted by name, and governors all over the then fledgling British Empire were ordered to capture him. On returning home to America, Kidd learnt of this decree, but apparently could not believe it, mistakenly trusting in his high-ranking, erstwhile supporters. He was duly arrested in Boston in July 1699 and hanged at Execution Dock, London, in May 1701.[13]

William Kidd is one eye-opening example of an individual who, like so many others, crossed the lines between trader, slave-trader (with and without concession), high-ranking officer on navy and merchant vessels, privateer with a license to attack enemy ships, and privateer to hunt down pirates and stamp out piracy, to become finally a pirate on the gallows himself. What is particularly remarkable in his case is how deeply entangled the activities of this merchant-turned-privateer-turned-pirate were with the activities of the political and economic elite in England and New England, without whose commissions and financial backing he could not have equipped and manned his ship. The fact that he did not manage to return to 'civilian' life was due less to what he actually did than to the fact that he attacked the wrong ships at the wrong time. When his erstwhile supporters from the heart of society and the politico-economic world came under public attack back home because of the dubious commissions they had authorized, they found it wiser not to support Kidd during his almost two years of imprisonment and legal struggle, but to let him hang and thus be silenced.

John Bowen

One prime case illustrating the fact that even freebooters and anarchists of a special kind needed a hub, and that islands such as Mauritius were ready to provide this function, can be found in the person of the Anglo-American pirate John Bowen. Bowen was born in Bermuda in 1660 and subsequently started his 'career' as a pirate in the Caribbean. At the turn of the century, he and his companions transferred the major field of their activities to the Indian Ocean. Here Bowen, on board a vessel called the *Speaker*, captured numerous English, French, Portuguese, and Arab vessels, especially along the west coast of India. That this coast of the Moghul empire was not only good for 'enter-prizes', but also for selling one's booty to local Indian and Dutch merchants and for re-equipping oneself through them is captured in the following lines of Defoe:

> The Pyrates here met with no Manner of Inconveniences in carrying on their Designs, for it was made so much a Trade, that the Merchants of one Town never scrupled the buying Commodities taken from another, tho' but ten miles distant, in a publick Sale, furnishing the Robbers at the time with all Necessaries, even of Vessels, when they had Occasion to go on any Expedition, which they themselves would often advise them of. (1972 [1724]: 452)

At one point, however, Bowen decided to abandon this bountiful region and to steer for the safer havens of Madagascar, where the following events, reconstructed by Piat (2007), took place:

> At the beginning of January 1702, the *Speaker* came up against a violent cyclone in the region of the Mascarene Islands and on 7 January captain BOWEN was in great difficulties off the south-east coast of Mauritius. Despite his efforts, he could not manage to save his ship from the raging seas and the *Speaker* was shipwrecked on the reef off the mouth of the Grand Rivière Sud Est, close to Roches islet. Aboard were 170 pirates and 30 Arab captives. They built rafts, and all made it to the shore in possession of their weapons. They set up camp a few kilometres from the lodge of the Dutch governor, Roelof Deodati and killed three oxen for dinner (. . .). In the meantime, the governor who had been informed of the situation, had to accept the obvious, that, with the 52 men at his disposal, he had very little margin for negotiation. The governor therefore authorized the Dutch colonists to sell food to the pirates and to behave 'as friends' towards them, lest the worst should happen. Treatment was provided to the injured as part of an impromptu understanding. (ibid.: 21, his emphasis)

In the words of Defoe, the hospitality of the Dutch appears to have been even more pronounced:

They met here with all the Civility and Good Treatment imaginable; *Bowen* was complimented in a particular Manner by the Governor, and splendidly entertained in his House; the sick Men were got, with great Care, into the Fort, and cured by their Doctor, and no Supplies of any sort wanting for the rest. (1972 [1724]: 452–3, his emphasis)

For his further journey west, the Dutch governor of Mauritius sold Bowen and his companions a boat and 'supply'd them with Necessaries for their Voyage (. . .) and gave them a kind Invitation to make that Island a Place of Refreshment in the Course of their future Adventures, promising that nothing should be wanting to them that his Government afforded' (ibid.: 453).

Some months later, after a brief stay on Madagascar, Bowen landed on Île Bourbon (Réunion), 'where on 19 August 1702, under pressure of numbers, the colonists supplied him with water and food for payment, in spite of Governor Villers' ban on trade with pirates' (Piat 2007: 23). In the early months of 1704, Bowen and his men once again chose to stay on Mauritius for several weeks. They did so close to the Dutch governor's fort, and again relations between the colonists and the pirates were peaceful, even amicable, during the pirates' two-month stay. 'All transactions were duly paid for', as Piat (ibid.: 21) emphasizes. One must ask why in this case the attitude of pirates towards the Dutch colonizers varied from that exhibited by Kidd and his men toward the inhabitants of the Laccadives. Was Kidd just more reckless and ruthless than Bowen and others? This must be doubted because in other instances Bowen and his fellow pirates did not hesitate to kill, torture, and rape as well. Were the Dutch colonialists and soldiers on Mauritius too powerful to be attacked and killed? This must also be doubted. Bowen and his men could easily have gained the upper hand had they wanted to. Was it less the force available locally which made the pirates hesitate to attack the Dutch settlers than the knowledge that all over the Indian Ocean the Dutch were represented by powerful ships and forts that could make pirate activity difficult and dangerous if Dutch citizens were harmed elsewhere, as on Mauritius? This is a possible explanation, especially given the occasional alliances negotiated between the Dutch and the English in the Indian Ocean. And the English, as also the French, would have taken the attack on Dutch settlers as a more general threat to their colonizing ambitions in the macro-region. But one must also assume that both sides, not only the pirates, had an interest in conducting and upholding the principle of proper and non-violent barter and trade on land, which was to their mutual benefit.[14]

In April 1704, Bowen and his men sailed from Mauritius to Île Bourbon, where they laid down their arms and agreed to several conditions demanded by Governor Villers with the intention of starting settled life there. One must assume that this move from (still) Dutch Mauritius to French Île Bourbon was not unprepared; maybe some communication about Bowen's plans had taken place beforehand. And the move was successful. Many of these former pirates settled down, married, and had children, their descendants being numerous and noticeable on Réunion up to the present day. Bowen himself, however, died without issue soon after settling down.[15]

Christopher Condent

A further example of how porous the boundaries between pirate crews and settler communities could prove to be is provided by the life story of Christopher Condent, yet another pirate of English origin. He first roamed the Caribbean Sea before he and his men made their way to the Indian Ocean around 1719. There he captured a number of English, Dutch, Arab, and Moghul prizes, using the isle of Sainte Marie in northern Madagascar as his base. At one point in this burdensome life, namely in 1721, it seems that he grew tired of being a pirate, so he sent a message to the governor of Île Bourbon, requesting him to grant an amnesty to himself and his 135 men (including their five dozen or so slaves). He stressed that they were willing to become good and loyal subjects of the King of France. The conditions upon which the governor and the council of Île Bourbon were willing to grant this amnesty were not acceptable to all the pirates. Apart from surrendering their weapons, they were asked to submit all slaves (except one per person) and to pay 20 piastres as a fine. In the end, apart from Condent, only 32 pirates accepted the offer. It appears that in the following year Condent acted successfully as a mediator between the governor and various pirates when it became necessary to negotiate the payment of ransoms for prisoners in pirate hands. On the island, he had a liaison with the governor's sister-in-law and even had a child with her. But in 1722 Condent eventually decided to go to France, where he married a woman from a respected merchant family of Lorient, henceforth leading a life as a wealthy *armateur* until his peaceful death in 1734. What is striking in Condent's example, then, is the fact that we find here a case of 'transnationalism': Condent, an English pirate, became a respectable French citizen. And this shift in national identity took place not on the periphery of the kingdom, i.e. on Île Bourbon, but in one of its then colonial centres, namely in the major port city of Lorient in Brittany.[16]

Oliver Le Vasseur

At around Condent's time, Madagascar and the Mascarenes also provided bases for the actions of one of the most myth-enshrouded of all pirates in the southwestern Indian Ocean during this period, the French pirate Oliver le Vasseur, also known as 'La Buse'. Like so many other pirates of his time, La Buse arrived in the Indian Ocean – in his case, in 1720 – from the Caribbean, with a short interim stay on the coasts of West Africa and Brazil. One of the most spectacular prizes he acquired was a magnificent vessel belonging to the Portuguese crown, the *Nostra Senhora de Cabo*. This ship, with immense riches on board, was lying in the harbour of Saint-Paul, Île Bourbon. While large numbers of the crew were on land, with the Portuguese captain and many other dignitaries of the vessel staying as guests with the island's French governor, Vasseur and another pirate captain named Taylor attacked the Portuguese vessel and made off with tremendous booty worth several million Euros if translated into today's currency. The Portuguese Count of Ericiera, who was also the Viceroy of Portuguese India at that time, was among those who were captured, but later set free for a rather modest ransom (negotiated through Condent). La Buse and Taylor took the Portuguese vessel back to Madagascar, where they divided up the spoils. They captured other vessels, including French ones, during the next couple of years, until the two men parted over a quarrel, with Taylor returning to the Caribbean, while La Buse stayed on in Madagascar and in the vicinity of Île Bourbon. When the Île Bourbon governor Boucher-Desforges offered him an amnesty in 1724, La Buse rejected it, by contrast to other pirates of the time and region who accepted similar offers. In 1727, a new governor, Pierre Benoist, decided to put an end to piracy. He sent a well-armed vessel under the command of Captain L'Hermitte to Sainte Marie with an order to arrest La Buse. This having been accomplished, La Buse was taken to Réunion and there sentenced to death by hanging, carried out in July 1730 in the public square of Saint-Paul. Walking towards the gallows, La Buse made hints to the crowd concerning the place where he had hidden his immense treasure. But these hints were so vague that, despite the feverish efforts of innumerable treasure hunters over many generations, this treasure has still not been found.[17]

PIRATES ON THE MASCARENES

These glimpses of the life histories of a few pirates operating in the southwestern Indian Ocean in the decades before and after 1700 must suffice at this point so that some more general, yet preliminary observations can be made, especially with regard to the entanglements of pirates with the early settler colonies of Île Bourbon (later Réunion) and Île de France (earlier and later Mauritius).

When on land, so it transpires from the preceding accounts, pirates preferred to stay in hidden and remote bays such as those provided by the Malagasy coasts or on small uninhabited or only sparsely inhabited islands like the Mascarenes.[18] In this southwestern part of the Indian Ocean there were as yet no strong states, native or foreign, which could endanger pirate activities too much, but quite frequently there were native communities or incipient settler colonies just around the corner. Often it was advantageous for both sides to trade with each other and to establish and maintain regular and 'friendly' forms of interaction. From the indigenous communities' and settlers' point of view, it was of course preferable to keep these heavily armed and militarily well-trained men at some distance (to keep them *at bay*, so to say). However, on land, pirates had the same needs as other seafarers after a long and hazardous journey. Their crews had to recover from the often Spartan and brutal life at sea, some of them needed medical treatment for wounds or sickness, and they had to be housed and provided with food, water, alcohol, and other amenities. Taverns and brothels were needed to offer physical and mental relief. Gambling provided a welcome opportunity to redouble one's booty or to lose it faster than it had been won. Warehouses of a kind opened, and landed merchants offered enticements and opportunities to spend or sell one's loot. The boats had to be careened for cleaning, caulking, and repair, for the execution of which local carpenters and other handymen offered their services; and, of course, before departure these vessels had to be equipped anew, not only with all the available basic and possibly some luxury provisions such as wine, but also with gunpowder and with new, booty-thirsty crew members for the next expedition.

All these 'necessaries' (as Defoe calls them) were regularly bought and duly paid for by the pirates, just as any other seafarers and merchants would have done. During their stays on land, then, these fierce individuals and communities, who did not hesitate to murder when at sea, were often remarkably observant of the rules that governed the more civil economic and social life on the fringes and in the interstices of the emerging colonial empires and the native Indian Ocean world. Trading and barter activities with pirates could give a considerable boost to the local economies, 'shadow' or otherwise, of the indigenous or settler communities involved. This economic impact acquired greater dimensions if one considers the fact that, in contrast to popular belief, pirates were not really in the habit of burying their treasure in places where no one could later find it again. The greater part of the booty of pirate activity was sold, used in exchange for goods that were needed, or invested in some way or another. Through further transactions by visiting traders, this booty, especially that consisting of gold, silver, pearls, luxury commodities, money, or spices, entered and dynamically stimulated long-distance commercial networks and thus the wider world of the Indian Ocean in this age of global mercantilism and commerce.

For the pirates, settled life was not without its attractions, especially the older and weaker they became. There are stories of whole pirate communities who attempted to settle down and establish fortified villages or even to create their own utopian free republics.[19] Repeatedly, we hear of European admiralties, local governors, or commanders-in-chief granting amnesties to whole groups of pirates who had laid down their arms, asked for pardon, and expressed their wish to return to respectable settled life. One must bear in mind that Île Bourbon, one of the incipient settler communities at that time and in this region offering such possibilities of retreat from a life of piracy, was only sparsely inhabited. The settler community consisted of some immigrants who had come directly from Brittany and other parts of France, while others were the remnants of French settlers who had had to flee from Madagascar in the 1670s after native onslaughts upon them. Occasionally, French settlers also returned from India to establish life on Île Bourbon. In this situation, governors, settlers, and the small slave population of that time were not in a very strong position and not always willing to offer any opposition to pirates appearing on their island. Some of these pirates just came to visit and replenish men and materials for further raids at sea, while others came to stay, as happened in 1687, when Avery and his crew, laden with gold and other riches (including a Moghul princess), made a stop at Île Bourbon. A number of them settled on the island, while Avery went on with his trade.[20] In 1695 and 1704, when two large groups of pirates disembarked – the latter, as already mentioned, led by John Bowen – they were granted an amnesty and became settlers.[21] These men not only provided sheer manpower to the island, namely their own labour and that of the slaves they brought with them and continued to bring in through their 'brethren' left behind on Madagascar, they also possessed much needed crafts and skills (including military skills and skills as mediators between white settlers and other pirates, as well as Malagasy natives). They also brought financial resources to Île Bourbon that could be invested in the infrastructure and, last but not least, they started families. All in all, the influx of 'pirate blood' into the embryonic colony of Île Bourbon was so substantial that it is estimated that 'around three-quarters of the present-day "white" population of Réunion have pirate forebears' (Carter 2009: 59). Establishing good relations with pirates, and even turning them into settlers, was thus a matter of killing two birds with one stone: to get rid of piracy, which was becoming increasingly detrimental to the colonializing project, and to find new settlers.

While the initial settlers on Île Bourbon were always eager not to fight the pirates arriving on their shores, but to conduct business with them and integrate them, the attitude of the island's governors was more ambivalent. Officially, they had to fight these men and forbid their settlers from dealing with them, but in practice they turned a blind eye to such interactions, tolerated them, and even tried to come to terms with the pirates themselves and conduct business with them. This ambivalence was reduced when, in 1716, the Navy Council back home in France also came to realize that pirates had potential in terms of France's colonizing ambitions and granted a general amnesty to those who were willing to lay down their arms.[22] It is remarkable that even Christian missionaries seem to have had a share in the shadow economy provided by the pirates, not to mention the fact that ex-pirates often adopted the Christian faith and became respected members not only of the settler communities, but also of the newly founded colonial parishes. When some of the Île Bourbon priests and missionaries objected to the general amnesty for pirates, they were reminded in no uncertain terms of these facts and thus made to look hypocritical.[23]

Around 1700, another only sparsely populated island was Dutch Mauritius. At any time there would not have been more than two dozen company servants and an even smaller number of slaves, besides the settler population of a few dozen. As we have seen, this island was also visited by pirates, who outnumbered and out-gunned the embryonic Dutch community. However, as long as they were left unmolested by *Vereenigde Oostindische Compagnie* officials and their soldiers, the pirates had little interest in overrunning the Dutch community. As already noted, this may have been out of fear that the *Vereenigde Oostindische Compagnie*, which was more aggressive elsewhere (especially at the Cape), might take revenge on them or even hunt them down. Furthermore, even from the most ruthless pirate's point of view it would have been disadvantageous to kill the colonists, who not only promised a temporary source of supplies then but also a constant supply in the future, and the colonists even welcomed the pirates to return. In any case, there was not much to gain: the Dutch colony itself was struggling hard to survive in the face of rats, cyclones, and absconded slaves, which posed various threats to its very existence. The *Vereenigde Oostindische Compagnie* continued to keep the island for fear of others making use of its undoubted strategic potential. However, in 1708 the Company's board, the *Heeren XVII* in Amsterdam, decided to give up the colony, a decree which, as mentioned before, was put into effect in 1710. In 1721, after a period of desolation, the French took over. In fact, the first colonizers on Île de France consisted of a small contingent of officials and settlers, including ex-pirates, from Île Bourbon.[24]

PIRATES ON MADAGASCAR

The history of piracy in the southwestern Indian Ocean cannot be told without making Madagascar the focus of attention. During the sixteenth century, the indigenous Malagasy population had already established some sort of trading contacts with Portuguese, Dutch, English, and French traders and sailors, who started to introduce cloth, silver, muskets, copper wire, glass beads, and other items into the island's economy. Madagascar had vital things to offer for the immediate needs of ships passing by: water, rice, beans, beef, yams, taro, poultry, lemons and oranges (soon found to be good remedies against scurvy), and many other much needed provisions, as well as wood and other materials for repairing the ships. However, the first European sailors during the sixteenth century, who were heading for India and the Spice Islands further east in search of only the greatest promises of wealth, were soon convinced that the island's other attractions and riches were too small (or even non-existent, as in the case of precious metals or spices) to compensate them for the heavy losses they made when trying to establish more permanent trading posts on the island. So, by the end of the sixteenth century and the beginning of the seventeenth, the Portuguese and the Dutch, after some rather fitful attempts to establish forts and trading posts on the world's fourth largest island, had still not managed to establish permanent trading posts or even forts and factories there.[25]

The seventeenth century saw various more serious endeavours by France and England to establish not only short-lived trading posts but permanent settler colonies on the island. All these attempts eventually failed and even ended in disaster for the colonizers, leaving thousands of them dead.[26] Malaria, dysentery, fever, extreme tropical humidity, unbelievable incompetence and arrogance in the colonial administration, and most of all the failure to create good relations with the neighbouring Malagasy communities were the main factors in not being able to establish lasting European settlements on the island. In addition, Europeans also had to face the fact that, in the second half of the seventeenth century, powerful kingdoms developed in the island's south and west, most notably the Sakalava kingdom, which were well able to demand high prices and/or expel unwelcome visitors and settlers. Ironically enough, this emergence of powerful opponents of European colonization was more or less the result of early contacts with the Arabian and European traders themselves. These contacts allowed some local rulers to achieve wealth and obtain firearms and thus to gain the upper hand against neighbouring chiefdoms and to unite the traditionally small and scattered local polities of Madagascar into larger politico-military units. Certainly, trade with Arabs and Europeans did not initiate fighting and cattle raids among the Malagasies, which seem to have been endemic on the island already, but it intensified and drastically changed the character of these quarrels and fights. Small-scale and brief feuds, fought against the background of an approximate equilibrium of power between structurally opposed petty polities, changed into warfare in which one opponent tried to defeat the other in order to extend his rule and dominion at the latter's expense.[27]

Yet, ever-increasing European settler colonies at the Cape, on the Mozambique coast, and most of all on the nearby Mascarenes, as well as the mounting traffic passing Madagascar on its way to and from India and Indonesia, led to several bays and harbours on Madagascar gradually developing into quite stable ports of call for European ships. Therefore, at the time of the arrival of Euro-American pirates in the second half of the seventeenth century, Madagascar had already become partially integrated into the Indian Ocean sphere of trade, commerce, credit, and socio-cultural exchange. This was even more the case because, apart from the basic provisions it had to offer to sailors and nearby colonies, Madagascar finally had a valuable commodity to offer in that it became an apparently unlimited reservoir for the Europeans' demand for slaves with whom to build up tropical colonies and plantation economies. In this trade with slaves, some

Malagasy rulers functioned as significant slave-raiders in the island's interior and as traders at their ports.[28]

Euro-American pirates from the Atlantic and Caribbean, arriving in their new ocean of choice, more often than not chose the northeast coast of Madagascar, especially the Bay of Antongil and the islet of Sainte Marie, for their bases.[29] This was one part of Madagascar where natural conditions were relatively good, both for those staying on land, seeking concealment and retirement of some sort, and for those wishing to arrive and depart safely with their marauding ships. Furthermore, in this part of the island neither the Sakalava nor the colonial powers had made their presence felt to such a degree as to seriously impede pirate activity. Take the example of Commodore Thomas Mathews, who in 1722 was sent by the English East India Company to Madagascar with four warships specifically to hunt down pirates. However, he found that the pirates' defences and fire power were too strong for him to overcome. Furthermore, and maybe more importantly, pirates had something to offer in terms of profitable trade. So, in another fine example of the entanglement of pirates with apparently more legitimate, even anti-pirate authorities, Mathews started trading rum and clothes for cattle and precious metals from the pirates and then returned to India a richer man.[30]

One indicator of the fact that, in the decade before Mathew's trade with them, the pirates of Île Sainte Marie had already begun to participate strongly in the long-distance, even global commercial networks of that time are the reports we have of American merchants living there in order to conduct their trade at the source of the profits, so to speak, thus seeking to avoid the restrictive tolls and policies of their English masters. According to Ellis:

> Some of the pirates who established themselves in Madagascar retained the links established during the heyday of Caribbean piracy with investors in New York, who had spotted in Madagascar's location a means of circumventing the monopoly on the supply of slaves to North America held until 1698 by England's Royal African Company. The leading financier of the Madagascar pirates was Frederick Philipse (1626–1702), a Dutchman who had settled in New York and had worked his way up to become one of its leading investors and entrepreneurs. In 1691, Philipse dispatched an agent, Adam Baldridge, to set up a trading-station in Madagascar on the island of

Sainte-Marie. Baldridge became a broker for many of the pirate networks. (2007: 445–6)

Baldridge is known to have turned from trader to pirate and even to 'little king' himself. On top of these activities he married Malagasy women and left 'mulatto' offspring on the island before returning to America.[31] On account of these direct involvements between pirates and American merchants, it might even be argued that Euro-American piracy in the southwestern Indian Ocean was heavily sponsored by New England. In this sense, pirates and their trading contacts were spearheading the proto-globalization of that time.[32]

The indigenous political situation that pirates confronted in the Bay of Antongil, as well as on the neighbouring littoral and island world, was characterized by the existence of segmentary lineage systems, similar to the 'model' so systematically described by Evans-Pritchard and others.[33] However, these Malagasy lineage systems were not acephalous. Rather, in the northeastern part of Madagascar, there had by now also developed a large number of local chiefdoms (emerging from and dominating the kinship-based clan-systems) headed by elders, local potentates, warlords, and even (little) kings. In contrast to the Malagasy kingdoms of the south and the Sakalava kingdom of the west, however, these local Malagasy polities in the northeast tended to be small, often consisting of no more than a few villages, and the power of their chiefs was rather limited.

For these northeastern Malagasy rulers of various kinds, pirates must at first have been barely distinguishable from the other foreigners who had reached their coasts earlier. They had the same demands for necessities as any seafarer after a long journey around the Cape. But in their wilder appearance and less disciplined behaviour, pirates will also have been visibly different from the captains and crews of Company ships and royal ships. Also, their precarious legal situation vis-à-vis the latter was quickly noticeable in their well-armed and fortified hide-outs, as well as in the sudden riches they continued to bring on to Malagasy shores. After some initial hesitation, barter and other more routine economic exchanges between the pirates and the indigenous communities started to flourish, with advantages for both sides. Local rulers provided food and also slaves who could be sold on by the pirates. The latter, in return, had not only weapons to offer the local rulers, but their own fierceness and fighting power as well, which could make a decisive difference to local potentates in their internal power struggles.

Socially and culturally, the entanglement between pirates and Malagasy locals grew day by day. Some pirates decided to stay on land for longer times or even permanently. They learnt the local language and acquired other bits of local knowledge, which helped them and their confrères in their dealings with the natives and which, in external matters, turned them into well-versed mediators between European and Malagasy agents. More and more pirates also started amorous and even marital relationships with Malagasy women, resulting in offspring and stable families of mixed pirate and Malagasy descent. The children of these unions became known as 'Zana Malata' or 'Mulatto Children'.[34] As not a few of the pirates' wives were the daughters of high-status local chiefs, in the indigenous kinship system Zana Malata came to acquire the status of daughters' sons, while the ever-growing community of Zana Malata chiefs had the traditionally supportive position of direct or classificatory maternal uncles to members of the indigenous population. While one could then well argue, with Bialuschewski (2005: 419), that the first decade of the eighteenth century saw 'the end of the pirate era' on Madagascar, their offspring with local women continued to wield considerable influence in the island's internal and external affairs.

KING RATSIMILAHOE AND PRINCESS BETI

The maritime trade in cattle, rice, fruit, and slaves, as well as the growing stability of pirate and especially Zana Malata life on the island, finally led to gradual changes in the equilibrium of power within the fragmented northeastern Malagasy political world. The weapons and gunpowder that were acquired by some local rulers, mostly by those who controlled regions with a port or at least a suitable place for anchorage, increased their military strength, which could be used against neighbouring contenders in their struggles for resources and power. So, internal Malagasy fighting over access to ports and thus to these lucrative new trading opportunities increased, with the result that the internal balance of power turned out to be to the advantage of those who profited more from the trade and military alliances with the pirates and Zana Malata. Consequently, ever larger, more centralized and more powerful chiefdoms, which could be labelled 'early kingdoms' or 'segmentary states',[35] arose in this part of the island, some of which were headed by Zana Malata.

As is so often the case worldwide, slow and gradual processes of state formation experience a sudden boost when military events and conquering ambitions come to a peak. In the early eighteenth century, this is what happened on the eastern shores of Madagascar, where the more important ports like Tamatave, Foulpointe, and Fénérive just south of the Bay of Antongil came under attack and were forcefully captured by a confederation of chiefs of the southern-based Bentanimena ethnic group, initially also known as Tsikoa ('The Invincible'). The political and military unification of the northern Antavaratra clans and chiefs, which became indispensable against these attacks from the south, was achieved by a young charismatic warrior named Ratsimilahoe, who in 1712 inflicted a decisive victory on the (now no longer) 'Invincibles', whose soldiers were killed or fled the area. But Ratsimilahoe was not only successful militarily. By a number of politically astute moves, he managed to incorporate allied chiefs, as well as formerly hostile chiefs of the Bentanimena, into a new kingdom founded under his rule, which eventually occupied approximately 600 kilometres of the east Malagasy coast. This socially, culturally and politically quite diverse and even heterogeneous kingdom was called 'Betsimisaraka' or 'The Indivisible-Many'. However, while this confederation thrived with Ratsimilahoe on its throne in its capital at Foulpointe, after his death in 1750 the multi-centred kingdom soon disintegrated into its component parts under his successors.[36]

Perhaps unsurprisingly, the founder and head of this kingdom, Ratsimilahoe, was a Zana Malata, the son of a local princess and an English pirate called Tom.[37] It seems that, in his youth, not only did Ratsimilahoe learn the ways of both the Malagasy and the pirates, but also that his father took him to England and India, where he received some kind of education. During the war against the southern invaders, as already noted, Ratsimilahoe proved himself most capable in fighting and in organizing the northern confederation into a powerful, united force. Thereafter, he and his allies (and some of his former enemies) formed a vigorous, though short-lived kingdom. In a clever move of internal diplomacy, Ratsimilahoe also married a daughter of the powerful Sakalava king Toakafo, with whom he had a son called Zanahary. In 1735, he also had a daughter, called Beti, with another local Malagasy woman.[38] At Ratsimilahoe's death the kingdom seems to have been divided between his son Zanahary, based in Foulpointe, and his daughter Beti, who had her 'palace' on Sainte Marie Island. Both vied, separately and jointly, for a closer alliance with the French colony on Île de France, which in the meantime had been chosen by the *Compagnie des Indes Orientales* as its *chef-lieu* in this part of the Indian Ocean. It was on account of this newly emerging and ever-growing French colony and its ever-increasing demands for provisions that the centre of the Malagasy trade in food and slaves had shifted during Ratsimilahoe's rule, from Swahili and Sakalava hands on Madagascar's northwestern coast to its more convenient north-eastern coast and thus into Betsimisaraka and Zana Malata hands.[39] Beti is reported to have offered her islet kingdom to the French as a new colony. It is reported that soon after some sort of agreement had been reached between Beti and twenty-nine Betsimisaraka chiefs, on the one hand, and a French deputation headed by the Company agent Guillaume Gosse, on the other, the leading French officer and fourteen of his companions were killed in a revolt by Betsimisaraka warriors against Beti's intentions.

After these events in September 1750, the further history of Princess Beti is shrouded in a degree of romantic mystery. It is reported that she started an affair with a French corporal called de Forval, who was sent from Île de France to northeastern Madagascar to take care of French interests there and re-establish peace. After an assault on his life by Betsimisaraka chiefs, who continued to oppose too direct an involvement of the French in their own political and economic affairs, Beti is even said to have saved the corporal's life, thereby putting her own life in danger and being forced to flee as de Forval's consort to the Île de France.[40] In the mid-eighteenth century the colonial community of Port Louis, the island's capital, had already experienced a degree of consolidation under the energetic colony-building efforts of Governor Mahé de Labourdonnais. He ruled the island from 1735 to 1740 and did much to improve its infrastructure and future prospects, including by drastically increasing the importation of slaves. However, while some progress was made, the settlers still lived in a rather shabby and unhealthy town. The colony could not yet be sure that it would survive. Life on Île de France was constantly threatened by cyclones, fires, epidemic diseases, rats, famines, company neglect, marooned slaves, and, last but not least, the on-going enmity with the English, whose warships more than once passed the island close by, threatening invasion.

Princess Beti's arrival and stay on the island from 1751 until her death in 1805[41] was quite remarkable and must have been a major topic of local gossip. Baron Grant, a French citizen of noble birth who was staying on Île de France in Beti's time, reports that 'her colour was certainly displeasing to the white people and her education did not qualify her to be a companion to such a man as her husband' (1801: 220–1).[42] But, as Grant continues, 'despite remonstrances of his friends, he lives happily with her' (ibid.), a blissful quasi-conjugal state which may also have been aided by the fact that Beti's 'figure was fine, her air noble, and all her actions partook of the dignity of one who was born to command' (ibid.). As Vaughan (2006: 106) puts the matter aptly: 'She was (. . .) of the right social class, even if she was of the wrong colour'.

Indeed, Beti fell between, or transgressed, all the colonial racial categories that were apparently needed to build up and administer an incipient settler colony at a time and place which was far from the current celebration of fluid identities, *créolité*, and cosmopolitanism. Beti was neither white nor black, but according to the categories in use on Mauritius at that time a member of the so-called '*gens de couleur*'. This group was small in size in Beti's time, but it was to grow ever larger the more frequent intimate relationships between white plantation owners and black slave women became. Furthermore, in a probably disturbing manner, the 'white' in Beti was, on closer inspection, not French but English in origin. In another ordering scheme, she was neither a slave nor a '*noire libre*' (i.e. there never was an act that 'emancipated' her from bondage), but born free and stayed so, just like the members of the white population of the island. In this respect, she belonged to the group of *civils blancs.* From the feudal perspective of the time, however, she was of a higher status than most of these free white citizens of Île de France, most of whom were *petits blancs,* while she was noble in blood and demeanour. For the slaves, freed slaves, and *gens de couleurs* on the island, Beti must have provoked ambivalent feelings. On the one hand she was a black woman, free and full of dignity, and thus holding a status and exhibiting a habitus which many of the black inhabitants of the island longed for and aspired to, mostly in vain. On the other hand, she was a representative of that Malagasy community which was instrumental in capturing and sending more and more slaves to the island, only to lead a most miserable life there. For the French islanders (to continue our attempt to locate Beti in the social world of her time), she posed a serious gender problem. She lived openly with a quite respected member of the French community, not just as a tacitly tolerated mistress leading a shadowy life alongside a lawful wife, as was so often the case on these 'fringes of empire' (Agha and Kolsky, eds. 2009). Instead, she was openly beautiful and self-confident, a childless woman of power and an 'Amazon' (as Grant called her) in a male-dominated settler society, in which the female ideal was to be submissive and gentle, and to bear a lot of children.[43] Furthermore, she was a heathen within an insecure and unstable natural, social, economic, and political environment, in which Catholicism soon came to play a leading social and religious role. Last but not least, she was the granddaughter of a pirate.

These and other ambiguities in the life of 'Princess Beti', as she is still remembered in Mauritius's historical imagination until today, were eventually smoothed over and even eliminated. By the time of her death, Beti had become a more suitable and more easily categorized member of Île de France colonial society. She seems to have married her French corporal, adopted the Christian faith, regularly attending church, and she acquired a considerable estate outside Port Louis, thus entering the ranks of the landed aristocracy in this newly emerging plantation economy. Finally, this granddaughter of an English pirate and a Malagasy woman was 'naturalized', that is, made a full French citizen, thus completing a three-generation translation from the 'existential mode' (Latour 2013) of a pirate into that of a Franco-Mauritian noble in exemplary fashion.[44]

PIRACY BEYOND EXCLUSION

By prominently using concepts like 'power', 'marginality', and 'exclusion' in the interpretation and analysis of piracy, as Alpers (2011) and others[45] have done, one may well be able to dispose of the essentializing view of piracy as an illegitimate activity per se. In its place, it might be possible to throw a new, more comparative and cross-cultural light on the causes of piracy and on piracy as a specific, dynamically changing figuration of maritime violence, in the production of which many diverse and even heterogeneous actors and factors are involved.

However, when piracy is seen chiefly and solely as representing the result of exclusion, one runs the opposite danger of romanticizing pirates. Piracy is then interpreted in a Hobsbawm-like manner as an expression of social banditry and as being anti-imperialist in nature, representing protest and resistance against oppressive states such as those of the Moghuls, or all too dominant maritime powers, like the Portuguese, the Dutch or the British.[46] However, this perspective and interpretational approach basically still retains the view of piracy as being outside and against the law and legitimate power. Moreover, this view obscures piracy's manifold positive and integral entanglements with those on the 'right' side of the law, i.e., exactly the sort of entanglements I seek to stress in this chapter.

Against the background of the ethnohistorical data and discussion presented above, looking at piracy as a phenomenon that lies strictly outside, and even operates against, the existing structures of power and law not only fails to grasp its complexity and ambiguity as such, it also implicitly tends to assume that the established structures of power are in themselves monolithic, homogeneous, and clearly identifiable. This, of course, is not the case. Take the state, an obvious candidate when it comes to identifying an actor that claims a monopoly of violence and thus plays perfectly what one might call for simplicity's sake 'piracy's other'. It is common knowledge – and studies from history, social anthropology, political science, and others have been at pains to show this in the minutest detail[47] – that what is regarded as *the* state is in fact a rather fragmented and multi-layered entity in which the different components more likely contest each other than work for the common good. The political situation in the macro-region of the Indian Ocean is even more complicated, not only on account of the fact that piracy typically operates on water and not on land, where the territorial integrity of one polity, and hence its traditional and legitimate realm of influence and power, is more easily defined. Rather, this ocean has connected a great number of polities, which are very different as far as their political, cultural, linguistic, economic, religious, and social constitutions are concerned.[48]

Compared to western models of mono-archy and the nation state, many of the Indian Ocean polities of the period in question are difficult to categorize when applying western models and ideals. Even on the Indian subcontinent, where the Moghuls had established a hitherto unknown concentration and spread of power, the land was still divided into numerous little kingdoms, many of which were vying to become great themselves.[49] Little kingdoms like Cochin or Calicut on the west coast of India, for example, were constantly in conflict not only with each other, but also with their 'greater' neighbours further inland. And sooner or later they tried to influence these power struggles in their favour with the aid of Muslim traders, European powers and, last but not least, pirates. Similarly in Madagascar, we find, as has been pointed out, a poly-archical system of tribes, chiefdoms, and mono-archies, in which some ethnic and neo-ethnic groups, like the Sakalava and Betsimisaraka, managed to greatly extend their dominions and spheres of influence due to contacts and trade with European powers, pirate or not.

On top of this multifaceted 'indigenous' picture of the Indian Ocean world overall, from the sixteenth century onwards various European powers entered the Indian Ocean. During the period under consideration here, these European powers, their East Indian Companies, and their settler colonies could not be at all sure that their endeavours to take part in the Indian Ocean trade and finally to establish colonies there would be successful. Even 'back home', these European kingdoms were far from stable themselves, nor was the overall political situation in Europe peaceful and settled but characterized by constant internecine dynastic wars. For a long time, the European powers and their agents in the Indian Ocean in no way represented a well-defined 'piracy's other' against the background of which piracy could unanimously be defined and dealt with.

Thus, the political arena as a whole, in which the Euro-American pirates of the southwestern Indian Ocean operated from around 1680 to 1750, was far from being unequivocal and stable. On the contrary, it was extraordinarily multilayered, polycentred, fragmented, competitive, and in great flux, both on land and at sea – in the Indian Ocean world as well as beyond. Piracy, and (ironically, but not contradictorily) the struggle against it and over the *Deutungshoheit* of who was a pirate and who was not, was one important element *within* this manifold and contested politico-economic field, *not outside* it. And within this 'within', identifying some manifestations of maritime violence as piracy (or else as not being piracy) was as complex and variable as was the world of the 'piracy's other'. This is clearly expressed by Carter when she writes:

> Pirates are one group in a range of characters inhabiting the fringes of empire whose activities are generally seen as antithetical to and obstructive of colonial state development. In practice, the role of pirates was more complex than this stereotypical appraisal suggests. At a time when European powers were vying for control of key territories in India, and yet had to establish fortified colonies along the Indian Ocean trade routes, the activities of pirates, while initially a source of harassment and irritation to settler communities, were often also harnessed to further the development of embryonic states.[50]

In strange, sometimes direct, often indirect but always dialectical ways, piracy therefore formed an integral part of the dynamically expanding early European colonization of the Indian Ocean around 1700, reflecting, of course, all the internal cleavages between the various seafaring European nations. And at least in this specific spatial-temporal context, piracy was a vital and stimulating force of 'connectivity in motion' of the Indian Ocean world and the world beyond.

SUMMARY AND CONCLUSION

(a) The life histories of pirates can only be grasped if 'the pirate' is not seen as an essentialized, outlawed manifestation of the person in the sense of the Maussian *personne morale* or of the 'social person' of orthodox British social anthropology.[51] Rather, to be a pirate or to be considered one was *only one* possible location in a conceptual space, with the statuses of pirate and governor representing the two extreme poles, while the labels privateer, freedom fighter, slaver, trader, sailor, captain, settler, merchant, and officer are some of the other possible intermediate locations in this space. For any one person or group of persons, movements within this space could quickly change direction, and he, she or they could end up at either pole or anywhere between them. The question of the legitimacy or not of a given *personne piratal* and his actions cannot be totalized, but depends on the different, situationally relative, and dynamically shifting points of view of those who had to cope with these actions and assess them.

(b) Some pirates were 'made' by the agents of colonial powers issuing *Kaperbriefe* or letters of marque authorizing some sailors to attack enemy ships, often under the obligation to hand over a specified part of the loot to those who authorized the commissions and financed the trips. These 'privateers' or pirates-turned-privateers then certainly had what could be called 'state-building' functions. At one point, however, it occurred that some of these 'privateers' could not be controlled any longer and did not function in the way that had first been intended, though the authorizing powers always had opportunities to 'un-make' these pirates and to turn them once again into privateers, legal sailors, or settlers, or else to hang them.[52]

(c) Up until the first decades of the nineteenth century, European traders and colonial officers made extensive use of pirates, remnants of former pirate communities, or descendants of pirates as local middlemen in their insatiable desire for slaves. Piracy in the south-western Indian Ocean (and elsewhere) was always linked with and ultimately turned into the slave trade, arguably the most essential trade for the early colonial project.

(d) Euro-American pirates operating in the region and period in question had many skills which were needed not only for the slave trade, but also for other, more routine commercial interactions between on the one hand local indigenous populations (as well as, of course, locally established traders of Indian, Arab, Persian, Armenian, Jewish, or other backgrounds), and on the other hand Western traders, company officials, and representatives of settler communities. Pirates, at least some of them, and later especially their mixed offspring, possessed the linguistic abilities necessary for these roles, being also experienced in the often weary and lengthy local rituals of bargaining, and they had acquired some social and political standing in the places of trade. In a nutshell, they were masters in cross-cultural encounters, possessing both the local knowledge, the status and the overseas knowledge and networks necessary to enable them to act as mediators in commercial and other affairs.[53]

(e) The settled (ex-)pirates' knowledge of indigeneity, so well exemplified by the Zana Malata on the Malagasy shores, was exploited not only in the slave and other trades, but also in achieving the wider ambition to establish colonies in new, hitherto unexplored or unconquered places, as when Princess Beti and French officers from Île de France conspired to incorporate Île Sainte Marie into the French overseas dominions.

(f) The boundaries and transitions between pirates and even pirate communities on the one hand, and European and Eurasian settler communities on the other, and thereby also the perceived borders between 'criminal' and 'legal' lives, were structurally blurred and offered many possibilities for economic and social 'transgressions' in both directions. Pirates could become respectable citizens in local indigenous or settler communities. Alternatively, ambitious young men in these communities, as well as disaffected or discharged sailors, ill-treated servants, and runaway apprentices and slaves – all in search of wealth and sometimes freedom – could join a pirate ship and become outlaws.

(g) The interaction between pirates (privateers, buccaneers, corsairs, freedom-fighters, etc.) and the representatives of the established colonial orders, both at home and in the colonies, was ambivalent, but in the end astonishingly often of mutual interest. Whole groups of pirates were granted royal pardons and thereby integrated (as individuals rather than as communities) into settler communities, where their descendants formed a substantial percentage of the population thereafter. In some cases, they were thus enabled to return to the European or North American heartlands. Pirates had many skills and assets to offer which were much needed in building up settler communities: simple labour power, the more elaborate skills of soldiers, artisans, and planters, and last but not least, considerable wealth in some cases that could be 'pumped' into the colonies' commercial transactions or into their infrastructure.[54]

(h) This usefulness of pirates also holds true for their nautical knowledge. Pirates are prime examples of trans-maritime motility, i.e., of the ability to move across the oceans and around the globe with an agility that could hardly be surpassed by any of their royal and company counterparts. They were able, sometimes very rapidly, to change their ocean of activity. In what became known as the 'pirate round', they also retained links with their erstwhile spheres of influence in the Caribbean and on the Atlantic coasts, thereby connecting the oceans through a sort of long-distance trade and socio-economic exchange: booty made in the Persian Gulf was brought to the shores and islets of Madagascar and from there sold to merchants from New England. The profits arising from these sales were exchanged for goods in high demand present and produced in the New World, such as cloths, medical supplies, food, alcohol, gunpowder, guns, and even ships. Alternatively, it might be invested 'back home'. Pirates thus formed a significant part of the maritime vanguard of proto-globalization.

To conclude, company and pirate ships alike – and the colonial officers, settlers, honest but ill-paid and badly-treated sailors, as well as despised pirates – made their way to the Indian Ocean containing and exhibiting various 'existential modes'. Occasionally, the modes of existence of pirate, trader, settler, or even indigenous littoral people existed side by side, so to speak; sometimes they swiftly changed their modalities in one direction or another, while at other times they were in conflict and even stark confrontation with each other. In the end, the confrontations certainly dominated, especially after the conflicts with the Moghuls over hijacked pilgrim ships increased. But to look at the various existential modes merely in confrontational and oppositional terms would not only mean misunderstanding the nature of the colonizing project and its moving forces, but also neglecting the vital and often integral role piracy played in this age of mercantilism and proto-globalization. One might well end this story with a quotation from Daniel Defoe, who was well aware of the hypocrisy entailed by moral statements on piracy in his own times. Asking himself whether pirates felt any remorse when dividing their spoils, Defoe held:

> I can't say, but that if they had known what was doing in England, at the same Time, by the South-Sea Directors, and their Directors, they would certainly have had this Reflection for their Consolation; viz.: that whatever Robberies they had committed, they might be pretty sure they were not the greatest Villains then living in the World. (1972 [1724]: 134)

NOTES

1. An earlier version of this article was first published as a *Max Planck Institute for Social Anthropology Working Paper*, No. 160. Halle/Saale: Max Planck Institute for Social Anthropology 2014, reprinted here with kind permission.
2. Risso defines maritime violence as 'the *indiscriminate* seizure of seaborne or coastal property, under threat or use of force. It sometimes involves also the holding of passengers or crew for ransom' (2001: 293–4, her emphasis).
3. See Alpers (2011: 19–21, 24–32) for a wide range of examples of maritime violence, including contemporary Somali maritime violence. See also Alpers (2014: 99–104); Antony (2013); Davies (1997); Dua (2020); Pennell (ed. 2001); Prange (2011, 2013); Risso (2001: 302–16); Rogozinski (1995); Nagel (2007: 59–64); North (2014: especially 103–9); Sellström (2015: 26–34).
4. After being brought on board ships, the stolen cargoes were often called 'prizes' (derived from the perfect form of the French verb *prendre*). One can detect here a nice approach to the etymology of the modern word 'enterprise', which still connotes a commercial undertaking with a degree of risk (and force?) involved.
5. A contemporary case of this shift to piracy is the first phase of Somali piracy (before it was taken over by organized criminals), when fishermen of the 'failed state' that was Somalia, which had no means of guarding its coasts, saw innumerable European and Asian boats first overfish their territorial waters and later illegally dump toxic wastes on the Somali coast. They then took matters into their own hands.
6. See Grotius (1916 [1609]).

7. In this respect, the Dutch East India Company was, of course, only following the example of the Portuguese, who introduced state-backed maritime violence into the Indian Ocean in their attempt to gain access to what had long been a rather peaceful free-trade zone. Prime targets for the Portuguese were Muslim ships of Arab, Persian and Indian origin, which dominated the trade in the Indian Ocean at that time. Attacking vessels of these 'denominations' could also be justified as a valuable religious action and as a continuation of the crusade against Islam known in Europe and West Asia, albeit with other means and in a new, more global arena. There is no need to emphasize that it was not only the Portuguese in the sixteenth and the Dutch in the seventeenth centuries, but also, a little later, the French and the English who resorted to attacking boats of Indian, Arab and East Asian origin. And these European ships, which could thus turn, from one minute to the next, from a merchant vessel into a warship or pirate vessel, also directed their weapons against the ships of their European rivals. These attacks against 'fellow Europeans' often reflected the existing state of peace or war between these nations back home in Europe. For examples of crown-, state-, and company-based piracy, see also Andrade (2005), Carter (2009: 48–9), Hanna (2017), and Lunsford (2005).
8. The Ming Chinese, to give but one example, tended to label those merchant communities and ports in the Malayan maritime world who had *not* submitted to their authority 'evil pirates', while those who acknowledged Chinese supremacy were regarded as 'peaceful merchants'. See Alpers (2011: 19), Dreyer (2007: 55–6).
9. See North (2014: 204–9).
10. The Dutch authorities at the Cape at that time estimated that, in 1705, i.e., in the heyday of pirate activities, there were more than 830 pirates in Madagascar. In offering their services to the King of Sweden in exchange for his royal protection, the pirates of that time and place themselves claimed to number 1,200 men. See Ellis (2007: 446) and Hooper (2011: 226).
11. For a contemporary collection of the life histories of several pirates of the period under consideration, see Captain Johnson, alias Daniel Defoe (1972 [1724]), though this work extensively mixes *res factae* with *res fictae*.
12. On Avery, see Defoe (1972 [1724]: 49–62). The serious problems created by these and other pirate attacks on Moghul vessels are described by Risso as follows: 'One of the ships belonged to Aurangzeb himself; it had been carrying Muslim pilgrims on their return from Mecca, as well

as valuable cargo. Rumours spread that some pilgrims had been killed and some women violated. At the ship's home port, Surat, angry locals tried to lynch any available English merchants, on the assumption that Avery's attack was somehow sponsored, condoned, or facilitated by the East India Company. The Mughal governor of Surat intervened to prevent lynching, but he also ordered his troops to occupy the East India Company's establishments in Surat and nearby Suwali, to incarcerate their sixty-three employees, and to stop their trade' (Risso 2001: 307–8, cf. also 317).

13. Kidd's fate is described by Defoe (1972 [1724]: 440–51). See also Brown (2006: 67–8), Risso (2001: 308), Ritchie (1986), and Rogozinski (2002).
14. There is undoubtedly a strong element of early racism. The men and women whom Kidd enslaved, tortured and abused were of Asian origin. This racism is also often reflected in the social compositions and hierarchies of the pirate crews and communities under consideration here. The higher strata were white, and only seldom does one find black, Asian or Creole pirates of some standing; by contrast, many of the non-white pirates were abducted from the ships that had been captured and simply taken over as slaves, servants, sailors and labourers in pirate communities. These, then, should not be romanticized as being free and egalitarian, despite their sometimes anarchistic and anti-authoritarian appeal and self-identification. On this, see also Carter (2009: 51).
15. On Bowen, see Piat (2007: 23), Brown (2006: 70–2), Defoe (1972 [1724]: 452–64).
16. Such changes in nationality may have been easier from British to French than vice versa, because the French government had a reputation among pirates of being more trustworthy than the British when it came to adhering to promising pardons, as Rogozinski (2002: 159) points out. In this specific case, the French were the obvious choice not only because Île Bourbon was nearby, but also because Condent's attacks on Moghul ships were detrimental to British rather than French interests in the Indian Ocean. On Condent, see Defoe (1972 [1724]: 581–4), Piat (2007: 26–7).
17. See Piat (2007: 34–9).
18. While Madagascar will be the focus of the next two sections, the Comoros cannot be dealt with here, though they certainly deserved attention. For this island group to the northwest of Madagascar, see Carter (2009: 57–8), Martin (1983).
19. In 1690, for example, an ex-Dominican priest and then pirate called Caraciolli and the Hugenot pirate Oliver Misson are rumoured to have

attempted to create a pirate's republic called Libertalia in northern Madagascar, near the Bay of Diego Suarez. See Brown (2006: 66), Defoe (1972 [1724]: 383–418), Piat (2007: 10), Schicho (2004: 230–1).

20. See Piat (2007: 14–17), Defoe (1972 [1724]: 49–63).
21. Moreover, in 1698, a royal decree of clemency by the British, with a general pardon and amnesty, was issued, and many pirates worldwide took advantage of the opportunity.
22. See Carter (2009: 59–60).
23. Here, one might add that the pirate Burgess, who remained for several years on nearby Madagascar, is reported to have had good relations with the Bishop of London and the Archbishop of Canterbury. See Defoe (1972 [1724]: 506–10).
24. See Carter (2009: 60–4). However, the history of piracy on the Mascarenes is not over yet. During the second half of the eighteenth century, Mauritius was a safe haven for pirates ('corsairs' to the French), like the famous Surcouf, who had great success in capturing numerous British East Indiamen. For an overview, see Piat (2007).
25. On this period of Malagasy history, see especially Brown (2006: 30–7). Consequently, as already indicated, the Dutch chose to establish a colony on Mauritius (between 1638 and 1710), only to find that settling an uninhabited island was no less difficult than settling one with a hostile native population.
26. As far as the English were concerned, these colonizing efforts failed in the southwestern Bay of Saint Augustine in 1646, after less than two years, and they also proved futile for the *Compagnie des Indes Orientales*, which abandoned its Malagasy colonizing project at Fort Dauphin in 1674 after almost three decades of almost incessant hostility with the surrounding population and a final massacre during a mass marriage ceremony of French settlers to French orphans sent there by Louis XIV (see Ogot, ed. 1992: 885). As a consequence, the French started to turn Île Bourbon into a port of call and colony for their Indian Ocean ambitions.
27. For an intimate description of these incessant wars among Malagasy chiefdoms, see the account by Robert Drury, who spent fifteen years as a shipwrecked sailor and then as a slave and mercenary in the south and southwest of the island at the end of the seventeenth century (Drury 1890 [1729]). In this context, it is therefore more correct to say that the trade with the Europeans was only beneficial to some Malagasy groups, and disastrous for others, as especially Bialuschewski (2005: 410–4) has argued with reference to the southern part of the island.

28. On Malagasy history in the seventeenth century, see especially Brown (2006: 38–49) and Hooper (2011: 218–26). On the Malagasy slave trade during the second half of the seventeenth century, see Bialuschewski (2005: 403–6, 414–8) and Campbell (2005).
29. For an overview on pirates in Madagascar, see Deschamps (1972).
30. See Brown (2006: 75–6), Carter (2009: 54–6).
31. Forty to fifty years later, French traders and officers visiting the Bay of Antongil encountered 'mulattos', who presented themselves as belonging to the Baldridge clan. See Ellis (2007: 450).
32. See also Bialuschewski (2005: 406–9); Brown (2006: 69–70); Carter (2009: 56–7, 65); Hooper (2011: 222–3, 227–8); Nutting (1978).
33. See especially Evans-Pritchard (1940), Evans-Pritchard and Fortes (eds. 1940).
34. On this, see Ogot (ed. 1992: 882), Piat (2007: 24).
35. I use these terms in the senses proposed by Kulke (1993) and Stein (1980). Here, it might also be apt to apply the concept of 'little kingdom', as developed from within the anthropology and historiography of India. The situation in Madagascar is then to be understood less as a conglomeration of *mono*-archies struggling for predominance than as a *poly*-archical system of kingdoms, many little and a few great, standing in politically and ritually expressed hierarchical relationships to each other. On the theory of the 'little kingdom', see Schnepel (2002: chap. I). State formation in Madagascar is discussed by several authors, in the piracy context especially by Ellis (2007) and Hooper (2011).
36. For more details of his rule, see Brown (2006: 78–82), Ogot (ed. 1992: 882–3).
37. It is disputed, and cannot be verified, whether the surname of this Thomas was White or Tew.
38. One important, though not undisputed source for the history of Ratsimilahoe is the Frenchman Nicolas Mayeur, whose *Histoire de Ratsimil-hoe* was written in the early nineteenth century. For the history of Ratsimilahoe, see also Ellis (2007: 447–51), Bialuschewski (2005: 422–3), and Hooper (2011: 233–4).
39. The economic and political impact of this 'Sakalava connection' is discussed by Ellis (2007: 451–3), who writes that 'he [Ratsimilahoe, B.S.] and his Sakalava allies made such a systematic use of Europeans as advisors and auxiliaries, and were so closely integrated into overseas systems of credit and trade, that they foreshadowed some developments often regarded as innovations of a later period' (ibid.: 442).
40. See Brown (2006: 83–4).

41. A stay only interrupted by two returns to Madagascar in 1757 and 1762.
42. De Forval actually seems to have been Grant's cousin.
43. Up to half a dozen children and even more was not at all exceptional in these days and places.
44. On Beti, see Grant (1801), MacMillan (ed. 2000 [1914]: 133–5), Vaughan (2006: 105–7), Piat (2007: 41–2), Brown (2006: 83–5). More generally, on the ambivalent status of 'free persons of colour' and '*gens de coleur*' in Mauritius, see especially Allen (1999: chap. 4).
45. See Carter (2009), Starkey (2001), Rediker (1987), Risso (2001), and Subramaniam (2007).
46. See, for example, Rediker (1987); the internet journal *Darkmatter: In the Ruins of Imperialist Culture*, 2009 issue; or Subramaniam (2007: 25) who argues: 'The advent of the Portuguese and the enforcement of their *cartaz*-based politics altered the situation in so far as it displaced small time merchants and forced them to resort to desperate measures (. . .) traders became pirates quite inadvertently'. Similarly, Pearson (2003: 126–7). See also Risso (2001: 316–9), who argues against such an interpretation.
47. For a classic introduction to the problem, see Abrams (1988).
48. This diversity still applies today, even after centuries of exchanges and globalization (see Bouchard and Crumplin 2010).
49. Estimates go up to 5,000. See Schnepel (2002: 1, and chap. I).
50. Carter (2009: 45). For a similarly pronounced view of the integral role of pirates, see Starkey (2001).
51. See Mauss (1938), Schnepel (1990).
52. It is most probable that piracy managed to thrive, first in the Caribbean and then in the Indian Ocean, on account of the fact that during the many intra-European wars and skirmishes, such as the 'Nine Years' War', so many letters of marque had been issued that the situation became close to anarchy and almost impossible to handle or judge. This was the case especially after these wars ended and peace treaties made these sailors jobless, as when, after the Peace of Utrecht in 1713, around 40,000 Royal Navy personnel were discharged. See Carter (2009: 46).
53. In the words of Hooper, 'The stability of trade on Madagascar, admired by European captains during the mid-eighteenth century, developed in part from contact with pirates in the previous decades' (2011: 230). The liminal or hybrid position of the pirate and Zana Malata mediators is also expressed by the fact that they often appeared in a mixture of French and local dress for the lengthy trade negotiations (see ibid.: 234).
54. See also Carter (2009: 62–3).

REFERENCES

Abrams, P. 1988. 'Notes on the Difficulty of Studying the State'. *Journal of Historical Sociology* 1(1): 58–89.

Agha, S.S., and E. Kolsky (eds.). 2009. *Fringes of Empire.* New Delhi: Oxford University Press.

Allen, R.B. 1999. *Slaves, Freedmen, and Indentured Laborers in Colonial Mauritius.* Cambridge: Cambridge University Press.

Alpers, E.A. 2011. 'Piracy and Indian Ocean Africa'. *Journal of African Development* 13: 15–38.

——, 2014. *The Indian Ocean in World History.* Oxford: Oxford University Press.

Andrade, T. 2005. 'The Company's Chinese Pirates: How the Dutch East India Company Tried to Lead a Coalition of Pirates to War against China, 1621–1662'. *Journal of World History* 15: 415–44.

Antony, R.J. 2013. 'Turbulent Waters: Sea Raiding in Early Modern South East Asia'. *The Mariner's Mirror* 99: 23–38.

Bialuschewski, A. 2005. 'Pirates, Slavers and the Indigenous Population in Madagascar, *c.* 1690–1715'. *International Journal of African Historical Studies* 39: 401–25.

Bouchard, C., and W. Crumplin. 2010. 'Neglected No Longer: The Indian Ocean at the Forefront of World Geopolitics and Global Geostrategy'. *Journal of the Indian Ocean Region* 6: 26–51.

Brown, M. 2006. *A History of Madagascar.* Princeton: Marcus Wiener Publishers.

Campbell, G. 2005. *An Economic History of Imperial Madagascar, 1750–1895: The Rise and Fall of an Island Empire.* Cambridge: Cambridge University Press.

Carter, M. 2009. 'Pirates and Settlers: Economic Interactions on the Margins of Empire'. In Agha and Kolsky (eds.) 2009: 45–68. New Delhi: Oxford University Press.

Davies, C.E. 1997. *The Blood-Red Arab Flag: An Investigation into Qasimi Piracy 1797–1820.* Exeter: University of Exeter Press.

Defoe, D. (alias Captain Johnson). 1972 [1724]. *A General History of the Pyrates.* London: Dover Maritime Publication.

Deschamps, H. 1972. *Les Pirates à Madagascar aux XVIIe et XVIIIe Siècles.* Paris: Editions Berger-Levrault.

Dreyer, E.L. 2007. *Zheng He: China and the Oceans in the Early Ming Dynasty, 1405–1433.* New York: Pearson, Longman.

Drury, R. 1890 [1729]. *Madagascar or Robert Drury's Journal, During Fifteen Years Captivity on that Island.* London: Unwin and Macmillan.

Dua, J. 2020. *Captured at Sea: Piracy and Protection in the Indian Ocean.* Los Angeles: University of California Press.

Ellis, S. 2007. 'Tom and Toakafo: the Betsimisaraka Kingdom and state formation in Madagascar, 1715–1750'. *Journal of African History* 48: 439–55.

Evans-Pritchard, E.E. 1940. *The Nuer: A Description of the Modes of Livelihood and Political Institutions of a Nilotic People.* Oxford: Oxford University Press.

Evans-Pritchard, E.E., and M. Fortes (eds.). 1940. *African Political Systems.* Oxford: Oxford University Press.

Ghosh, D., and S. Muecke (eds.). 2007. *Cultures of Trade: Indian Ocean Exchanges.* Newcastle: Cambridge Scholars Publishing.

Gilroy, P. 1993. *The Black Atlantic: Modernity and Double Consciousness.* Cambridge: Harvard University Press.

Grant, C. 1801. *The History of Mauritius or the Isle of France and the Neighbouring Islands.* London: W. Bulmer and Co.

Grotius, H. 1916 [1609]. *The Freedom of the Seas.* New York: Oxford University Press.

Hanna, M. 2017. *Pirate Nests and the Rise of the British Empire, 1570–1740.* Chapel Hill: University of North Carolina Press.

Hooper, J. 2011. 'Pirates and Kings. Power on the Shores of Early Modern Madagascar and the Indian Ocean'. *Journal of World History* 22: 215–42.

Kulke, H. 1993. *Kings and Cults: State Formation and Legitimation in India and Southeast Asia.* Delhi: Manohar.

Latour, B. 2013. *An Inquiry into Modes of Existence: An Anthropology of the Moderns.* Cambridge: Harvard University Press.

Lunsford, V.W. 2005. *Piracy and Privateering in the Golden Age Netherlands.* New York: Palgrave Macmillan.

MacMillan, A. (ed.). 2000 [1914]. *Mauritius Illustrated. Historical and Descriptive Commercial and Industrial Facts, Figures and Resources.* New Delhi: Asian Educational Services.

Martin, J. 1983. *Comores: Quatre Îles entre Pirates et Planteurs*, 2 vols. Paris: L'Harmattan.

Mauss, M. 1938. 'Une Catégorie de l'esprit humaine: la notion de personne, celle de "moi"'. *Journal of the Royal Anthropological Institute* 68: 263–82.

Nutting, P.B. 1978. 'The Madagascar Connection: Parliament and Piracy, 1690–1701'. *American Journal of Legal History* 22: 204–9.

Ogot, B.A. (ed.). 1992. *General History of Africa*, Vol. V: *Africa from the Sixteenth to the Eighteenth Century*. Oxford: Heinemann.

Pearson, M. 2003. *The Indian Ocean*. London: Routledge.

Pennel, C.R. (ed.). 2001. *Bandits at Sea: A Pirates Reader*. New York: New York University Press.

Piat, D. 2007. *Pirates and Corsaires of Mauritius*. Mauritius: Christian Le Comte.

Prange, S.R. 2011. 'A Trade of No Dishonor. Piracy. Commerce, and Community in the Western Indian Ocean, Twelfth to Sixteenth Century'. *American Historical Review* 116: 1269–93.

——, 2013. 'The Contested Sea. Regimes of Maritime Violence in the Pre-Modern Indian Ocean'. *Journal of Early Modern History* 17: 9–33.

Rediker, M. 1987. *Between the Devil and the Deep Blue Sea: Merchant Seamen, Pirates, and the Anglo-American Maritime World, 1700–1750*. Cambridge, MA: Harvard University Press.

Risso, P. 2001. 'Cross-Cultural Perceptions of Piracy: Maritime Violence in the Western Indian Ocean and Persian Gulf Region during a Long Eighteenth Century'. *Journal of World History* 12(2): 293–319.

Ritchie, R.C. 1986. *Captain Kidd and the War against the Pirates*. Cambridge (MA): Harvard University Press.

Rogozinski, J. 1995. *Pirates, Brigands, Buccaneers and Privateers in Fact, Fiction, and Legend*. New York: Facts on File.

——, 2002. *Honor among Thieves: Captain Kidd, Henry Every and the Pirate Democracy in the Indian Ocean*. Pennsylvania: Stackpole Books.

Rothermund, D., and S. Weigelin-Schwiedrzik (eds.). 2004. *Der Indische Ozean: Das afro-asiatische Mittelmeer als Kultur- und Wirtschaftsraum*. Wien: Promedia Verlag.

Schicho, W. 2004. 'Die französische Kolonisierung der Inseln im Indischen Ozean: Der Mythos vom Glück und der leichten Liebe'. In Rothermund and Weigelin-Schwiedrzik (eds.) 2004: 227–46.

Schnepel, B. 1990. 'Corporations, Personhood, and Ritual in Tribal Society: Three Interconnected Topics in the Anthropology of Meyer Fortes'. *Journal of the Anthropological Society of Oxford* 21(1): 1–31.

——, 2002. *The Jungle Kings: Ethnohistorical Aspects of Politics and Ritual in Orissa*. Delhi: Manohar.

Sellström, T. 2015. *Africa in the Indian Ocean: Islands in Ebb and Flow*. Leiden: Brill.

Starkey, D.J. 2001. 'Pirates and Markets'. In Pennel (ed.) 2001: 107–24.

Stein, B. 1980. *Peasant State and Society in Medieval South India*. Delhi: Oxford University Press.

Subramaniam, L. 2007. 'Of Pirates and Potentates: Maritime Jurisdiction and the Construction of Piracy in the Indian Ocean'. In Ghosh and Muecke (eds.) 2007: 19–30.

Vaughan, M. 2006. *Creating the Creole Island: Slavery in Eighteenth-Century Mauritius.* Durham: Duke University Press.

CHAPTER 4

Infections on the Move: Epidemic Diseases in the History of Mauritius and Beyond

INTRODUCTION

Of all the things that have crisscrossed the Indian Ocean throughout its long history as a maritime contact zone, diseases are certainly among the most unwelcome. Like stowaway passengers, the various pathogens and their diverse carriers have used the same points of departure and arrival, and travelled the same routes, that commercial cargoes and human passengers have taken. Once having disembarked, these stowaways come out into the open and start to develop an agency of their own accord. To humans their activities have spelled immeasurable suffering, often reaching epidemic and even pandemic proportions, which over the centuries have killed millions in the Indian Ocean world. This chapter addresses the issue of 'infections on the move' across the Indian Ocean world from an ethno-historical perspective.While sticking to the Indian Ocean world as the spatial frame within which epidemic diseases will be considered, I start by focusing on the small island of Mauritius.

As far as this island is concerned, there is no doubt that the repeated loss of thousands of lives, sometimes amounting to a large percentage of the island's population, due to what at the time were mysterious and dreadful infections on the move, had a traumatic effect on the island's population. This is attested in reports by the island's visitors, as well as its inhabitants, whose accounts also testify to other catastrophes, such as the cyclones and large-scale fires that befell the island with unflinching regularity, causing significant mortality and widespread social and economic damage. Mauritians were never certain whether they would survive as individuals, families or communities, or whether the colony itself could be maintained. Moreover, these traumatized states of mind also caused a great variety of disputes concerning the causes of epidemics, as well as the best means to prevent their further spread. It also led to allegations, often racist in kind, concerning the actual spreaders of disease, a well-known and deplorable fact even during contemporary pandemics. Given, then, that these health-related issues heavily influenced and certainly constituted a vital part of Mauritian life, a case can be made for examining the island's medical history, which constituted such a disruptive, but also integral part of the life experience of the island's population.[1]

A CHRONOLOGY OF DEATH

The first major epidemic in Mauritius occurred in 1754 with an outbreak of smallpox, which caused the deaths of so many labourers that the much-needed construction works in the island's capital and port came to a temporary halt.[2] In 1770 smallpox reappeared, this time accompanied by an epidemic of anthrax, which killed about a quarter of the slave population. Smallpox hit the island again in December 1772. A decade later, in June 1782, it was reintroduced to the island by the crew of a French naval squadron on its way to India. Poor sanitary conditions in Port Louis exacerbated its impact, which was devastating. Toussaint remarked: 'The town of Port Louis represented a horrible sight. The cemetery was still unfenced, and the pigs went in and rooted out the dead bodies, and wandered through the streets with scraps of human flesh. This plague delayed the expedition to India by six months, and reduced its manpower by a third' (1973: 43). Smallpox struck again, precisely a decade later, in June 1792, this time probably introduced by a group of infected slaves from India. It hit ordinary white labourers as well, but as always African and Indian slaves suffered the highest casualties. Negligent burial practices – some corpses were simply thrown into the bush to be eaten by dogs and pigs – furthered the spread of the disease. The few hospitals on the island became overcrowded with the sick, prompting the construction of a new hospital, intended especially for victims of infectious diseases, on Tonneliers Island, just north of the harbour. This action, and the stepping up of traditional, albeit disputed inoculation measures 'in the charged atmosphere of war and revolution' (Vaughan 2000: 412), gradually checked the epidemic, but not before it had killed 8 per cent of the island's population, which was about 60,000 at that time. Another smallpox epidemic in 1811 was checked by the adaptation of Jennerian vaccination measures using cowpox lymph by the new British authorities, who took over the island in 1810. Thereafter, smallpox ceased to be the greatest disease threatening Mauritius.[3] In 1813 the island was struck by rabies, introduced by pet dogs belonging to the British troop commander. As there was then no vaccine against rabies, many people died terrifying deaths. All that could be done to check the spread of the disease was to kill every dog on the island. In October 1819, another new disease, namely cholera, hit the island: Almost 7,000 people, most of them slaves, died, and so many people fled Port Louis that life in the capital came almost to a standstill.[4]

The situation worsened rather than improved in the mid- to late nineteenth century, despite the fact that successive British governors introduced ever harsher and stricter regulations to prevent the spread of infectious diseases. In April 1850, a ship carrying workmen from India reached Port Louis with cholera on board. The mayor of Port Louis ordered it to stay out at sea, leaving its passengers to their fate. In May 1854, another ship landed with 'coolies' from India, again with cholera on board, but this time the authorities reacted too late, and the highly infectious disease spread rapidly through Port Louis. In panic, about 10,000 people left town to seek shelter in the countryside. In January 1856, two cholera-infected ships arrived from Calcutta, one shortly after the other, and the disease quickly spread not only within Port Louis, but all over the island, claiming around 3,500 victims. Three years later, in September 1859, cholera appeared once more, again arriving on board a ship from Calcutta. In December 1861, yet another cholera epidemic struck the island, introduced by a ship which was allowed to disembark its cargoes and passengers after only one day in quarantine.[5]

In 1865, a cyclone struck the town. The floods which came with it are reported to have drowned 30 people. But things got even worse. The dirty and infectious flood waters, which remained in the town for a considerable time after the cyclone, contributed decisively to the impact of another, initially mysterious disease, which spread throughout Mauritius in epidemic form from 1866 to 1868. This epidemic lasted longer, and caused more deaths, than any previous one. It is estimated to have killed 50,000 people, over 33,000 in Port Louis and its immediate environs alone: it affected particularly the quarters inhabited by Indian 'coolies' and the poorer Creoles. This epidemic, unknown at the time, was later discovered to have been caused by malaria, transmitted by anopheles mosquitos that flourished in the brackish water that remained after the cyclone of 1865.[6]

In 1891, due to the neglect or inefficiency of vaccination, smallpox unexpectedly erupted again in Mauritius, infecting 3,500 and killing at least 650. In 1893, more than 500 people died of influenza. In between these two epidemics, in 1892, Port Louis experienced one of the worst cyclones ever, one that destroyed almost a third of the town's buildings, killing 600 people and injuring more than a thousand. In 1899 the plague appeared in Mauritius, probably introduced by boat from the port city of Tamatave in Madagascar. Although its presence in Madagascar had been noted for several years, the Mauritian authorities neglected to adopt adequate preventive measures, letting ships from Tamatave freely enter the harbour of Port Louis. Consequently, the plague spread throughout the island, reaching epidemic proportions between September and December every year, most devastatingly in 1921 and 1922. Not until 1932 was plague eradicated. In addition, in 1905 and 1913 smallpox reappeared in Mauritius, as did influenza in 1906 and again in 1919 when, in the form of the (in)famous 'Spanish influenza', which killed millions worldwide, it left more than 4,000 dead in the island.[7]

GLOBAL ROOTS AND ROUTES

Each of the epidemics briefly enumerated here had its own distinctive micro-history, its own set of causative agents, its own pattern of dispersal and counter-measures, and its specific impact on Mauritian society. But these diseases were far from being isolated, insular events:

they were clearly embedded in more widespread manifestations of infections on the move, with Port Louis and its surroundings constituting only one point along the multiple interlocked disease routes across the Indian Ocean world and wider afield. In other words, all the *epi*demics that reached Mauritius and rapidly spread through its population were *pan*demics, that is, parts of larger dispersals of these diseases across national and continental borders and over vast tracts of sea. Locally some of these diseases became so entrenched that they became *en*demic. Take smallpox, for example, which caused human-to-human infection through the so-called *variola* virus. Smallpox, as we have seen, dominated the history of infectious diseases on the island during the eighteenth and sporadically the nineteenth centuries. It probably reached Mauritius for the first time in the early eighteenth century on ships which not only carried sailors and traders, but also thousands of African slaves, as well as large contingents of soldiers heading for the battlefields of India and further on. These human carriers were both the victims and the transmitters of this disease.

The ever-increasing movements that took place in the age of European mercantilism and colonialism by traders and sailors, colonial officials and troops, pilgrims, migrant labourers and adventurers facilitated the introduction and rapid spread of new diseases throughout the Indian Ocean world. Cholera, a bacterial disease transmitted from person to person either through the oral induction of bodily liquids or through food and especially water contaminated with infected human faeces, won for itself the dubious reputation of being one of the most widespread and deadly diseases of the nineteenth century.[8] Cholera demonstrated a particular 'predilection for the poor and undernourished' (Arnold 1986: 123), due to the fact that the unsanitary housing conditions of the rural and urban poor and their low level of health, aggravated by malnutrition and even famine, helped promote transmission of the disease in these underprivileged communities. As already noted, cholera made its first appearance in Mauritius in 1819, in the middle of a severe global cholera pandemic (1817–22) that affected the Indian Ocean world and beyond. Cholera's 'endemic home' (Arnold 1991: 10) is reported to have been Bengal, from where it made its way across the ocean, developing, as it did so into a 'crowd disease'. As Arnold points out:

It moved with traders and troopships eastward from Bengal into Burma, Malaya, Thailand (where an estimated 100,000 people perished in 1819), Java (leaving 125,000 dead in 1821), and the rest of island Southeast Asia, and on to East Asia, reaching Japan in 1822. It ran through peninsular India to Sri Lanka, or swept southwest from Calcutta and Madras to Mauritius . . . and to Zanzibar and the East African coast. (ibid.: 8)

Some cholera outbreaks were closely connected with major British military campaigns in 1817–18 and 1857 in India, 1819 in Malacca and the 1840s during the Opium War in China.[9] In the case of Mauritius, however, especially in the 1850s, the main human carriers were neither soldiers nor Muslim or Hindu pilgrims (the other main factor in the spread of diseases on the Indian subcontinent and in the Indian Ocean world as a whole), but 'coolies', that is, indentured labourers who arrived on the island from Calcutta, Madras and Bombay in great numbers from the 1840s.[10]

Indian migrant labour also accounted for the mass dispersal of malaria and the 'great fever epidemic' caused by this disease throughout the island in the late 1860s. As far as malaria is concerned, Mauritius certainly did not represent what epidemiologists call a 'virgin soil population'.[11] Many people who arrived on the island as African slaves or Indian 'coolies' or as their 'masters' will have carried malarial fever in their bodies, and significant numbers died of this disease on the island prior to the 1860s. Those carrying fever increased dramatically with the mass arrival of Indian immigrants from the 1840s. So, the vexed question in this regard is not how malaria-stricken people arrived on Mauritius, but how the disease could be transmitted on the island itself and become an endemic 'crowd disease'. This question relates to the then unknown vector, the anopheles mosquito. How did anopheles mosquitos get to Mauritius, given that their life-cycle is short and that they require stagnant water to breed and proliferate? Various hypotheses have been put forward, which have been discussed by Alpers (2020). To start with, it is possible that anopheles mosquitos arrived on the island aboard steamboats in the 1860s, when malaria first erupted in Mauritius in epidemic form. The sheer number of new arrivals in terms of both infected human beings and the right kind of mosquitos thereafter caused a catastrophic increase in malarial infection. The fact that there was stagnant water left over from cyclones, and major deforestation due to the large-scale clearance of land to create sugar plantations and roads, significantly increased the breeding grounds for mosquitos in Mauritius and thus contributed to the disease's rapid spread. Secondly, however, one might also surmise that anopheles mosquitos, like other mosquitos, were already present on the island and thus that their voyaging over vast stretches of sea was already possible even in the age of sail. This might be explained by the phenomenon of 'island hopping', that is, a relay method of transporting material and immaterial things across the Indian Ocean. A final hypothesis emerges from Alpers's comparison of recent epidemiological findings concerning *chikungunya* on contemporary La Réunion and Mauritius with malaria on Mauritius in the mid- to late nineteenth century: Mauritius's endemic species of mosquito might have undergone some kind of transmutation and adaptation, being transformed from non-vector to malaria-carrying mosquitos, possibly in association with the great demographic and environmental change that the island experienced during the second half of that century. In other words, a combination of human and environmental factors may have led to mutations in the endemic parasite-vector world of Mauritius.[12]

Furthermore, the plague that reached Mauritius in 1899, which recurred periodically up to the 1930s, was likewise embedded in the wider global movement of this disease from the 1890s onwards. This plague pandemic is reported to have originated in inland southern China, from where it made its way to the two highly frequented port cities of Canton and Hong Kong. Carried by fleas ('travelling' on rats or in travellers' clothes and baggage), the plague entered steamboats and sailing vessels in these ports, carrying it to all parts of the globe: Sydney and San Francisco, Java and other islands of the Malay Archipelago, ports in the African and Arab worlds, and South America. By the close of the nineteenth century it had reached India, affecting especially Bombay and surrounding areas of the west coast. The plague may have travelled to Mauritius from India, or from Madagascar, where several outbreaks had occurred, to which it might have travelled via Cape Town.[13] In the case of plague, as with smallpox and malaria, the infection moves easily and rapidly along the established maritime circuits and hubs of the Indian Ocean world. Its vectors (rat fleas) accompanied commercial goods (rats were especially keen on grain and rice) and their traders, as well as soldiers, migrant workers, pilgrims and other passengers. The increasing European colonial penetration, not only of the littoral, but also of the hinterland of the Indian Ocean world, which notably brought improvements to inland routes in the form of roads and railroads, facilitated the rapid spread of the plague and other diseases into and from the interior on caravans, trains and lorries.[14]

Globalization, then, also took place in the realm of diseases; some authors even speak of a 'unification of the globe by disease'.[15] A notable example was the worldwide influenza epidemic, which started at the end of World War I and caused millions of deaths in 1918–20, more deaths than were caused by the war itself. In contrast to cholera, the plague and malaria, the 'Spanish flu' did not have its origins in the global south,[16] but in European battlefields and military barracks. From there, and especially from North America (rather than Spain, as the nickname of the epidemic suggests), this influenza rapidly moved along the same routes as its predecessors had done, only in the opposite direction, that is, from the west to the rest.[17] Finally, one other disease which seems to have arrived in the Indian Ocean world, especially its port cities, from the west was syphilis, also known as 'the Frankish/French disease'.

LOCAL BREEDING GROUNDS

So far we have identified the possible places of origin, transmitters and routes of the pandemic diseases that entered Mauritius by sea. We have also looked at the longer routes on which they arrived in Mauritius (and possibly continued to move on), as well as the imperial infrastructure that facilitated these movements. This perspective on dispersal, however, leaves several questions unanswered. How and why could these diseases, once they had arrived on Mauritius, cause such tremendous losses so often? Why could the germs sometimes linger on, reappearing every now and again, for decades? In other words, what were the local causes and conditions that encouraged the acceptance, massive spread and persistence of such diseases on Mauritius? These questions lead us to a consideration of the social, cultural, political, economic, sanitary and medical environments in which diseases established themselves and became epidemic.

To start with, and again in the words of Arnold, 'the periodic peregrinations of infectious or crowd diseases like cholera, smallpox or plague needed relatively dense human populations for their survival and onward transmission' (1991: 4). Consequently, some of the best breeding grounds for pathogens in the Indian Ocean world, and some of the most dispersal-effective hubs of virulent diseases, were to be found in the urban environments of port cities. While this holds true throughout Indian Ocean world history, it was especially the *colonial* port cities that constituted the most active hosts and onward carriers of these diseases. Colonial port cities, with their depots for soldiers, migrant labourers and pilgrims, were usually overcrowded. In the words of Pearson: '. . . it was not new diseases which affected populations around the ocean so much as faster communications, and increased density of people in certain places: examples of the hordes congregated for the hajj, and the increasing populations of the port cities' (2003: 169). More often than not, these places had only contaminated water supplies, bad sanitation, sewerage and drainage, and insufficient medical institutions and expertise, or were simply not equipped to deal with large numbers of unhealthy or infected travellers and populations.

The 'capital of disease' was Calcutta, the centre of British colonial ambitions in the global south from the mid-eighteenth century onwards. This city was made unhealthy by the very nature of its location in the swampy, mosquito-breeding region of the Ganges delta, close to the cholera-endemic zone of rural Bengal. From the nineteenth century, Calcutta's capacity to breed and circulate germs was catapulted by the sheer numbers of seafarers who reached its port from all over the world and by the tens of thousands of inland workers who migrated to the city in order to make a living there. These numbers increased substantially during the great rural depressions caused by British colonial rule and revenue ordinances, when large numbers of Indians abandoned the towns and villages of its hinterland. These people often originated from districts that had experienced poverty, malnutrition and famine and, consequently, crowd diseases. Many of these often physically weakened or even infected persons did not see any alternative to escaping their misery but to let themselves be shipped to the world's plantations as indentured labourers. Their health worsened further on long, cramped and unsanitary sea voyages, and many died during the voyage.[18] Colonial port cities like Calcutta, Bombay, Cape Town, Singapore and Hong Kong, as well as many of the port cities that served as stops along the pilgrimage route to Mecca, such as Jeddah or Karachi, then 'performed much the same function in epidemiological terms as they did in commercial ones. They were disease entrepôts: the principal points of entry for arriving pathogens' (Arnold 1991: 10).

In all these respects, Port Louis, from its beginnings until modern times, was neither better nor worse than most of the other port cities of the Indian Ocean. For quite some time, first French and then British colonial officers even considered the island to be a comparatively healthy location, well suited to recuperating from life in the more insalubrious places of their respective empires.[19] Such views were not totally unfounded when one considers that privileged officials would have shunned the shabby, unsanitary parts of Port Louis and hence would be less prone to be affected by epidemics.

In the eighteenth century, the overwhelming majority of people living in Port Louis were slaves or manumitted slaves of African origin. In the nineteenth century these groups were joined by Indian indentured labourers or 'coolies'. In both centuries, people from Europe represented a clear minority of the island's population, albeit one wielding enormous political and economic power. In addition to this continually growing and socially, religiously and ethnically heterogeneous settled community, Port Louis was always stretched to its limits by those who were just passing through but who nevertheless often spent some considerable time on the island. In this regard, there were of course sailors and traders on their way to other shores, leaving their boats to undertake commercial activities or just to recuperate. Some of these entered the island's hospital, even when there was no epidemic disease involved, to be cured, for example, of scurvy. In the second half of the eighteenth century, when the fight for predominance in the Indian Ocean world between England and France heightened and eventually (in the final days of Napoleon's rule) came to a showdown with the British take-over of Mauritius in 1810, the islanders had to host so many transient soldiers that food, water and other resources became scarce. These soldiers, moreover, waiting in the port city's barracks or on the boats, not only strained the island's resources, they also introduced deadly diseases. This observation also holds true, as has been noted, for the migrant labourers who reached Port Louis harbour from India in great numbers from the 1840s and spent some time in the harbour's depots before being moved to the island's plantations.

These diverse and unequal population strata were not distributed evenly across the town. From the very beginning, Port Louis's cityscape was characterized by segregation according to race and colour (as understood by the colonial administrations of that time). While the French and British elites lived in better and more sanitary housing conditions in the centre of the town, slaves, freed slaves, 'coolies', vagrants, *petits blancs* and soldiers lived in more cramped and unsanitary conditions in separate quarters to the east and west of the city centre (Camp de Noirs Libres and Camp des Malabars).[20] Generally, these groups were poor and consequently less well-nourished and less healthy; access to food and clean water was difficult, and medicines and medical care were often too expensive or simply not available to them. Finally, they did not have the means to flee the town and live inland when health conditions in the populous port city deteriorated. Not surprisingly, therefore, the casualties suffered by Port Louis's inhabitants during epidemics were not distributed evenly over the population at large. While no one on the island was totally safe, the lower and poorer strata were invariably affected by epidemic diseases to a much greater degree than the better off. For example, during the smallpox epidemic of 1754 around half of the slave population died, the 1782 smallpox epidemic mostly killed soldiers and slaves, and the 1792 smallpox epidemic killed about a third of the slave population.[21]

Despite regularly occurring epidemics, Port Louis experienced substantial increases of population under British rule. From 1851 to 1861 alone, the population grew from 50,000 to 75,000, notably amongst the city's Asian inhabitants, whose numbers increased in the same decade from 11,000 to 27,000. Only after the great malaria epidemics that occurred from the mid-1860s, when large numbers of its inhabitants fled Port Louis permanently, did the capital cease to be the most populous part of the island. Subsequently, towns in the Plaines Wilhems District, such as Quatre Bornes, Rose Hill and Curepipe, grew rapidly, extending in an area along the central plateau at lower elevations and up into the central mountains.[22] This new pattern of settlements outside the capital city and port, which was also a consequence of the new and increasingly large sugar plantations, was backed by the steady extension of the road network and the construction of a railway line from Port Louis across the island to Mahébourg between 1864 and 1875.[23] Ironically, while road and rail facilitated travel in and out of the town and escape from the insalubrious environment of the port city, they also promoted the rapid spread of disease from Port Louis to other parts of the island, affecting almost every corner of it.[24]

HEALTH-CARE MEASURES

The ability of the authorities to prevent diseases from entering Mauritius or to inhibit their dispersal depended on a number of factors, including the state of contemporary scientific knowledge or popular and religious beliefs concerning the causes, carriers and remitters of disease.[25] Smallpox stopped being the greatest threat to the island after the British takeover in 1810 on account of the widespread vaccination measures undertaken by the British authorities throughout the Indian Ocean world.[26] The inhabitants of Mauritius, like most people elsewhere in the British Empire, were initially sceptical about the treatment. They were especially concerned as to whether the infection could spread after inoculation through human-to-human contact, and significant numbers refused it. Others, especially those in the remoter parts of the island and among the slave, ex-slave and indentured populations, were simply not reached by the government vaccinators.[27]

While the causes of smallpox and the means of its dispersal were known relatively early on, any more basic knowledge about crowd diseases such as cholera, malaria or the plague was limited until the great discoveries in virology from the late nineteenth century onwards. As Dr Montgomery, after making extensive investigations into the spread of cholera in Mauritius, exclaimed in 1854: 'The disease is of so mysterious a nature as to be beyond the search of human investigation; that rests with the Divinity alone' (cited from Anderson 1918: 112). Before these scientific breakthroughs, several 'theories' circulated among both experts and lay circles concerning diseases and their transmitters. As we know today, some of them were simply false, while others only captured a part of the truth. One very common notion about diseases in premodern times was that they are airborne, being transmitted, so it was thought, by gases emanating from sewage and other decomposing matter, and even by the sea breeze (which hence had to be avoided). That this 'miasma' view was not restricted to the Indian Ocean world is shown by the word 'malaria', which has its roots in the medieval Italian expression *male aria*, a reference to the 'bad air' emanating from swamps (which, of course, are perfect breeding grounds for mosquitos).[28] This miasma theory led to several ineffectual attempts to find a remedy. For example, when cholera erupted on Mauritius in 1819, the island's governor and his aides thought it right to dispel the 'something' that was believed to have caused the disease by firing cannon balls into the air and fumigating the town. The citizens of Port Louis were also advised to visit the island's more elevated interior to breath in the better air found there. However, the belief that the emanations of foul air were the carriers of this disease also led to some indirectly effective measures, as when cemeteries were moved out of town and ordinances were issued to remove sewage.[29]

From foul air emanating from swamps and the sea, it is only a short logical step to the notion of water as a further possible cause of disease. And indeed, polluted water was always suspected of being a transmitter of disease, a theory which, as we now know, was close to the truth with regard to most stomach diseases such as dysentery, diarrhoea or cholera.[30] The contentious and, at least from the point of view of the present day, almost farcical issue of the drainage system in Port Louis, of which Toussaint (1973: 115–6) reports, is quite illustrative in this regard: The need to construct a sewerage system and to supply the city with clean piped water had been on the agenda of the colonial authorities from the beginning of Port Louis's transformation from a camp into a colonial capital in the 1730s. The issue became especially urgent after the major malaria epidemic of 1866–8, when brackish cyclone waters exacerbated its lethal force. However, due to the common belief that the epidemic was caused not by mosquitos breeding in these waters, but rather by mysterious agents lying dormant in the soil, the town was divided into 'drainers' and 'anti-drainers'. 'So it is not surprising', as Toussaint writes, 'that when the proposal was made that the soil in the capital should be opened up for laying sewers, large numbers of people should be horrified at the idea' (1973: 103). Only in 1895, almost three decades later, following heated debates between 'drainophobes' and 'drainomaniacs', as Toussaint calls them, did the government finally put the scheme into effect, though in the teeth of heavy opposition. Nevertheless, sanitation in Port Louis continued to be unsatisfactory until after World War II, and it was only around 1950 that malaria, at least in its endemic form, could be said to have been banished from the island.[31]

Many Europeans on Mauritius also saw the source of tropical illnesses in the climate and landscape of their new expatriate home. Thus, Governor Gomm, in office in the 1840s, was sure that a change in weather conditions would stop the cholera epidemic of that time.[32] These widespread natural-ecology theories of disease sooner or later led to, and included, notions that the native populations were vectors of disease and therefore that intimate contact with Africans or Indians should be avoided. In nineteenth-century Mauritius such ideas sometimes existed alongside, sometimes in stark opposition to, the miasma theory. The Franco-Mauritian elite in particular adhered to a 'contagion theory' and advocated the establishment of *cordons sanitaire* and quarantine stations, while the British favoured a less costly and restrictive miasma theory.[33] Fear of contagion by the 'coloured races', especially Indians, was directly coupled with other, more general racist beliefs and practices. As Boddhoo states:

> Although the British came across many diseases in India which existed in Britain, they were nonetheless suspicious of Indians, associating them with outbreaks of smallpox, plague, cholera and malaria. The fear of catching native diseases provided them a pretext to stay aloof and withdraw from closer social contact and they built their residences away from native reservoirs of disease such as bazaars and slums.[34]

The contagion theory of disease, therefore, both resulted from and gave further impetus to the hardening of racist ideology and practice under European colonialism. Proponents of this theory held indigenous peoples as such, rather than the bad sanitary conditions or insufficient health care they had to suffer, responsible for the outbreak of epidemic diseases. Thus, Gomm attributed the high mortality rate among Indian indentured labourers to their promiscuous character, their ignorance and superstition, their abuse of alcohol and cannabis, and their other 'peculiar habits'.[35] Their 'deficiencies', the authorities held, could and should be rectified through certain laws (regulating marriage, for example), the introduction of western medicines and other 'civilizing' measures, for example, in matters of hygiene.

One means of checking diseases which was very much in accordance with notions of contagion, but which ran against the British ideology of free trade, was drastic quarantine measures. Initially, ships with a disease on board were simply not allowed to enter port.[36] They and their unfortunate passengers had to anchor some way off Port Louis, preferably on the leeward side so as to prevent the foul air presumably issuing from them from reaching the land. Their crews and passengers were sometimes left for weeks without provision of water or food from the land. A policy of isolation was also implemented, in a somewhat milder but still highly inhuman form, by establishing quarantine stations on the small islets lying off Mauritius: Tonnelier Island just north of the harbour, the Gabriel and Flat Islands further north,[37] and the Île aux Benitiers to the southeast. Later, two quarantine stations were established on the main island, one near Pamplemousse north of Port Louis, the other to the south of the city. The island's hospitals also started to set aside separate wards for those suffering from contagious diseases.[38]

One example that illustrates both the inhuman dimension and the ineffectiveness of quarantine measures as enacted at that time and place occurred in 1856. In January that year, two ships, the *Hyderee* and the *Futtay Mobarrack*, arrived in Port Louis from Calcutta carrying respectively 273 and 380 Indian 'coolies', many of whom were ill (forty had already died on board ship). Fearing the possible spread of disease, British colonial officers in Port Louis, and even more so local citizens, hesitated to let the passengers and crew on to the island. The local population had recently been suffering badly from a cholera epidemic, and smallpox was a constant threat. Consequently, the ships were forbidden to enter the harbour and were ordered to Flat Island (Île Plate) and Gabriel Island (Îlot Gabriel), two small barren islets lying approximately ten kilometres off the northern cape of Mauritius, where some 500 Indians were disembarked. However, the islets had no housing or other basic amenities, nor any medical staff. Within a short period, half the 'coolies' had died of cholera, other diseases and general fatigue. Moreover, despite these rigorous and inhumane measures, cholera spread to the Mauritian mainland, killing 3,000 people, two-thirds of them in Port Louis. The cholera either came from the ships which had been allowed to enter Port Louis after discharging their human cargoes without being disinfected, or from those commuting back and forth to the islets in the early days of their occupation.[39]

While the European elite in Mauritius took care to avoid intimate or frequent contact with Indian 'coolies', the authorities did little to prevent diseases from spreading among these new inhabitants of the island. Their main concern was initially to ensure the provision of enough 'young, able bodied and healthy' labourers to satisfy the plantations' labour requirements.[40] Only in the wake of the frequent and virulent epidemics of the mid-nineteenth century did government officials introduce some health measures. However, they initially lacked the will and capacity to enforce these new regulations.[41] It was only in the 1880s, under Governor Pope Hennessy, that sanitary measures, including piped water, were implemented in some parts of Port Louis. By the end of the nineteenth century, the colonial government and the Catholic Church had both started to build new hospitals (including two asylums for lepers who had hitherto been shipped to remote islets in the Chagos archipelago and the Seychelles), to establish homes for the poor and sick, and to provide dispensaries all over the island.[42] Locally based scientists also energetically researched the causes of and remedies for cholera and malaria. Nevertheless, the influx of boats and people from Asia was simply too rapid for the authorities to be able to check the arrival of shipborne diseases in Port Louis. 'Health measures', as Boodhoo points out, 'did not keep pace with population growth and economic development' (2010: 28).

CONCLUSION

There have been a number of substantial anthropological and historical studies of hazards and disasters as events (or processes) resulting from destructive combinations of natural, technological and human factors.[43] These make it evident that investigations of port cities and small islands cannot be conducted without taking full account of the frequent catastrophes that tend to befall these two especially vulnerable bio- and socio-topes.

The history of epidemic diseases in Mauritius was closely interspersed and sometimes fatally linked with the occurrence of other catastrophes such as cyclones or fires that inflicted death and havoc to infrastructure. Cyclones struck the island with varying degrees of intensity. For example, on 1 February 1771, a cyclone sank two of the ships lying in Port Louis harbour, threw most of the others ashore, and inflicted great damage on the town. Another cyclone struck only a month later, in March 1771. Two years afterwards, in April 1773, a cyclone cast 30 ships ashore and destroyed over 300 buildings in Port Louis, including the parish church. There were further damaging cyclones in 1784, 1785, 1786 and 1788. In 1818, a cyclone sank eight vessels in Port Louis and cast the rest ashore. Further severe cyclones damaged Port Louis in 1819, 1824, 1834, 1836, 1840, 1844, 1848 and 1865. In 1869 four successive cyclones blew over the town, destroying a great number of houses. Other particularly destructive cyclones occurred in 1879 and 1884. Port Louis, which consisted of close concentrations of timber buildings and had inadequate water supplies and fire-fighting facilities, was also badly affected by fire. In one night in September 1816 a fire, reportedly started inadvertently by a slave-maid, destroyed about one-fifth of the capital's buildings, valued at over seven million Spanish dollars. Other great fires broke out in 1838, 1877, 1893, 1895 and twice in 1896.

Many of these disasters, whether man-made or natural, hit Port Louis at the same time as or shortly before epidemic disease, for which they also sometimes prepared the ground. Sometimes the interdependencies between natural catastrophes and epidemics were more indirect, as when hospitals and other infrastructure were destroyed by cyclones or proved otherwise insufficient to cope with the scale of a disease or natural disaster. Other factors that exacerbated the impact of diseases, cyclones and fires in Port Louis included insanitary and overcrowded dwellings, especially among the poor, inadequate or contaminated water supplies, insufficient sanitary and medical care and deficient scientific knowledge, combined with sometimes fantastical popular beliefs about the real causes and vectors of disease. Additionally, the French and British were in an almost constant state of war in the second half of the eighteenth and early nineteenth centuries. French Mauritius was faced with the constant threat of invasion by the British, a situation often combined with economic depression and restrictions, and even with malnutrition and famine. Political neglect and politico-economic agendas that accorded population health only a secondary level of priority added further to the misery. It is apparent that Mauritius was affected by both natural and human factors when it came to turning a disease into an epidemic. Epidemics, then, were caused by the successful interplay of manifold and heterogeneous human and non-human actants. They were not merely a product of the germs and pathogens which underlay disease: they were also caused and spread by specific types of careless person-to-person communication and inadequate human surveillance of animal carriers such as fleas and mosquitos or of contaminated water or food. Added to this are the social, political, economic, cultural, mental and historical circumstances that infections encounter when on the move. Also, the occurrence and spread of diseases are closely linked to transport improvements, such as the introduction of steamships or the building of roads and railways.

Furthermore, diseases are not just part of the medical histories of certain times and places, they also are part of, and offer deep insights into, the imperial authorities' attempts to control and classify their subjects.[44] Colonial disease prevention policies were implemented in a world in which 'free trade' and the rapid circulation of commercial goods constituted cherished ideals, at least among the British. Such policies had to focus especially on the port cities and islands of the Indian Ocean world, where boats and their passengers, as well as the vectors and pathogens of diseases, arrived and from where they departed. There then arose situations in which the desired everlasting flow of cargoes had to be stopped in an attempt to interrupt the movements of the pathogenetic stowaway passengers who accompanied them. It is these disruptive moments in 'connectivity in motion' across the Indian Ocean world that this chapter has sought to add to the overall picture of this maritime region's history and present.

NOTES

1. In what follows I am especially indebted to Anderson (1918), Toussaint (1973), and Boodhoo (2010), as well as a number of other studies mentioned in the text.
2. See Toussaint (1973: 25).
3. On these points, see Anderson (1918: 154–9), Toussaint (1973: 47–8).
4. See Toussaint (1973: 67–9, 75).
5. See Anderson (1918: 111–53), Boodhoo (2010: 60–2, 143–9), Kalla (2001: 99–102).
6. See Toussaint (1973: 95–9), Boodhoo (2010: 172–93), Kalla (2001: 103–4).
7. On this paragraph, see Toussaint (1973: 103–6).
8. Cholera's leading position in this regard during the first half of the century was challenged from the mid-nineteenth century onwards by the plague, malaria and influenza. Other diseases, 'seriously undercounted in official statistics' (Klein 1973: 643), such as respiratory diseases or diarrhoea, also took an enormous toll, as did travelling diseases like elephantiasis (probably moving from Southeast Asia to Africa), leprosy and hookworm infection. On attempts to quantify the impact of certain diseases (in India), see ibid. and Arnold (1986: 120–3).
9. It is estimated that, in the first half of the nineteenth century, roughly 8,500 British troops died of cholera in the Indian Ocean world, while many others succumbed to venereal diseases. See Arnold (1986: 126–8), Arnold (1991: 10), and Boodhoo (2010: 32).
10. On cholera in British India, see Alpers (2014: 125–7), Arnold (1993: 159–93).
11. See Shlomowitz and Brennan (1990: 85).
12. On malaria in Mauritius, see Anderson (1918: 160–216), Ross (1908), Hurgobin (2016), and Alpers (2020).

13. See Arnold (1991: 11–12).
14. On the plague in British India, see Arnold (1993: 200–39).
15. See Arnold (1993: 2).
16. While smallpox, cholera, malaria and the plague were all diseases known and feared in Europe as well, from the nineteenth century onwards they became, in the eyes of European commentators, 'tropical' and 'native' diseases and as such started to constitute an integral part of an Orientalist and European hegemonic discourse. See especially Arnold (ed. 1988).
17. See Arnold (1991: 12).
18. On the health situation and death tolls in the depots and places of embarkation, as well as on the dreadful sea journeys, see especially Boodhoo (2010: chap. 5).
19. For some statements in that direction, see Boodhoo (2010: 22, 28), Kalla (2001: 93–4).
20. For further demographic details, see especially Teelock (2018), and here Chapter 5.
21. See Boodhoo (2010: 57–9).
22. See Toussaint (1973: 91–2).
23. See Teelock (2001: 265).
24. See Boodhoo (2010: 43). Also Klein (1973: 645–51), on the considerable impact of modern transport and irrigation systems – roads, railways, canals and dams – on the dispersal of diseases, not only by enabling human vectors to move further, faster and in greater numbers than before, but also through the creation of new pools of stagnant and therefore contaminated or mosquito-breeding water and infected working populations housed in slums on construction sites and routes.
25. For an account of local Hindu responses to smallpox and cholera on the Indian subcontinent, see Arnold (1986: 128–35).
26. The difficulties in implementing smallpox vaccination in nineteenth-century India, as well as the implications of these measures for the stability of the colonial power, are impressively discussed by Arnold (1993: 116–58).
27. On the socio-political implications of smallpox vaccination in Mauritius, see Boodhoo (2010: 58–9, 129–36) and Vaughan (2000: 415–7).
28. Beyond Mauritius, as Arnold (1986: 143–5) has shown, British colonial officials concerned with diseases in India, almost up until the end of the nineteenth century (when Robert Koch discovered the cholera vibrio in a Calcutta tank, thus opening the way for the 'victory' of the water-borne and germ theories of infections), clung to the view that cholera was transmitted through 'aerial highways' and through sudden climatic

or environmental changes. See also Shlomowitz and Brennan (1990: 89–92). The connections between 'miasma theories' of disease and wider scientific theories concerning the interdependence of deforestation, desiccation and weather changes, as well as climate and environmental change, are pursued in great detail by Grove (1996).

29. See Boodhoo (2010: 46).
30. On these points, see Boodhoo (2010: 32–6).
31. On debates concerning sanitation, sewerage and water supply in Port Louis, especially within the Port Louis camps of 'vagrant' Indian labourers, see Anderson (1918: 84–94), Kalla (2001: 104–9).
32. See Boodhoo (2010: 84–5).
33. Boodhoo (2010: 138–40, 154–66), Kalla (2001: 104–5, 109–12).
34. Boodhoo (2010: 32). On these points, see also ibid. (16, 22, 33).
35. See Boodhoo (2010: 87).
36. This denial of entry to the port found its counterpart on land, when, at the height of the epidemics, some districts of the island resorted to preventing people, especially those coming from disease-ridden Port Louis, from freely entering their locality, a measure which ran counter to the highly appreciated value of freedom of movement (at least for whites). See Vaughan (2000).
37. See Boodhoo (2010: 149–53). A vivid literary account of the quarantining of a ship with Indian 'coolies' on these islands is given by Le Clezio (1995).
38. On the politics of quarantine, see Boodhoo (2010: 44, 129–33, 138–43).
39. For more details, see Boodhoo (2010: 150–1).
40. For this and similar statements, see Boodhoo (2010: 79–82).
41. In this context, it is important to see how British colonial officers in Mauritius and Calcutta, often in conflicts of interest against each other rather than cooperating together, soon started to worry (more for commercial than for humanitarian reasons) about the high rates of ship mortality on immigrant ships. The measures taken from the mid-nineteenth century onwards to improve the situation in the immigrant depots of Calcutta, Bombay and Madras, as well as on the ships were, of course, also meant to reduce the number of sick passengers and thereby the risk of infections on the island through them. See Boodhoo (2010: 70–3, 103–28). Deerpalsingh and Carter (1996) dedicate Chapter 3 of their *Select Documents* to 'Shipping and Quarantine Issues', first with an insightful essay (ibid.: 171–80), then with a reprint of a substantial number of documents and enclosures pertinent to this matter (ibid.: 181–260). See also Carter (1995: 120–50).

42. See Boodhoo (2010: 63–4, 89–93).
43. See the review by Oliver-Smith (1996). See also two especially insightful studies in this context by Horden and Purcell (2000: chap. VIII) and Davis (2001). On the spread of diseases across the Indian Ocean, see Echenberg (2018); Winterbottom and Tesfaye (eds. 2016); Campbell and Knoll (eds. 2020).
44. See Agamben (1998). For a 'neo-Foucauldian view' of British colonial health policies and attempts to 'colonize' the bodies of their Indian subjects, see Arnold (1993: 1–115, 240–94).

REFERENCES

Agamben, G. 1998. *Homo Sacer: Sovereign Power and Bare Life*. Stanford: Stanford University Press.

Alpers, E.A. 2014. *The Indian Ocean in World History*. Oxford: Oxford University Press.

——, 2020. 'Chikungunya and Epidemic Disease in the Indian Ocean World'. In Campbell and Knoll (eds.) 2020:211–36.

Anderson, D.E. 1918. *The Epidemics of Mauritius with a Descriptive and Historical Account of the Island*. London: H.K. Lewis.

Arnold, D. 1986. 'Cholera and Colonialism in British India'. *Past and Present* 113: 118–51.

——, 1991. 'The Indian Ocean as a Disease Zone, 1500–1950'. *South Asia* 14: 1–21.

——, 1993. *Colonizing the Body: State Medicine and Epidemic Disease in Nineteenth-Century India*. Berkeley: University of California Press.

Arnold, D. (ed.). 1988. *Imperial Medicine and Indigenous Societies*. Manchester: Manchester University Press.

Boodhoo, R. 2010. *Health, Disease and Indian Immigrants in Nineteenth Century Mauritius*. Port Louis: Aapravasi Ghat Fund.

Campbell, G., and E.M. Knoll (eds.). 2020. *Disease Dispersion and Impact in the Indian Ocean World*. Cham: Palgrave Macmillan.

Carter, M. 1995. *Servants, Sirdars and Settlers: Indians in Mauritius, 1834–1874*. Delhi: Oxford University Press.

Davis, M. 2001. *Late Victorian Holocausts: El Niño Famines and the Making of the Third World*. London: Verso Books.

Deerpalsingh, S., and M. Carter. 1996. *Select Documents on Indian Immigration, Mauritius 1834–1926*, Vol. II: *The Despatch and Allocation of Indentured Labour*. Moka, Mauritius: Mahatma Gandhi Institute.

Echenberg, M. 2018. *Africa in the Time of Cholera: A History of Pandemics from 1817 to the Present.* Cambridge: Cambridge University Press.

Grove, R.H. 1996. *Green Imperialism: Colonial Expansion, Tropical Island Edens and the Origins of Environmentalism, 1600–1860.* Cambridge: Cambridge University Press.

Hookoomsing, V., R. Ludwig, and B. Schnepel (eds.). 2009. *Multiple Identities in Action: Mauritius and Some Antillean Parallelisms.* Berlin: Peter Lang.

Horden, P., and N. Purcell. 2000. *The Corrupting Sea: A Study of Mediterranean History.* Oxford: Blackwell Publishing.

Hurgobin, Y. 2016. 'Making Medical Ideologies: Indentured Labor in Mauritius'. In Winterbottom and Tesfaye (eds.) 2016: 1–26.

Kalla, A.C. 2001. 'Health and Urban Environment in Mauritius (1850–1900)'. *Journal of Mauritian Studies* 1(1): 93–120.

Klein, I. 1973. 'Death in India, 1871–1921'. *Journal of Asian Studies* 32(4): 639–59.

Le Clezio, J.M.G. 1995. *La Quarantaine.* Paris: Editions Gallimard.

McPherson, K. 2009. 'Mauritius: Mirror and Model of History'. In Hookoomsing, Ludwig, and Schnepel (eds.) 2009: 31–44. Berlin: Peter Lang.

Oliver-Smith, A. 1996. 'Review: Anthropological Research on Hazards and Disasters'. *Annual Review of Anthropology* 25: 303–28.

Pearson, M. 2003. *The Indian Ocean.* London: Routledge.

Ross, R. 1908. *Report on the Prevention of Malaria in Mauritius.* London.

Schnepel, B., and E.A. Alpers (eds.). 2018. *Connectivity in Motion: Island Hubs in the Indian Ocean World.* New York: Palgrave Macmillan.

Shlomowitz, R., and L. Brennan. 1990. 'Mortality and Migrant Labour in Assam, 1865–1921'. *The Indian Economic and Social History Review* 27: 85–111.

Teelock, V. 2001. *Mauritian History: From its Beginnings to Modern Times.* Moka, Mauritius: Mahatma Gandhi Institute.

——, 2018. 'A Hub of "Local Cosmopolitans": Migration and Settlement in Early Eighteenth- to Nineteenth-Century Port Louis'. In Schnepel and Alpers (eds.) 2018: 209–29.

Toussaint, A. 1973. *Port Louis: A Tropical City.* London: Allen and Unwin.

Vaughan, M. 2000. 'Slavery, Smallpox, and Revolution: 1792 in Île de France (Mauritius)'. *Social History of Medicine* 13(3): 411–28.

Winterbottom, A., and F. Tesfaye (eds.). 2016. *Histories of Medicine and Healing in the Indian Ocean World, Volume Two: The Modern Period.* Basingstoke: Palgrave Macmillan.

CHAPTER 5

'Little India' or 'Creole Society'?[1] Demography, Contested Identities and Heritage Politics in Contemporary Mauritius

INTRODUCTION

Mauritius has had a long history of 'unfree labour'. French plantation owners, settlers and colonial officials, who built the colony in earnest from 1735 onwards, were only able to survive, settle down amicably and develop the island by installing two exploitative labour regimes, which followed each other without interruption: first, slavery, with an overwhelmingly African workforce; and secondly, after the abolition of slavery in 1835, 'indentured labour' with contract workers from India until 1914. These individuals, who were put to work in unfree and/or extremely coercive conditions, built the island's infrastructure, provided the necessities for the colony's subsistence, served in the households of the rich, and finally made Mauritian sugar plantations a long-running economic success. The history of slavery and indentured labour decisively shaped the island's society as it exists today. Let us therefore look briefly at the demographic dimensions of these two historical labour regimes before considering demography, identities and heritage politics in contemporary Mauritian society.

In absolute terms, the number of slaves who were forcefully brought to Mauritius steadily increased during the century in question, namely from 650 in 1735 to 25,000 in 1777 to 65,000 in 1835.[2] Of these slaves, 45 per cent came from Madagascar, 40 per cent from Mozambique and other parts of East Africa, 2 per cent from West Africa and 13 per cent from South and Southeast Asia. During the period from 1735 to 1835 a total of approximately 150,000 slaves arrived in Mauritius, two-thirds of them male. Even in the intermediate period between the prohibition of the slave trade in 1807 ('Slave Trade Act') and the abolition of slavery itself in 1833 ('Slave Abolition Act'), approximately 30,000 Africans continued to be brought to and enslaved in Mauritius clandestinely, often via Zanzibar or the Seychelles. It is unlikely that this could have been done without the connivance of Farquhar, the first British governor, and his men. In relative terms, the numbers of slaves 'living' (and dying) on the island far outnumbered the number of French settlers and colonial officials, usually constituting around 80 per cent of the total population throughout the century in question here. Thus, if ever there was one, Mauritius during French rule and the first decades of British rule was a slave society par excellence.

The dichotomy between 'masters' on the one hand and slaves on the other represented the key social relation and the lynchpin around which the colony was ordered and organized. However, the social and racial barriers between these two sides soon proved fragile and porous. First, on the French side, not all settlers had slaves or land and/or were powerful: on the contrary, large numbers of settlers hailed from the poorer and lower strata of French society and had fled their homes to escape the misery of their lives in France. Although these *petits blancs*, unlike the slaves, were legally free, their living conditions were often characterized by poverty, malnutrition, sickness, exploitation and despotism on behalf of government officials and the holders of the great estates. Furthermore, within the category of slaves there soon arose a new social category, which, from the 'whites' point of view, was awkwardly located in between the free 'white' category and the enslaved 'black' population, namely manumitted slaves or so-called 'freedmen'. Until the abolition of slavery in Mauritius in 1835, the number of ex-slaves, with their freely born offspring, continually rose, until it reached some 20 per cent of the total population. Not a few of these ex-slaves were females who had been the mistresses and concubines of slave owners and had even had children with them. These children of mixed biological and social provenance constituted yet another hybrid category within the colonial system of racial classification, namely the *gens de couleur.*

Like the 'freedmen' (and freed women), legally these 'coloureds' were free, though socially and economically they were disadvantaged and often impoverished when compared with their 'white' half-brothers and half-sisters.[3] Finally, there existed yet another social category on Mauritius, namely that of runaway slaves or *marrons*, who, despite all endeavours by special detachments of police and armed planters to track them down, were growing to quite substantial numbers. It is estimated that at any point in time during the period of slavery discussed here, about five to 10 per cent of the slave population absconded, at least temporarily; some of them even managed to form stable communities, especially in the island's rather impenetrable south. When slavery was abolished by the British, therefore, around four-fifths of the population (according to the colonial colour system) consisted of 'blacks' (ex-slaves, ex-freedmen, and ex-*marrons*) and 'coloureds'. 'White' colonial officials and French settlers (*petit* as well as *grand*) were in a clear minority throughout the colony's history, but they always wielded power, and many of them grew wealthy.

This demographic situation changed swiftly and substantially within three to four decades, when the first indentured labourers or 'coolies', as they were disparagingly called,[4] started to arrive in Mauritius on ships from India.[5] In 1834 the first ship reached the island from Calcutta with 75 male labourers; until the end of the scheme in the early twentieth century, almost half a million Indian immigrants were to follow.[6] From the middle of the nineteenth century at least 40 per cent of these arrivals, it was officially decreed, had to be women, many of whom were unmarried or widows that were intended to be (re-)married in the island. 'In this way', Carter observes, 'the recourse to Mauritius was for many Indian women not a search for work at all but rather a marriage migration' (1996: 140).[7] Indian indentured labourers disembarked in Port Louis at the so-called 'Aapravasi Ghat' – today a UNESCO World Heritage Site – with contracts that bound them to work (and live) on sugar plantations, usually for a period of three or five years, and under conditions that initially were not much better than those of slavery. However, legally these 'coolies' were free, and their working and living conditions, as well as their political and economic situations, improved slowly but steadily during the period in question. As a result, in the end around 70 per cent of the 'coolies' who had been transshipped from India to Mauritius opted to stay on the island, creating families there and producing island-born offspring. Much to the dismay of colonial officials and plantation owners, most of these ex-coolies or 'old immigrants' (as labourers who had served their contracts were called) refused to be re-indentured and opted to make a living in Mauritius outside the indenture system instead.

The continuing in-flow of Indian labourers, as well as the fact that many of them stayed on the island and created families, resulted, as already noted, in a significant demographic change on the island. The descendants of African slaves or 'Creoles' (as 'blacks' and 'coloureds' together were labelled), who for over a century had constituted the majority of the Mauritian population, came to be outnumbered by the Indian immigrants. Already in 1835, roughly 35 per cent of the island population had been of Indian origin; by 1860 this number had risen to 60 per cent, while in 1870 almost 70 per cent of the Mauritian population hailed from India, reaching the percentage level that still obtains today.[8]

The following sections of this chapter will investigate and assess to what extent, and with what consequences, this colonial history has influenced demographic, socio-cultural and political matters on the island today. In particular, it will be asked what kind of society contemporary Mauritius represents, not only from an external analytical perspective, but also from the points of views of the various population groups living on the island today. For these actors, the questions of where they come from (both historically and in terms of their terrestrial belonging), who they are and who they wish to be (or become) are not merely academic ones, but vital for how they see themselves and act accordingly.

LITTLE INDIA

Pursuing this line of inquiry, one may well start by looking at the Indian part of the Mauritian population, i.e. at the Indo-Mauritians or 'Persons of Indian Origin' (PIOs).[9] A first feature that has strongly influenced the situation of Indian immigrants on Mauritius, and improved their chances of establishing a life for themselves on the island, relates to the fact that their new Mauritian homes were *relatively* close to their old ones. These simple geographical and quantitative facts were probably more important in the 'age of sail' than they are in the contemporary age of jet planes and the internet, but the actual distance between 'mother country' and diasporic community has continued to play a role. In the 'age of sail', first of all, 'coolies' were better off than African slaves, who had been forcibly deported in chains, in terrible hygienic conditions and subjected to severe penal regimes. The average death toll on the slave ships had been roughly 10 per cent. The death toll on vessels transporting Indian labourers, by comparison, was 'better', namely at around three to 5 per cent. Certainly, this percentage is bad enough, and therefore only relatively advantageous. Not unlike African slaves, moreover, the indentured labourers were crammed into inhuman and unhygienic spaces on board often old and unsafe vessels at risk of shipwreck, and they were prone to spread epidemic diseases on board.[10] The disruptive journey through which family, neighbourhood and friendship ties were severed for a long time, if not forever, as well as their harsh, bleak and insecure lives in an unknown and often hostile world, placed a severe mental burden on those who journeyed across the 'black waters' (*kala pani*) to new shores.

Even when they had safely arrived, communication with and remittances to families back home in India were uncertain, and a return journey would only be possible, if at all, after the standard five-year contract had been completed. As far as distance is concerned, a journey to Mauritius took around eight weeks from Calcutta and six weeks from Madras or Bombay.[11] The passage to Mauritius was therefore long and hard compared to those to Ceylon and Burma, where Indian plantation workers also went in great numbers. From Sri Lanka and Burma, then, it was easier to return to India frequently and to maintain some ties with home. It was also possible to be joined by members of one's family, caste, village or subregion on a larger scale. At least it was possible to try and mirror one's socio-cultural life at home, with all its established networks of solidarity and its traditional caste-based social organization. This socially more integrated system of migration was known as *kangani*.[12] In contrast, trips to Mauritius were mostly made by individuals, rather than being family, sub-caste or village affairs. While on board, one might meet neighbours or friends, or make new acquaintances. These new relationships became known as *jehaji bhai* or 'ship brothers', and on the island, subsequently, they could assume the character of quasi-kinship bonds.[13]

Compared to other destinations in the worldwide indentured labour scheme, however, Mauritius was still relatively close to home. Destinations in the Caribbean or Fiji were so much further away (namely, nineteen to twenty weeks on board) that these longer distances made a significant qualitative difference. Indo-Mauritians who had completed their time as contract labourers could return to India, and about a third did so. However, many of these returnees did not stay in India, but re-emigrated to Mauritius, this time bringing their wives and families with them. The *relative* proximity of Mauritius to the Indian homeland, accompanied by the gradual improvements in postal communications and maritime transport, therefore enabled a sort of circular or chain migration to develop. All this gradually resulted in the establishment of more traditional forms of social cohesion among Indo-Mauritians.

As far as the Indian diaspora in contemporary Mauritius is concerned, it is clearly many-sided and even heterogeneous in its social, caste, class, religious and linguistic aspects, as well as regarding its places of origin on the Indian subcontinent. Most of the Indians who were shipped as 'coolies' to Mauritius came from rural areas and belonged to the lowest and poorest castes and classes on the Indian subcontinent.[14] Only later in the nineteenth and twentieth centuries were the first immigrants joined by clerks, priests and merchants from the higher castes and better-off strata of Indian society. As for their geographical roots, almost two-thirds of immigrant labourers came from the north of India, mainly Bihar and Uttar Pradesh. These individuals were and are known in Mauritius as Biharis, and they spoke and sometimes still speak Bhojpuri, a local north Indian variant of Hindi. Approximately the remaining third came from the south of India, being further divided into Tamil- and Telugu-speaking groups of roughly equal size.[15] The merchants and petty traders mainly came from western India, so that today 3 to 4 per cent of Indo-Mauritians are Marathis or Gujaratis, who tend to retain their own group consciousness and language affiliations.[16] Looking at religion, around 65 per cent of Indo-Mauritians are Hindu, 25 per cent Muslim and 10 per cent Christian, with many Tamils especially having converted to Christianity. Within these categories there are also various, sometimes quite important further sub-distinctions, such as those between orthodox and Arya Samaj Hindus,[17] Sunni and Shiite Muslims,[18] and Catholics, Protestants and Pentecostals among the Christians. Following Hollup (1994), one could also attempt a categorization according to what he sees as some sort of ethnic affiliation. According to this author's estimates (based on the 1972 and 1982 censuses), Hindus make up 40.2 per cent of the total Mauritian population (58 per cent of PIOs), Tamils 7.3 per cent (10.5 per cent), Telugus 3 per cent (4.3 per cent), Marathis 2.1 per cent (3.1 per cent) and Muslims 16.6 per cent (24 per cent). These various regional backgrounds, mother tongues and religious as well as ethnic identifications combine dynamically with other identity-making criteria, such as education, rural or urban residence and differences in economic success and professional standing.[19]

All in all, it requires caution in speaking about *the* Indian diaspora in Mauritius, as if it were a homogeneous group. Rather, we should think of a plurality when it comes to describing and analysing the *internal* socio-cultural, politico-economic and religious dimensions of the Indo-Mauritian diaspora(s). However, more important than these statistics, with their various categorizations as starting points and ordering schemes, is that Indo-Mauritians themselves often strategically emphasize and adopt different identifications in different situations. Thus, in some circumstances – namely, in structural opposition to the non-Indian inhabitants of Mauritius, as well as to the island's Indo-Muslims – some PIOs may stress that their 'ancestral language' is Sanskrit and their religion Hindu, while in other situations Hindus and Muslims may point to their common Indian origins as opposed to fellow Mauritian nationals with African, Chinese or French roots. In other situations, when it comes to defending their social, educational and economic privileges, well-off or well-educated Indians may ally with *gens de couleur* and/or Franco-Mauritians of similar standing at the expense of solidarity with rural and poor Indo-Mauritians. In yet other situations, internal differences may peter out, not only within the community of Indo-Mauritians, but also between all ethnic groups and other communities living on Mauritius, as when Mauritius plays an important soccer match against Réunion, or when relations between Mauritians and tourists are at stake. In a nutshell, PIOs in Mauritius adopt multiple, overlapping and situationally shifting 'fusion and fission' forms of identification, both within the category of Indo-Mauritians and when transcending this category. Some of these identifications, namely those derived from one's region of origin on the Indian subcontinent, or those referring to the three main religions, appear to be more important from the actors' points of view than others, and therefore tend to be 'essentialized' more strongly.[20]

MIGRATION PATTERNS

It is estimated that more than twenty million Indians live abroad today, as reflected in the statistics shown in the table below. Two major historical waves of Indian emigration are largely responsible for these numbers.[21] The first wave consisted of migration in the nineteenth century to the plantation economies in southern, subtropical parts of the world. The second wave, starting after 1945, has brought Indians to the industrialized countries of North America and Europe, as well as to Australia and, for several decades now, to the oil-producing Arab world. By and large, the descendants of those who came with the first wave are today regarded as 'Persons of Indian Origin' while substantial numbers of those who came with the second wave and their descendants are often labelled as 'Non-Resident Indians' or 'NRIs'.

A closer look at Table 5.1 shows that the Indian diaspora in Mauritius is substantial in absolute terms (716,000) and was exceeded in this respect only by the Indian diasporas in Britain (1.2 million), Canada (850,000), Malaysia (1.6 million), Myanmar (2.5 million),[22] Saudi Arabia (1.5 million), South Africa (1 million), the United States (1.7 million) and the United Arab Emirates (950,000). However, only Malaysia and Myanmar – two countries with their very own special migration histories – have larger 'first-wave' immigrants (still as Malaya and Burma). Furthermore, with reference to the total population,

TABLE 5.1: ESTIMATED SIZE OF OVERSEAS INDIAN COMMUNITY[23]

Country	*Persons of Indian Origin (PIOs)*	*Non-Resident Indians (NRIs)*	*Total*
Australia	160,000	30,000	190,000
Bahrain	nil	130,000	130,000
Canada	700,000	150,000	850,000
Fiji	337,000	nil	337,000
France	55,000	10,000	65,000
Germany	10,000	25,000	35,000
Great Britain			1,200,000
Guadeloupe	40,000	nil	40,000
Guyana	392,000	nil	392,000
Italy	36,000	36,000	72,000
Jamaica	60,000	1,500	61,500
Kenya	85,000	15,000	100,000
Kuwait	1,000	294,000	295,000
Malaysia	1,600,000	15,000	1,615,000
Mauritius	705,000	11,000	716,000
Myanmar	2,500,000	2,000	2,502,000
Netherlands	200,000	15,000	215,000
Oman	1,000	311,000	312,000
Qatar	1,000	130,000	131,000
Réunion	220,000	nil	220,000
Saudi Arabia	nil	1,500,000	1,500,000
Singapore	217,000	90,000	307,000
South Africa			1,000,000
Surinam	150,000	nil	150,000
Tanzania	85,000	5,000	90,000
Thailand	70,000	15,000	85,000
Trinidad & Tobago	500,000	nil	500,000
United Arab Emirates	50,000	900,000	950,000
USA			1,700,000
Yemen	100,000	1,000	101,000

i.e., in relative terms, globally the Indian diaspora in Mauritius holds *the* top position, with more than two-thirds of the Mauritian population having an Indian background. With the gradual democratization of Mauritian society from the first half of the twentieth century and the granting of full electoral and citizenship rights to all the island's adult inhabitants today, this demographic dominance has allowed

Indians great political influence, and even assured their dominance within the Mauritian political system.[24] Indeed, with the exception of Paul Berenger, a left-wing Franco-Mauritian who led the country from 2003 to 2005, all Mauritian prime ministers have had an Indian, and more specifically a Hindu background. This numerical and subsequent political superiority was accompanied, if not also decisively triggered and supported, by the gradual economic liberation and upward social mobility of PIOs in Mauritius. Today, substantial numbers of Indo-Mauritians are well-off, highly educated, 'upwardly mobile' citizens. Therefore, the standing of contemporary Indo-Mauritians has improved greatly when compared not only with their initial state of 'coolitude', but also with the state of affairs of their former relatives and neighbours (and their descendants) who chose to stay behind in India.[25] Furthermore, in recent decades the relationships and cooperation between Mauritian PIOs and India have been strengthened through measures which 'Mother India' has been implementing globally to regain the interest and support (in terms of remittances and investments) of those of her 'children' who live permanently abroad. Especially the introduction of a 'Person of Indian Origin Card' in the early 1990s, offering many advantages to Mauritian PIOs in their travels to India and their financial dealings with Indians and Indian institutions, has strengthened the ties between members of the Mauritian diaspora and their homeland.[26]

THE MAURITIAN POPULATION AS A WHOLE

While the Indian diaspora in Mauritius is the most important one, it is not the only one. According to the 1982 census (the last of its kind, and probably out of date as far as accurate numbers are concerned, but still representative in terms of relative percentages), the population of Mauritius totalled 1.2 million people and was broken down as follows: Hindus 52 per cent; Muslims 16 per cent; Sino-Mauritians 3 per cent; and General Population 29 per cent. Mauritius, then, seems to be a multi-ethnic and poly-religious society. This diversity is expressed by the twenty annual nationwide holidays which demonstrate that most religious and ethnic groups on the island are equally acknowledged, and that their interests and self-

Figure 5.1: The Mauritian Flag

esteem are respected. Another symbol of plurality (and unity in diversity) is the national flag, which features an abstraction of the colours of the rainbow and stands for a *nation arc-en-ciel*.[27]

If we look at the categories used in the 1982 census more carefully, however, some inconsistencies appear. The distinction between Hindus and Muslims is obviously a religious one, and we have already noted that the ancestors of both Hindus and Muslims in Mauritius today originally came from India, especially North India. However, given that various Muslim groups on the island have recently started to claim that they originate from the Arabian Peninsula, these common local roots in India should again be emphasized: Both Hindus and Muslims are *Indo*-Mauritians and were labelled as such in censuses until 1947, the year of India's independence and the partition of India. The third largest census group, 'Sino', is not a religious categorization but rather one based on region of origin, namely China or East Asia. Finally, subsumed under the categorization of 'General Population' are such heterogeneous groups as white Franco-Mauritians (accounting for 2 per cent of the population) and 'Creoles' (including *gens de couleur*, with around 27 per cent).

Strikingly, then, the descendants of former slaves and those of their former masters find themselves in the same demographic melting pot, namely, one called 'General'. This indicates that in post-colonial Mauritius the descendants of indentured labourers had become such a majority by the mid-twentieth century that they could be split into two religious groups, as well as being distinguished from the East Asian 'Sino' group. The unified category of 'General Population', made up of the two distinct groups that first populated the island in the eighteenth century, can therefore also be defined *ex negativo*, namely, as all those who do not come from Asia.

Other categorizations in the census would obviously have produced different figures. Using regions of origin as a basis, for example, could have identified macro-groups as Indian, Chinese, African and European, or even just Asian, African and European. If one took religious affiliation in all instances (and not only in the first two) as the criterion, the state of affairs would have looked different again. Not only are all sub-groups of the 'General Population', no matter whether 'black', 'coloured' or 'white', Christians, but so are large numbers of Mauritians hailing from South India, as well as most Sino-Mauritians.[28] Taking yet another criterion, namely that of language, would have 'shuffled the cards' yet again in other ways. Officially, fifteen languages are spoken in Mauritius, including English, French, Kreol, Bhojpuri, Hindi, Urdu, Tamil, Telugu, Marathi, Arabic, Hakka and Cantonese. However, in almost all interactions, a French-based Kreol is spoken. Indeed, many Mauritians also speak excellent French, in which most of the national media also communicates. The official national language, however, is neither French nor Kreol, but English. If one views language less as a means of communication than as a symbolic marker of identification and belonging, another dimension is added. Asked about their 'ancestral language' or 'mother tongue', Indo-Mauritians tend to mention languages such as Sanskrit, Hindi, Urdu and even Arabic – languages which they do not master now and which even their ancestors could barely have spoken when they arrived. As Eisenlohr comments: 'It thus seems that for a language to be considered ancestral in Mauritius, it should not only have origins outside Mauritius but should not be used in everyday action' (2006: 31).[29]

In Mauritius, then, we find multiple, sometimes overlapping, sometimes structurally opposed identities in action and motion. The island hosts a quite heterogeneous conglomeration of groups, which can be classified in a number of ways, according to country or continent of origin, phenotypical characteristics, languages spoken, (claimed) ancestral languages, religious denominations, and various sociocultural or economic characteristics. Among these various groups on the island, PIOs constitute the majority, namely, about two-thirds when all Indo-Mauritians are considered, and still more than 50 per cent when only Hindus are counted. These PIOs can be further differentiated or divided along various lines when different criteria are applied, not only analytically (i.e. from the point of view of an outside observer), but also by the actors themselves in their dynamic and strategic responses to various situations. This fluid and shifting situation applies not only to the PIOs, but also to other groups on the island. In Eriksen's words: 'The main theoretical point here is that ethnicity is, in practice, not an inert, categorical property of persons (although folk models tend to depict it as such), but a property of the relationship between agents acting in situations and contexts and as such, its meaning changes with the context' (1998: 98–9).[30]

DIASPORIC CONSCIOUSNESS, ETHNICITY AND NATIONHOOD

Each and every sector of the Mauritian 'rainbow society' has come from elsewhere. This means that no single group living in Mauritius today can claim indigeneity and hence demand rights or privileges arising from such a claim. Some groups may have been there (shortly) before others. However, any such claim to first-comer status is less important than sheer numbers, which eventually translate into political power. The absence of any aboriginal population or officially acknowledged 'first-comers' makes present-day inter-ethnic negotiations and identity politics in Mauritius somewhat unique. No group there can make a 'native' claim to possession or at least to privileged access to a resource like land, as one might in Australia or the United States; or in Fiji, where some native groups have sought to bar the descendants of Indian 'coolies' from acquiring landed property on the basis that only ethnic Fijians are the 'sons of the soil'; or in Trinidad, where Afro-Trinidadians claim political privileges on account of having arrived on the island first.[31]

Although, or maybe exactly because, everyone on the island came from abroad, the idea and ideology of an original home *elsewhere* remains pertinent in the lives of most Mauritians. In other words, apart from being Mauritians and Mauritian nationals (which the islanders are and consider themselves to be), all sections of Mauritian society also consider themselves, sometimes quite emphatically, as having diasporic roots and continuous diasporic links to their real and/or assumed 'homelands'. Consequently, in both ideology and practice they exhibit and are guided by a diasporic consciousness.[32]

Against this background, the Mauritian postcolonial state – from its beginnings till now – has been confronted with the task of accommodating two apparently contradictory issues: a multiplicity of ethnic identities on the one hand, and the need to establish a national identity capable of transcending sectional interests in an effective and peaceful manner on the other. As far as the former is concerned, ethnic politics are supported, not obstructed, by the Mauritian state in both its internal and external policies. For example, the state has subsidized institutions like the 'Mahatma Gandhi Institute', the 'Nelson Mandela Centre for African Culture' and the 'Centre Charles Baudelaire'. Many diasporic traditions, such as the Hindu *Maha Shivaratri*, have been turned into national holidays, while on 12 March, 'Independence Day', national unity is usually staged as a multicultural show of dances, songs and colourful dress.[33] Furthermore, the state has strongly espoused the teaching of 'ancestral languages' in school, while *Créole Morisyen*, the vernacular language spoken in everyday interactions by all, was long neglected and has only recently found a permanent place on the school curriculum.[34]

Hence, in Mauritius the idea of nationhood differs radically from the early modern European prototype of (ideally) 'one culture/one language/one religion/one nation/one territory/one state'. Certainly, this ideal was seldom if ever achieved. In Mauritius it was not even attempted; rather, the endeavour to build a nation and unify its diverse elements into both a working unit and a sentimental entity were pursued in accordance with slogans like 'Unity in Diversity' and

'The Rainbow Nation'. In fact, the 'unity in diversity' paradigm also guides post-colonies like Kenya, India, and Indonesia. The reason for this is simply that after independence many of the emerging postcolonial nation states found either that their territorial borders had been arbitrarily drawn, cutting across existing ethnic and cultural borders, or that, within the framework of the new nations, a multitude of heterogeneous groups had become mingled, also, like in Mauritius, through migration. To many postcolonial states, then, the 'unity in diversity' paradigm offered a possible way of dealing with such a plural and often heterogeneous arrangement as far as nation-building measures were concerned.[35]

While the Mauritian state's policy in this respect is therefore not unique, it can only be understood fully in its own terms if one considers two further Mauritian peculiarities. First, as has already been emphasized, all *ethnic* identifications on the island are closely combined with, and based on, a *diasporic* consciousness. In other words, ethnic discourses in Mauritius always emphasize links to other parts in the world, to other 'homelands'. The second peculiarity, which will be discussed in the remainder of this section, relates to the dominance of a diasporic role model which in essence is Hindu.

Nation-building activities and national ideology in Mauritius are based on the idea of the legitimate existence of a number of different ethnic groups. *All* of these share a diasporic consciousness and logic in which the following elements are esteemed and valued:

- an established link to a homeland outside Mauritius
- an ancestral language
- an ancient and essentialized 'ancestral culture'
- a religion that is conceived as 'traditional' and is performed in everyday rituals and annual festivities
- a history, or better a heritage, of one's own.

While all ethnic groups in Mauritius claim to have some such diasporic markers, and all, more or less, cherish them, these elements can most convincingly be referred to and invoked by the Indian diaspora in Mauritius. In other words, the Indo-Mauritian version of diaspora has become so dominant in heritage politics that it serves as the role model and ideal for other ethnic groups as well.

Let us look at these elements once again, this time with a focus on the Indian diaspora:

- Indo-Mauritians can clearly identify 'Mother India' as their land of origin
- Hindi and Sanskrit are conceived of and propagated as mother tongues representing purity and even sacredness
- Indian philosophy, literature, music and dance are considered ancient and sacred
- Hinduism, with its daily rituals and major religious festivals, plays an important role in Mauritian public life
- the history of India is considered very ancient, and great parts of its past are seen as glorious.

It will have been noted that, in this Indo-Mauritian logic of diaspora, the Hindu aspect is dominant, while Mauritian Muslims find themselves either excluded (e.g., as far as religion is concerned), or at best encompassed. As Eisenlohr writes:

> Though relative latecomers in the process of settling the island, Hindu Mauritians, who compromise the largest and politically dominant ethnic community of Mauritius, have legitimized their central place in a Mauritian nation not in terms of an imagined state of indigenousness but by the construction of diasporic ancestral cultures. (. . .), they have established the hegemony of a diasporic notion of cultural citizenship according to which Mauritians are primarily defined as subjects having origins in other parts of the world with continuing commitments to putative ancestral traditions. (2006: 5)

The ideal of an Indo-Mauritian diaspora, which is actually manifold and heterogeneous in itself, is a Hindu diaspora.

'LITTLE INDIA' AND 'CREOLE SOCIETY'

While the Hindu model of diasporic values represents the ideal against which all other diasporic communities are measured, it can hardly be achieved by them all. This is evident not only as far as Mauritian Muslims are concerned, but even more so in how Mauritians of African origin, or 'Creoles', fare in these respects. As a country of origin, Africa is too large to qualify as a sentimental 'home country'.

The violent abduction of Africans from their territorial roots and the policy of slavers to extinguish the identities of their slaves have severed any factual links to specific African countries and have also dampened any emotional or ideational attachments to them. Moreover, in the media contemporary Africa is typically represented as a place of poverty, misery, corrupt regimes, and war, making it even more difficult for Afro-Mauritians to attach positive evaluations to a putative 'ancestral home'. In terms of language identification, slavery has also cut the ties to any mother tongue. Certainly, Mauritian Creole or '*Créole Morisyen*' contains significant Bantu elements, but even its practitioners conceive of it (wrongly or not) as a derivative form of French rather than a suitable 'ancestral language'. Therefore, *Créole Morisyen* hardly qualifies as an ethnic language marker for Afro-Mauritians, let alone a sacred one. In religious matters, moreover, most Creoles are Christians today. By contrast to Brazil and other American countries, however, there are few 'African' elements in Christian beliefs and practices on the island. Culturally, Mauritians clearly identify the *Séga* dance as 'island-born', rather than as African in origin. They see it as a performative genre that only emerged in Mauritius under the harsh conditions of slavery.[36]

From the point of view of Hindu nationalists and their dominant idea of diaspora, then, the Mauritian descendants of former African slaves serve as an example of how culture and cultural identity can be lost if one's roots are severed and/or forgotten. All in all, then, the second largest group in Mauritius, the Mauritian Creoles, is generally seen as a deficient and incomplete version of the (Hindu) ideal of diaspora. This is strikingly expressed by the categorization of Creoles in past censuses under 'General Population' (as pointed out above), rather than being recognized as an independent and clearly identifiable entity in its own right. In Megan Vaughan's words, 'The Creoles in contemporary Mauritian terms are those who are *not*: they are neither Hindus nor Muslims nor Tamils nor Chinese nor "whites" of either the Franco or Anglo variety. The Creole community is the residue of these racial/ethnic/cultural categories, a residue that purportedly lacks a distinct culture and suffers from what is known as "la malaise créole", a "disease" not only of poverty, but of social marginality and abjection' (2005: 3).[37]

In conclusion, with Srebrnick (2000) one could ask: 'Can an Ethnically-based Civil Society Succeed?' The numerical predominance of PIOs in Mauritius, the opening of India to PIOs and NRIs, and the ever-increasing economic power and attractiveness of India in a globalized world have led to 'Indian-ness', especially in its dominant form of 'Hindu-ness', increasing in strength in Mauritius. Has Mauritius, then, become a 'Little India' after all, a society in which a pluri-ethnic nationhood is on its way to becoming replaced by an ethnonationalism in which all groups, other than the Indian, become underprivileged minorities? Or is there actually a tendency in Mauritius towards establishing a 'Creole Society'? In this context, 'Creole' is meant to be understood in the emphatic postcolonial sense, namely as depicting a creative '*metissage*' of diverse elements and abilities that produces something innovative which is more than just the sum of its parts.[38] There are scholars who predict that, in these times of ever-increasing mobility and worldwide interconnectedness, those individuals and communities that have what could be called 'globality' will have a decisive advantage and fare better.[39] In fact, Mauritius's relative success in various sectors of the world market is based on it promoting itself as a cosmopolitan 'hub society', which the islanders are performing and delivering accordingly.[40] At this point in time, however, it is difficult to predict whether communalism or cosmopolitanism will prevail in Mauritius. It must therefore suffice to suggest that Mauritian society as it exists today can best be characterized by changing the main title of this chapter from 'Little India' *or* 'Creole Society' to 'Little India' *and* 'Creole Society', and by characterizing present-day Mauritians as 'local cosmopolitans'.[41]

NOTES

1. Some such contrapositions of 'Little India' and 'Creole Society' have occupied a number of authors before. See especially Eisenlohr (2006: chap. 1), Hookoomsing (2009), and Vaughan (2005: chap. 1).
2. On slavery in Mauritius, see especially Allen (1999: 1–54), Barker (1996), Mann (2012: 53–66), Noel (1991), Nwulia (1981), Teelock (1998), and Vaughan (2005). In the following paragraphs on slavery, I am indebted to these publications.

3. *'Gens de couleur'* were barred from inheriting their father's estates, but they often received better education and other privileges, allowing them to climb the social ladder. Numerous *gens de couleur* today are lawyers, teachers, surgeons, journalists or managers, or occupy similar middle-class positions.
4. There have been attempts to re-evaluate this term positively. See Carter and Torabully (2002).
5. On 'indentured labour' in the nineteenth-century colonial world as a whole, see especially Tinker (1974) and Northrup (1995). As far as Mauritius in particular is concerned, the best studies of indentured labour are those by Carter (1994, 1995, 1996). See also Allen (1999: 55–75) and Teelock (2014).
6. Globally, from 1835 to 1914 more than 1.5 million Indians left their homes to start working on plantations (except Mauritius) in Ceylon, Burma, Fiji, Natal, and various Caribbean islands. For further details of these migratory movements, see Carter (1996: 20–2) and Tinker (1974: 62, 114).
7. The situation of women in Mauritius is especially dealt with by Carter (1994, 1996: 137–49).
8. On these numbers, see Allen (1999: 16–17, 55–8) and Carter (1996: 149).
9. The Indian diaspora in Mauritius has been thoroughly studied and analysed by a great number of scholars in its historical, ethnohistorical and sociological dimensions. See, among others, Beejadhur (1995), Benedict (1961), Bissoondoyal and Servansing (eds. 1986), Boodhoo (1999), Carter (ed. 2000), Deerpalsingh and Carter (eds. 1996a, eds. 1996b), and Hazareesingh (1966, 1977). I have dealt with these matters before in Schnepel (2018), an essay substantially reconsidered and rewritten here.
10. See Carter (1996: 45–51).
11. See Carter (1996: 32).
12. On the *kangani* system of importing labour, see Jain (1993: 6–11).
13. The issue of caste in Mauritius deserves a separate discussion that would go beyond the scope of this chapter. Here it suffices to state, with Hollup: 'Among the Hindus of Mauritius, there is no system of hierarchically ordered groups, but caste populations still exist as kinship groups, although the endogamous groups have undergone considerable change' (1994: 298). See also Hollup (2000).
14. On the situation of emigrants in India, see Carter (1992) and Prakash (1992).

15. On Telugus and Tamils in Mauritius, see, among others, Link (2002), Meisig (1999), and Nirsimloo-Anenden (1990).
16. On Gujarati merchants in Mauritius, see Kalla (1987).
17. On the Arya-Samaj in Mauritius, see Hollup (1995) and Ramsurrun (ed. 2001).
18. On Muslims in Mauritius, see Donath (2009), Hollup (1996) and Jahangeer-Chojo (1997, 2002).
19. In addition, an estimated 5 per cent of Indian emigrants to Mauritius were *adivasis* or tribals. See Hollup (2000: 222).
20. The general point about plural and dynamically shifting identities in Mauritius is best studied and exemplified ethnographically in Eriksen's seminal work, *Common Denominators* (1998).
21. For overviews, see among others Jain (1993), Schnepel (2005), van der Veer (ed. 1995), and Vertovec (2000).
22. These figures have been selected from the more detailed information 'Estimated Size of Overseas Indian Community: Countrywise', found in *Ministry of External Affairs* (2002: xlvii–xlx).
23. These numbers will have changed substantially after the enforced Rohingya exodus over the last decade.
24. On democratization processes and ethnic politics in Mauritius, see Brautigam (1997), Carroll and Carroll (1999 and 2000), Mathur (1997), and Mukonoweshuro (1991).
25. For the economic development of Indo-Mauritians, see Allen (1999: chap. 6), Carter (2002), Carter, Deerpalsingh and Govinden (2000), and Srebrnik (1999).
26. On the politics of 'Mother India', see Kantowsky (2002).
27. On the demographic development of Mauritius, see Dinan (2003), Lutz (ed. 1994), and Royle (1995). The difficulty of categorizing sections of the Mauritian population into clearly defined and 'politically correct' groups is expressed by the fact that, during more than a century of state-run census activities, a number of different criteria were tested and rejected until, in 1982, all such endeavours were discarded. See Christopher (1992).
28. On religion as an 'identity marker', see especially Eriksen (1998: 90–7).
29. Several studies discuss the importance of language identification in contemporary Mauritius. See, among others, Baker (2009), Eisenlohr (2002, 2004, 2006, 2009), Hookoomsing (1986), Eriksen (1990, 1998: 75–90), and Ludwig and Schnepel (2009).
30. On the issues in this section, see also Eriksen (1998: 14–21, 47–74, 97–101).

31. On this point, see Carroll (1994), Eriksen (1992), Kelly (1991), and Srebrnik (2000: 10–11).
32. This matter has experienced another twist, since, after several decades of secondary migrations starting from Mauritius, there are now also *Mauritian* diasporas all over the world, most prominently in Australia, South Africa, England, and France.
33. See Eisenlohr (2006: 28–9).
34. See Waldis (2017).
35. The issue of nation-building in Mauritius against the background of ethnic plurality and strong ethnic consciousness is discussed in Eriksen (1998: especially 137–66; and 1992). See also Chazan-Gillig (2000).
36. On Séga, see below, Chapter 8.
37. On this and other aspects of the so-called 'Creole malaise', see especially Miles (1999) and Boswell (2006).
38. See Bernabé, Chamoiseau, and Confiant (1995).
39. For a more recent voice, see Khanna (2021).
40. See next chapter.
41. For this term, see Ho (2006). With reference to Mauritians, see Teelock (2018).

REFERENCES

Allen, R.B. 1999. *Slaves, Freedmen, and Indentured Laborers in Colonial Mauritius.* Cambridge: Cambridge University Press.

Baker, P. 2009. 'Some of the Things that Social History and Old Texts Can and Cannot Tell us about the Evolution of Creole Languages'. In Hookoomsing, Ludwig, and Schnepel (eds.) 2009: 45–66.

Barker, A.J. 1996. *Slavery and Antislavery in Mauritius, 1810–1833. The Conflict between Economic Expansion and Humanitarian Reform under British Rule.* New York: St. Martin's Press.

Beejadhur, A. 1995. *Indians in Mauritius. Quatre Bornes.* Mauritius: Pandit Ramlakhan Gossagne Publications.

Benedict, B. 1961. *Indians in a Plural Society: A Report on Mauritius.* London: Her Majesty's Stationery Office.

Bernabé, I., P. Chamoiseau, and R. Confiant. 1995. *Eloge de la Créolité.* Paris: Gallimard.

Bissoondoyal, U., and S.B.C. Servansing (eds.). 1986. *Indian Labour Immigration.* Moka, Mauritius: Mahatma Gandhi Institute.

Bock, M., and A. Rao (eds.). 2000. *Culture, Creation, and Procreation: Concepts of Kinship in South Asian Practice.* New York: Berghahn Books.

Boodhoo, S. 1999. *Bhojpuri Traditions in Mauritius.* Port Louis: Mauritius Bhojpuri Institute.

Boswell, R. 2006. *Le Malaise Créole. Ethnic Identity in Mauritius.* Oxford: Berghahn Books.

Brautigam, D. 1997. 'Institutions, Economic Reform, and Democratic Consolidation in Mauritius'. *Comparative Politics* 30(1): 45–62.

Carroll, B.W., and T. Carroll. 1999. 'The Consolidation of Democracy in Mauritius'. *Democratization* 6(1): 179–97.

——, 2000. 'Accommodating Ethnic Diversity in a Modernizing Democratic State: Theory and Practice in the Case of Mauritius'. *Ethnic and Racial Studies* 23(1): 120–42.

Carroll, T. 1994. 'Owners, Immigrants and Ethnic Conflict in Fiji and Mauritius'. *Ethnic and Racial Studies* 17(2): 301–24.

Carter, M. 1992. 'Strategies of Labour Mobilisation in Colonial India: The Recruitment of Indentured Workers for Mauritius'. *Journal of Peasant Studies* 19(3–4): 229–45.

——, 1994. *Lakshmi's Legacy. The Testimonies of Indian Women in 19th Century Mauritius.* Mauritius: Editions de L'Ocean Indien.

——, 1995. *Servants, Sirdars, and Settlers: Indians in Mauritius, 1834–1874.* Delhi: Oxford University Press.

——, 1996. *Voices from Indenture: Experiences of Indian Migrants in the British Empire.* London: Leicester University Press.

——, 2002. 'Subaltern Success Stories: Socio-Economic Mobility in the Indian Labour Diaspora: Some Mauritian Case Studies'. *Internationales Asienforum* 33: 91–100.

Carter, M. (ed.). 2000. *Across the Kalapani: The Bihari Presence in Mauritius.* Port Louis: Centre for Research on Indian Ocean Societies.

Carter, M., S. Deerpalsingh, and V. Govinden. 2000. 'The Making of a New Community: Socio-Economic Change and the Bihari Hindus'. In Carter (ed.) 2000: 101–18.

Carter, M., and K. Torabully. 2002. *Coolitude. An Anthology of the Indian Labour Diaspora.* London: Anthem Press.

Chazan-Gillig, S. 2000. 'Ethnicity and Free Exchange in Mauritian Society'. *Social Anthropology* 8(1): 33–44.

Christopher, A.J. 1992. 'Ethnicity, Community and the Census in Mauritius, 1830–1990'. *The Geographical Journal* 158(1): 57–64.

Deerpalsingh, S., and M. Carter (eds.). 1996a. *Select Documents on Indian Immigration. Mauritius, 1834–1926*, Vol. 2: *The Despatch and Alloca-*

tion of Indentured Labour. Moka, Mauritius: Mahatma Gandhi Institute.

——, 1996b. *Select Documents on Indian Immigration. Mauritius, 1834–1926*, vol. 3: *Living and Working Conditions under Indenture*. Moka, Mauritius: Mahatma Gandhi Institute.

Dinan, M. 2003. *Mauritius in the Making: Across the Censuses, 1846–2000*. Port Louis: Nelson Mandela Centre for African Culture.

Donath, F. 2009. 'Islamic Fundamentalism and Western Modernity among Muslims in Mauritius'. In Hookoomsing, Ludwig, and Schnepel (eds.) 2009: 135–61. Frankfurt/Main: Lang.

Eisenlohr, P. 2002. 'Language and Identity in an Indian Diaspora: "Multiculturalism" and Ethno-linguistic Communities in Mauritius'. *Internationales Asienforum* 33: 101–14.

——, 2004. 'Temporalities of Community: Ancestral Language, Pilgrimage, and Diasporic Belonging in Mauritius'. *Journal of Linguistic Anthropology* 14(1): 81–98.

——, 2006. *Little India: Diaspora, Time and Ethnolinguistic Belonging in Hindu Mauritius*. Berkeley: University of California Press.

——, 2009. 'An Indian Ocean "Creole Island"? Language and the Politics of Hybridity in Mauritius'. In Hookoomsing, Ludwig, and Schnepel (eds.) 2009: 87–108.

Eriksen, T.H. 1990. 'Linguistic Diversity and the Quest for National Identity: The Case of Mauritius'. *Ethnic and Racial Studies* 13(1): 1–24.

——, 1992. *Us and Them in Modern Societies: Ethnicity and Nationalism in Mauritius, Trinidad and Beyond*. Oslo: Scandinavian University Press.

——, 1998. *Common Denominators: Ethnicity, Nation-Building and Compromise in Mauritius*. Oxford: Berg.

Geisenhainer, K., and K. Lange (eds.). 2005. *Bewegliche Horizonte: Festschrift zum 60. Geburtstag von Bernhard Streck*. Leipzig: Leipziger Universitatsverlag.

Hase, Y., H. Miyake, and F. Oshikawa (eds.). 2002. *South Asian Migration in Comparative Perspective: Movement, Settlement and Diaspora*. Osaka: National Museum of Ethnology.

Hazareesingh, K. 1966. 'The Religion and Culture of Indian Immigrants in Mauritius and the Effect of Social Change'. *Comparative Studies in Society and History* 8(2): 241–57.

——, 1977. *History of Indians in Mauritius*. London: Macmillan.

Hermann, E., and A. Fuhse (eds.). 2018. *India Beyond India: Dilemmas of Belonging*. Göttingen: Göttinger Reihezur Ethnologie.

Ho, E. 2006. *Graves of Tarim: Genealogy and Mobility across the Indian Ocean*. Berkeley: University of California Press.

Hollup, O. 1994. 'The Disintegration of Caste and Changing Concepts of Indian Ethnic Identity in Mauritius'. *Ethnology* 33(4): 297–316.

——, 1995. 'Arya Samaj and the Shaping of "Egalitarian" Hindus in Mauritius'. *Folk* 36: 27–39.

——, 1996. 'Islamic Revivalism and Political Opposition among Minority Muslims in Mauritius'. *Ethnology* 35(4): 285–300.

——, 2000. 'Kinship and Marriage in the Construction of Identity and Group Boundaries among Indians in Mauritius'. In Bock and Rao (eds.) 2002: 219–39.

Hookoomsing, V.Y. 1986. 'Langue et Identité Ethnique: Les Langues Ancestrales à Maurice'. *Journal of Mauritian Studies* 1(2): 117–37.

——, 2009. 'Mauritius: Creole and or Multicultural?' In Hookoomsing, Ludwig, and Schnepel (eds.) 2009: 19–28.

Hookoomsing, V., R. Ludwig, and B. Schnepel (eds.) 2009. *Multiple Identities in Action: Mauritius and Some Antillean Parallelisms.* Berlin: Peter Lang.

Jahangeer-Chojo, A. 1997. 'The Muslims in Mauritius: A Case Study in Ethnicity'. *Eastern Anthropologist* 50: 165–70.

_____. 2002. 'Islamisation Processes among Mauritian Muslims'. *Internationales Asien Forum* 33: 116–26.

Jain, R.K. 1993. *Indian Communities Abroad: Themes and Literature.* New Delhi: Manohar.

Kalla, A.C. 1987. 'The Gujarati Merchants in Mauritius *c.* 1850–1900'. *Journal of Mauritian Studies* 2(1): 45–65.

Kantowsky, D. 2002. 'Mother India ruft ihre Kinder. Bemerkungen zur Persons of Indian Origin Card besonders in Mauritius'. *Internationales Asien Forum* 33: 127–43.

Kelly, J.D. 1991. *A Politics of Virtue. Hinduism, Sexuality, and Counter Colonial Discourse in Fiji.* Chicago: Chicago University Press.

Khanna, P. 2021. *Move. Das Zeitalter der Migration.* Berlin: Rowohlt Verlag.

Link, H. 2002. 'Belonging, Longing and Constructed Identity: The Temple at the Centre of Politics of Tamil Identity on Mauritius'. In Hase, Miyake, and Oshikawa (eds.) 2002: 153–91.

Ludwig, R., and B. Schnepel. 2009. 'Some Ideas on Communication, Culture and Society in Mauritius: Multiple Identities in Action'. In Hookoomsing, Ludwig, and Schnepel (eds.) 2009: 9–16.

Lutz, W. (ed.). 1994. *Population – Development – Environment: Understanding their Interactions in Mauritius.* Berlin: Springer.

Mann, M. 2012. *Sahibs, Sklaven und Soldaten. Geschichte des Menschenhandels rund um den Indischen Ozean.* Darmstadt: Verlag Philipp von Zabern.

Mathur, R. 1997. 'Parliamentary Representation of Minority Communities: The Mauritian Experience'. *Africa Today* 44: 61–82.

Meisig, M. 1999. 'Tamilischer Hinduismus auf Mauritius. Der Minaksòi-Tempel in Port Louis'. *Mitteilungen für Anthropologie und Religionsgeschichte* 14: 251–74.

Miles, W.F.S. 1999. 'The Creole Malaise in Mauritius'. *African Affairs* 98(391): 211–28.

Ministry of External Affairs. 2002. 'Report of the High Level Committee on Indian Diaspora'. New Delhi: Government of India. Accessed October 02, 2017. http://indiandiaspora.nic.in/contents.htm.

Mukonoweshuro, E.G. 1991. 'Containing Political Instability in a Poly-Ethnic Society: The Case of Mauritius'. *Ethnic and Racial Studies* 14(2): 199–224.

Nave, A. 2000. 'Marriage and the Maintenance of Ethnic Group Boundaries: The Case of Mauritius'. *Ethnic and Racial Studies* 23(2): 329–52.

Nirsimloo-Anenden, A.D. 1990. *The Primordial Link: Telugu Ethnic Identity in Mauritius.* Moka, Mauritius: Mahatma Gandhi Institute.

Noel, K. 1991. *L'esclavage à l'isle de France, Île Maurice, de 1715 à 1810.* Paris: Edition Two Cities.

Northrup, D. 1995. *Indentured Labor in the Age of Imperialism, 1834–1922.* Cambridge: Cambridge University Press.

Nwulia, M.D.E. 1981. *The History of Slavery in Mauritius and the Seychelles, 1810–1875.* Rutherford: Farleigh Dickinson University Press.

Prakash, G. 1992. *The World of the Rural Labourer in Colonial India.* Delhi: Oxford University Press.

Ramsurrun, P. (ed.). 2001. *Glimpses of the Arya Samaj in Mauritius.* New Delhi: Sarvadeshik Prakashan Ltd.

Royle, S.A. 1995. 'Population and Resources in Mauritius'. *Geography Review* 8: 35–41.

Schnepel, B. 2005. 'Inder auf Reisen'. In Geisenhainer and Lange (eds.) 2005: 165–84.

——, 2018. 'Guests without a Host. The Indian Diaspora(s) in Mauritius'. In Hermann and Fuhse (eds.) 2018: 131–50.

Schnepel, B., and E.A. Alpers (eds.). 2018. *Connectivity in Motion. Island Hubs in the Indian Ocean World.* New York: Palgrave.

Sheriff, A., and E. Ho (eds.). 2014. *The Indian Ocean: Oceanic Connections and the Creation of New Societies.* London: Hurst & Company.

Srebrnik, H. 1999. 'Ethnicity and the Development of a "Middleman" Economy on Mauritius: The Diaspora Factor'. *The Round Table* 88 (350): 297–311.

——, 2000. 'Can an Ethnically-Based Civil Society Succeed? The Case of Mauritius'. *Journal of Contemporary African Studies* 18(1): 7–20.

Teelock, V. 1998. *Bitter Sugar. Sugar and Slavery in 19th Century Mauritius.* Moka, Mauritius: Mahatma Gandhi Institute.

——, 2014. 'Indentured Labour in the Indian Ocean and the Creation of New Societies'. In Sheriff and Ho (eds.) 2014: 151–83.

——, 2018. 'A Hub of "Local Cosmopolitans": Migration and Settlement in Early Eighteenth- to Nineteenth-Century Port Louis'. In Schnepel and Alpers (eds.) 2018: 209–29.

Tinker, H. 1974. *A New System of Slavery: The Export of Indian Labour Overseas 1830–1920.* London: Published for the Institute of Race Relations by Oxford University Press.

van der Veer, P. (ed.). 1995. *Nation and Migration: The Politics of Space in the South Asian Diaspora.* Philadelphia: University of Pennsylvania Press.

Vaughan, M. 2005. *Creating the Creole Island: Slavery in Eighteenth-century Mauritius.* Durham: Duke University Press.

Vertovec, S. 2000. *The Hindu Diaspora: Comparative Patterns.* London: Routledge.

Waldis, B. 2017. *Das ethnische Kaleidoskop Mauritius. Multikulturalismus beim politischen Einführungsprozess des Schulfachs Citizenship Education.* Münster: LIT Verlag.

CHAPTER 6

Dead as a Dodo? Mauritius's Path as Hub from Port of Call to Cyber Island[1]

INTRODUCTION

Lying roughly halfway between the Cape of Good Hope and India, in the age of sail Mauritius provided a welcome intermediate anchoring point and shelter in the vastness of the Indian Ocean. Against this geostrategic background, in this chapter I will argue that the primary function and most basic characteristic of this island was, is and will continue to be that it is a 'hub'. In other words, it is the *raison d'être* of Mauritius as an island, and especially its port city of Port Louis, to be a 'hub', while Mauritian society, then and now, is best characterized as a 'hub society'. Furthermore, I will argue that, from originally being a *maritime* hub, the expertise and functions the island acquired and developed in this capacity were gradually transferred to various *non*-maritime domains as well, where sooner or later they began to lead an independent life.

Hubs, to briefly recall earlier attempts to define them, are best seen as highly connected nodes that are instrumental in the circulation of 'things'.[2] In order to be or become a hub, it is not necessary to own or produce the cargoes that are being transported through the hub.[3] Indeed, there are numerous hubs in the Indian Ocean world which had or have nothing to offer themselves apart from providing a suitable geostrategic location for the circulation of things and being able to offer all the services to store these things and eventually move them on. Hubs, then, are seldom start or end points of mobility. However, as intermediate points of movement they strongly determine the speed, direction, intervals and interruptions of connectivity in motion across the Indian Ocean. Furthermore, it will be recalled that hubs also change the things they accommodate, if only temporarily, while passing by. Hubs therefore have agency when it comes to translating, transforming and transvaluating all the things that pass through them and that invariably stay in them for a while. This gives them a salient inner life and significant internal dynamics of their own.

This chapter will discuss Mauritius's history as a hub and the changes that have taken place during this history, starting from the island's early status as a naval base up to its present role as a cyber island. In discussing contemporary manifestations of Mauritius's global role as a hub, I shall also show that the etic term, together with the theoretical and methodological implications elaborated here, finds a particular emic correspondence in Mauritius itself. In other words, Mauritians themselves use the term 'hub' frequently, though of course not all Mauritians do so, and not in the same way as social theorists. In addition, in this chapter I shall also look more specifically at the transformative, value-enhancing processes that take place within the Mauritian hub before finally arguing that, for an understanding of Mauritian society and culture, it is no longer viable to look at it merely as a plantation society, as it is a hub society as well.

MAURITIUS AS AN EARLY MARITIME HUB

It is obvious that Mauritius, in essence, is a 'maritime hub' hubbing its cargoes across an ocean, with all the particularities in terms of technology, transport and transformation that this maritime dimension brings with it. These oceanic elements – the special kinds of vessels, modes of travel and cargoes; the physical characteristics of the ocean and its coasts and islands; the currents and winds; the patterns of the monsoons; the vastness of a seemingly endless ocean; the riches of the blue economy within the ocean, and its fluid and terrestrial boundaries – all need to be considered. This is the case even for those modern, contemporary periods in which it has become at least partially possible to ignore and transcend the ocean's fluidity, whether by using steamships, flying over the sea, transmitting messages via cables beneath it, or communicating by satellites in the sky.

While the Dutch tried, in the end unsuccessfully, to establish a small settlement and port of call on the island during the seventeenth century, the more serious attempts of the French to do so gradually led Mauritius to acquire its extraordinary capacity to circulate persons, animals, material objects and ideas across the Indian Ocean in all directions.[4] The island and those who stayed there built, ran and defended a port of call for the French navy and for their ships, captains, sailors, officers, soldiers, administrators and traders traversing the Indian Ocean to and from Asia, especially India. Originally, for the directors of the *Compagnie des Indes* in Paris, Mauritius (then, of course, Île de France) was meant to be no more than an intermediate military base and a port of call for the repair, renewal and re-invigoration of both ships and men, and for re-equipping them with food and water for the long and arduous journeys and battles that lay ahead.[5] Several times in the early history of the colony, when it was considered a burden to the *Compagnie*, its directors, like the Dutch VOC-Heeren before them, thought of abandoning the island. But the island's good bay and harbour in the northwest and its favourable geostrategic position between Africa and India soon led to plans to abandon the colony being discarded. As Vaughan remarks: 'Throughout the century . . . disappointment with this colonial outpost would periodically surface, and someone would suggest that perhaps it was not worth holding on to. But always this argument was rebutted with a few hard facts about weather and navigation' (2005: 37).

In this early phase, some of the cargoes landed on Mauritius were intended for the needs of the settlers and soldiers, while conversely other provisions from the island, like ebony wood or turtles, were loaded on to ships leaving the island. While sick sailors and travellers left incoming ships to be taken care of, those who had recovered embarked on ships passing by in order to move on themselves. Nonetheless, these embarkations and disembarkations were nothing but a means to an end, being intended merely to enable the ships and their passengers to reach their final destinations to the east or west. Mauritius itself had nothing much to offer in these early days except timber, water, seafood and its strategic location. This dimension of the maritime hub of Mauritius consisted in just the hubbing of ships and their crews. Mauritius, first and foremost, was a 'naval hub'.

This rather passive and fleeting role of Port Louis, and of the island of Mauritius as a whole, is made manifest by the fact that throughout its history the island hardly ever had a significant maritime force itself. Certainly there were periodic plans to provide it with one. Mahé de Labourdonnais (governor, to recall, between 1735 and 1746) had serious plans to equip Mauritius with a significant mercantile flotilla of its own, for he wanted to establish 'une marine des îles', as he called it. In a memorandum to the heads of the French East India Company back home in Paris, he considered the following fleet of merchant vessels necessary and desirable for Mauritius: one boat of 500–600 tons for procuring rice and bullocks from Madagascar; another of 150–200 tons for slaves from Madagascar; a third of 400–500 tons for slaves from Mozambique; two boats of 80 to a 100 tons plying regularly between Mauritius and La Réunion (then Île Bourbon); two boats of up to 100 tons for collecting sea turtles from Rodrigues; and finally two larger boats for the trade with India. These plans for a Mauritian flotilla were not welcomed in Paris and were never realized. Even under British rule, from 1810 onwards, things did not change, so that from their beginnings until today Mauritian governments and the island's mercantile class could never boast of a substantial indigenous or 'creole' merchant navy. Wherever Mauritius conducted trade, whether as a nation or in the form of Mauritian-based merchants or corporate groups, this was done less with ships of its own than by chartering foreign ships or opportunistically using ships that were just passing by.[6]

French endeavours to build and safeguard Mauritius's port and to be able to provide the services and provisions needed for passing ships sooner or later required the establishment of a small permanent settlement and garrison around the port. The French Company had to build up an island community able not only to feed itself, but also to accommodate the ever-increasing demands of ships and crews visiting the island. It also needed the military capacity to frighten off the occasional British flotilla monitoring the island. The very existence of this settlement was continuously threatened by hunger, cyclones and epidemic diseases, by runaway slaves hiding in the island's wilder parts, and by pirates somewhere out there on the sea, but occasionally also in a bay just around the corner. However, sooner or later, and almost against the express will of the directors of the *Compagnie,* Mauritius gradually developed into more than just a port of call. For many of those who arrived on the island, a majority of whom hailed from Saint-Malo or other parts of Brittany, Mauritius eventually became an island on which to start a new life, a place which *in itself* promised a decent living, and even riches. Consequently the port and its settlement, in its early years significantly known as 'Le Camp', grew into the port city of Port Louis, which later spread out into the island's interior. In addition, sugar plantations and new settlements were founded across the rest of the island. Mauritius thus developed into a colony with its very own needs, but also its own potentials and affordances, which emerged in addition to and sometimes independently of its function as a naval hub. Having started as a naval hub of merely passing significance, Mauritius, with its natural bay at Port Louis, developed into a fragile but thriving colony. It eventually became the French East India Company's and later the Crown's *chef-lieu* in the Indian Ocean world, outstripping first its rival Mascarene sister of Bourbon (Réunion) and then even Pondicherry on the southeast Indian coast.

Because of this functional extension and differentiation, the main dimension in the activities of the Mauritian maritime hub, namely naval hubbing, was refined and extended into other spheres of economic, sociocultural, technological and political life. One of the first extensions and refinements of the status of a naval hub arose out of the necessity to provide the island and its inhabitants with food, construction materials, tools and mostly unfree manpower. The need to import necessities as well as some luxuries (such as wine from France) soon developed into another kind of activity. Slowly but surely, Mauritius developed into a hub for merchandise and trade. Consequently, some of the foodstuffs and other goods that were brought on to the island and taken off it were somewhat mysteriously transformed into commodities, allowing Franco-Mauritian merchants to realize a profit by buying, storing and selling them. Thus, the island stopped being just a port of call and developed into a 'mercantile hub'.

For a long time, instead of producing food for passing sailors and soldiers, the islanders found themselves in dire need of importing staple foods such as rice, meat and grain just to satisfy their own needs. When the French took the island over from the Dutch, all the dodos had been killed and eaten, and the giant turtles were also on the verge of extinction.[7] It took some time to establish agriculture and horticulture on the 'island of rats', sufficient to cope with the increasing demands of the settlers and the ships passing by. Food scarcity was aggravated at times when, for strategic and military reasons, sailors and soldiers did not just stop over briefly but were staying for extended periods of time. Thus, during the Seven Years War between the major European powers from 1756 to 1763 and the American War of Independence of 1775–83, Mauritius became an important naval base for the French in their struggle with the British for hegemony in India and beyond. Hundreds and at times as many as 15,000 soldiers and sailors were stationed on Mauritius and had to be accommodated and fed while they waited for their orders and while their ships were being overhauled. This task brought the island, with a population then of hardly more than 50,000 (almost two-thirds of them slaves), to the brink of ruin and starvation.[8]

In its function as a regional mercantile hub for necessities and other goods, there were four main destinations for Mauritian merchants and sailors, namely Madagascar, Réunion, Rodrigues and the Seychelles. From its early days, Mauritius was much involved in trade with local Malagasy chiefs and Zana Malata traders from the *Grande Île* some 800 kilometres to the west, from which it imported mainly rice and beef. In addition, Madagascar was the Mascarenes' main source of slaves. Initially, this trade took the form of barter between independent entrepreneurs and local chiefs, but friction and even skirmishes often broke out, leading to several periods in which Malagasy chiefs closed their harbours to Mauritian ships. As far as Réunion is concerned, during the period of French colonial dominance of this part of the Indian Ocean, Mauritius and Réunion, lying roughly 160 kilometres from each other, were treated as sister islands. Réunion was settled first, from the mid-seventeenth century, by people arriving directly from France, fleeing from massacres in Madagascar, or exchanging existence as a pirate for that as a settler. Thus, for several decades, the then Île Bourbon was the French East India Company's main base in this part of the Indian Ocean. By the mid-eighteenth century, however, the Île de France gained the upper hand, basically on account of its better natural harbour at Port Louis. From then on, movements between Île de France and Île Bourbon took the form of trade between two colonial dependencies, the former being more important than the latter, which it now administered. The goods and personnel that landed on Réunion were directed through Île de France first. As a result, the political and mercantile class on the latter gained the upper hand and could dictate prices, customs and taxes to Île Bourbon.[9]

Communications between Île de France and its dependency of Rodrigues, lying approximately 650 kilometres to the east of Mauritius and settled since the 1750s, were bad for a long time. There were times during the eighteenth century when no ship from Île de France had visited Rodrigues for several years. The goods that were brought to this small island, inhabited by French planters with their proportionally much more numerous Malagasy and African slaves, were similar to those brought to Île Bourbon, though overall consisting even more of basic produce. Rodrigues had nothing much to offer except products of the sea such as turtles and fish. Plans to turn the island into a provider of beef cattle never worked out. The Seychelles Archipelago, finally, was settled from Mauritius from the 1770s onward. First under Franco-Mauritian, then Anglo-Mauritian rule, the archipelago was treated as a dependency of the colony of Mauritius and administered from there. Only in the early twentieth century did the Seychelles start to be administered separately, which brought some advantages to its inhabitants. Consequently, for a long time, the Seychellois had the same concerns and complaints regarding Mauritius that the other two dependencies had: communications were irregular or even non-existent until very late, and commercial and other exchanges were unequal, if not exploitative, favouring Mauritius and its merchant class over the dependencies. The Seychelles were mainly exploited as providers of timber and turtles, which on and around Mauritius had become scarce, and of coconut oil, plantations of which were established.[10]

From the mid- to late-eighteenth century onward, sugar became the main export and source of income for Mauritius under French rule. This is not the place to retrace the economic or even sociocultural history of sugar in Mauritius.[11] However, given the present chapter's focus on the hubbing qualities of this island and its inhabitants, one needs to emphasize the obvious: sugar is not native to Mauritius. Different varieties were brought to the island, often under secretive and dangerous conditions, from India and Southeast Asia and then tested out in the island's botanical garden or sugar plantations, until the most profitable and hardiest species for cultivation under Mauritian conditions were identified. Sugar and its derivatives like rum were then produced and exported by the island's planters and merchants. Sugar is therefore a prime example of an item which was brought to the island and transformed there before being exported and becoming a cargo with commodity value.

Another, rather special kind of trade that was instrumental in turning Mauritius into a mercantile hub of some consequence arose out of acts of piracy. During the decades before the British takeover of the island in 1810, Port Louis provided a safe haven for several dozen French pirates or corsairs, who acquired substantial wealth from their commercial raids on English, Dutch, Moghul and Marathi ships. The notorious Robert Surcouf alone is said to have boarded and captured forty-seven 'Indiamen', among them the *Kent*.[12] English historical sources report that between 1807 and 1809 – that is, at the very end of French rule on the island – eighteen mercantile ships fell into the hands of corsairs on their way to or from India.[13] Returning from their raids, the corsairs unloaded their prizes and divided their spoils between the captain and the crew, save for an obligatory share for the government at fixed rates. Instead of burying their treasure underground or hiding it in caves, as common pirate folklore has it, the corsairs sold or traded their quite substantial booty to merchants operating in or from Port Louis. Only a small proportion of the newly acquired wealth in gold, diamonds, pepper, fine cloth, spices or porcelain remained on the island in the coffers of the white Franco-Mauritian elites; the greater part of it was inserted into international commercial and financial circuits. With merchants and whalers hailing from the newly independent United States of America and from Denmark the booty was exchanged for money, naval supplies and even ships built in shipyards in Maine and Massachusetts.[14]

To understand the mechanics of this globalization of pirate loot, it should be realized that Port Louis had already become a well-frequented free port several years earlier, after the bankrupt French East India Company had ceded the island to the French Crown in 1767. This move opened up the possibility for all French citizens, and not only company officials, to start overseas trade from Mauritius. The rise of Mauritius to become a flourishing mercantile hub was exacerbated even further through the granting of trading rights to Americans in 1784.[15] Three years later, Port Louis was declared a 'free trade port', as a result of which it developed into an attractive commercial stopover for many ships from Europe (except British ones) and North America. By the late eighteenth century Mauritius had thus become a fully-fledged mercantile hub. Opening up the port to worldwide commerce in this way, the trade with Mauritius increased so steadily that in 1803 alone 350 ships dropped anchor in Port Louis. Apart from dealing in corsair 'prizes', then, Mauritius acted as an entrepôt and distribution centre for the products of regular trading activities in goods such as spices from Indonesia, textiles from India, traditional medicines from Sri Lanka, porcelain from China and slaves from Africa.[16] However, due to the blockade of the sea routes leading to Port Louis by the powerful Royal Navy and ultimately to the British conquest of the island in 1810, this trade boom came to an end. Henceforth, the island's future and prosperity were to be based on sugar plantations rather than on commerce.[17]

One of the basic skills needed for naval and mercantile hubbing is the steady and speedy reception, processing and dissemination of news, information and knowledge about incoming boats, their cargoes and the prices of these goods in other markets; about captains, crews and passengers; and about the state of peace, or war, out there in the world across the ocean. Given the island's important role as a stopover in the Indian Ocean, it may not be solely by chance that the world's most famous stamp hails from this island. Admittedly, 'Blue Pennies' were created mainly for intra-insular postal communication, but in 2014, in the Blue Penny Museum on the Caudan Waterfront in Port Louis, I viewed another artifact which exemplifies Mauritius's role as an information and/or communicative hub even more impressively: an artificial banyan tree, made of paper mâché, with a number of jugs fastened to its twigs. The text on the wall reads:

The first recorded letters from Mauritius were those from the Dutch Moluccan fleet and date back to June 1601. They were found by Willem von West-Zanen, the Enkhuizen's captain, when his vessel called at the island in June 1602. In the remote days of first stopovers in this uninhabited country, it was usual for ships' captains to leave messages in sealed jugs, hung upside down, on trees in Kuipers Eyland . . . at the entrance to Noord Western Haven, present day Port Louis Harbour.

With colonization, the receiving, digesting, enhancing and disseminating of knowledge increased to become a crucial aspect of the island's role as 'knowledge hub'. There was, to start with, the challenging task of determining the most advantageous techniques in the production of sugar on the basis of plant subspecies brought to the island from South and Southeast Asia. Other specimens of flora and fauna, such as nutmeg, cloves, indigo, cotton, pepper, fruit trees, palm trees, vegetables, Malagasy cattle or Javanese deer, were also tried out for their survivability and agricultural utility.[18] A crucial role in these attempts to trans-plant and settle new species of flora on the island was assumed by the Botanical Garden at Pamplemousse. This horticultural laboratory was headed and visited by some of the internationally most highly reputed botanists and scientists of the time, to mention only Pierre Poivre. Poivre first stayed on the island in 1746 and 1750, each time for a few months only, then again from 1753 to 1756, as botanist in Pamplemousse, trying to acclimatize valuable spices, some of which he had himself 'stolen' from the Dutch Moluccas, and then finally for five years from 1767 onward, having been sent there by the King as 'Intendant' in order to effect the island's administrative transition from company rule to the crown.[19] Another famous person who stayed on Mauritius at that time was Bernardin de Saint-Pierre, whose *Voyage à l'Isle de France* (1773) and *Paul et Virginie* (1788) are still widely read today.[20] In addition, in the Age of Enlightenment, Port Louis was made the seat of a number of learned societies pursuing philosophical, nautical, astronomical, geographical, botanical, arboricultural, cartographical and other kinds of research. These societies hosted several outstanding scientists, lay and professional, who sooner or later disseminated their insights back to Paris and London, and who in return were keen to learn about the latest scientific discoveries from these metropolitan centres. Individual scholars or scientific group expeditions, like that led by the famous Louis Antoine de Bougainville, who arrived on Mauritius in 1768, or the less fortunate explorer Jean-François de La Perouse, who stayed on the island for six years in the 1770s and went missing in the Pacific in 1789, also regularly passed through from east or west, taking the opportunity of a visit to undertake some research on the island itself.[21]

THE PRESENT-DAY 'SERVICE HUB': MAURITIAN VOICES

I shall now make an admittedly abrupt jump from the colony's founding and stabilizing phase to the present day in order to show that in contemporary postcolonial Mauritius the social, institutional and mental foundations of its status as a hub have experienced further extensions and refinements into spheres in which the maritime dimension is virtually absent. Independent Mauritius has developed into a 'service hub', achieving economic success by offering the amenities that are required in today's global markets. To show what is meant by this, it is time to let Mauritians speak for themselves. I shall therefore examine some Mauritian print and Internet media to acquire an idea of how the issue of being a hub or wanting to become one is represented and conceived in Mauritian society today.

In one the island's leading newspapers, one finds an article entitled 'Maurice se positionne comme hub financier entre l'Inde et l'Afrique'.[22] This piece informs the reader about a scheme by the Mauritian Standard Chartered Bank to use its financial services as a gateway to Africa. The Bank's CEO argues that, like Singapore and Hong Kong in their respective regions, Mauritius is ideally situated between Africa and Asia. The nation offers investors, it is argued further, a stable economic and political environment, a solid legal system and a qualified and dynamic workforce, which can be used as a 'portail pour investir en Afrique'. In a similar statement, namely an Internet announcement by Deutsche Bank's Mauritian Branch, one reads: 'Mauritius started to offer financial services in 1992 and has since built a solid reputation as a world-class international centre, providing operational security and commercial flexibility to investors. As an independent sovereign nation strategically located in the Indian Ocean, Mauritius offers political and economic stability, highly respected regulatory frameworks with common law structures and a tax-neutral environment. It benefits from a well-educated, multilingual workforce and its convenient time-zone for Asia, the Middle East and Africa.'[23] And finally, with regard to the role of Mauritius as a 'financial hub', in a brochure entitled *Guide to Global Investment*, the Mauritian Board of Investment asks why foreigners should invest in Mauritius, immediately answering: 'A business-friendly environment with a long history of hospitality; a safe country with enduring social and political stability; a culturally diverse, multilingual and highly educated workforce; strategically located between Asia and Africa; a convenient time zone; well-developed air and sea links to the rest of the world.'

Some services of this kind are known globally these days, quite tellingly, as 'offshore banking'. And indeed, most of the Mauritian institutions that work in this branch of finance, i.e. providing tax havens, are located directly on the Caudan Waterfront in Port Louis, the new gateway to the world. The port itself, however, has not com-

Figure 6.1: Port Louis as Seen from a Boat

pletely lost its original role, as the following statements referring to the present 'Free Port' of Port Louis make clear. During recent decades, the *Annual Reports of the Mauritius Port Authority* have reported sharp increases in almost all performance criteria, from cargoes arriving and departing to profits earned. In various newspapers, one reads of the construction of a substantial 'prolongement du quai' or of plans to continue extending the docking capacities of the free port even further, especially renewing the cranes in the port's increasingly important container section.[24] Furthermore, one repeatedly reads in newspapers about the free port's economically important function as a 'Seafood Hub' or 'Plateform de fruits de mer'.[25] This label refers to the port's role in offering substantial capacities in cold-storage warehouses to hoard the catches of the numerous Taiwanese junks that arrive in Port Louis daily, their holds full of tuna. This endangered pelagic species, incidentally, is not eaten or even processed in Port Louis. Rather, after being kept in storage for a time, the tuna are collected by larger transport vessels, which take their cargo to the Heinze factory and other factories on the Seychelles, or even as far away as Puerto Rico, from where they enter American or European stores in cans. But it is not only fish that are hubbed in Port Louis: increasingly cruise passengers are as well. Having recently completed a new terminal for cruise ships of all sizes, Mauritius was awarded the title of 'The Indian Ocean's Best Cruise Port 2012.' From this cruise terminal, one major Italian company has started regular luxury cruises stopping at major scenic ports in the southwestern part of the Indian Ocean as far as Zanzibar in the north and Cape Town in the south. Other cruise ships make intermediate stops on longer routes, using Mauritius as an entry and exit point for those tourists who only wish to do part of the journey and who arrive or depart by plane.[26]

Apart from being a seafood hub and international cruise destination, Mauritius and foreign investors have undertaken major investments to turn the port into a hub for liquefied petroleum gas (LPG). In 2010, the Mauritian government commissioned Petredec Investments Ltd to construct a 15,000-metric-ton storage terminal in the western corner of Port Louis's container port. This terminal, which cost 24.8 million Euros to construct, was completed and became operational in March 2014. It consists of three large tanks built in Italy topped by a concrete mound for security, and it features import and export pipelines leading some hundreds of metres out into the sea for the tank vessels anchoring there, as well as a modern control and administration building next to the tanks. On the one hand, this terminal is meant to cover the island's own needs and hence to supply approximately 65,000–67,000 metric tons per annum to the State Trading Corporation of Mauritius. On the other hand, however, it was built at this size so that 'the terminal will also act as a trading hub allowing the re-export of LPG in excess of 100,000 metric tons per annum to regional markets located in the Indian Ocean region.'[27] As the *Indian Ocean Times* writes: 'This project is designed to transform the port-franc into a vast gas-hub serving the entire region of the Indian Ocean.'[28] Mauritius's airport has also been extended to become a regional 'airport hub' comparable to those found in the Middle East, like Dubai. The CEO of Airports of Mauritius Co. Ltd, which had just completed the building of a new grand airport terminal (including a runway able to take the A380), assessed the impact of these new developments on tourism as follows: 'Owing to this economic [world] crisis, a gap has been noted in the projections made so far. However, I am confident Mauritius will be welcoming two million tourists in the years to come. This new terminal will be an additional marketing asset that will help in better selling our destination as a regional hub.'[29]

In the field of communications, which represents one of Mauritius's first and most basic hubbing functions from the period even before its settlement (remember the jugs hanging in trees), *Le Mauricien* for 5 April 2012 reported the installation of 'Lion 2'. LION stands for 'Lower Indian Ocean Network' and refers to a high-quality fibre-optic cable connecting the island underwater with Réunion, Madagascar, Mayotte and Kenya, eventually stretching over a distance of 3,000 kilometres. This cable, the reader is informed, will also be connected to three other underwater cables: (1) EASSY, which runs for approximately 10,000 kilometres between South Africa and Ethiopia, also connecting the Comoros, Tanzania and the Sudan; (2) a cable known as 'The East African Marine System' (TEAMS); and of course (3) 'Lion 1', inaugurated by the prime minister of Mauritius in 2009. In the same newspaper, two days later, one can read that, in the *Global Information Technology Report* of the World Economic Forum, Mauritius is ranked 53rd globally in terms of Network Readiness. This 'bonne performance', it is claimed, puts the country at the head of all the countries of Sub-Saharan Africa, including even South Africa and Nigeria. The report states: 'Therefore, continued and sustained efforts to bring down the costs of international connectivity, to improve the quality of the workforce, and to promote a business-friendly environment will further ensure that Mauritius becomes a preferred platform and solutions provider in the global ICT / BPO realm.'[30]

The distribution of information and knowledge go hand in hand. In this respect, it is not surprising to find attempts to turn Mauritius into a hub in this latter field as well. In 2005, the Mauritian Ministry of Education and Scientific Research launched a fifty-page government agenda and policy outline entitled *Developing Mauritius into a Knowledge Hub and a Centre for Higher Learning*.[31] These policy guidelines, which were devised by a high-ranking committee of ministers, state secretaries and personalities from industry and the public, state: 'The Government has decided that, henceforth, knowledge-based industries will be an increasing source of value added for the economy and a significant component of the new economic model. To that end, it is promoting a Knowledge Hub agenda . . .' (ibid.: 4). In this agenda the government commits itself to further strengthening the country's university and other places of higher learning, especially in the priority areas of 'information and communication technologies', 'medicine and allied health sciences', and 'business, finance and financial services'. Elsewhere one reads: 'A feature of globally competitive knowledge-based economies is that governments, institutions of higher learning and industries work together in those economies to create knowledge hubs. A knowledge hub is concerned with the process of building up a country's capacity to better integrate with the world's increasing knowledge-based economy' (ibid.: 3). These statements in the report are followed by two pages describing 'the Singaporean Model', Singapore being 'a country similar to Mauritius in terms of small land mass and lack of natural resources' (ibid.).

Finally, Mauritius is positioning itself in central roles in various international organizations that are striving to enhance cooperation and development within the Indian Ocean region. In 1997, Mauritius was among the founders of this macro-region's only all-encompassing association, namely the *Indian Ocean Rim Association for Regional Cooperation* (IOR-ARC).[32] Since then, it has been the seat of this organization's secretariat, and for a long time its Director General was a Mauritian. Furthermore, there is the *Commission de l'Océan Indien* (COI), which, launched in 1984 and with its headquarters in Mauritius, aims to increase cooperation within the francophone island world of the southwest Indian Ocean that is, between Mauritius, Réunion, Madagascar, the Seychelles, French Mayotte and the Comoros.[33]

Without going into greater depth or even exploring the credibility of the claims being made in these extracts from print and Internet media, it transpires that being a hub (or wanting to become one) is a vital part of Mauritian public discourse. Different kinds or dimensions of hubs are identified, with the 'seafood hub' perhaps being the most genuine type of hub for a small island society like Mauritius. But this very same island also wishes to become, or claims to be, a 'financial hub', an 'LPG hub', a 'tourist hub' and a 'knowledge hub'. Nothing material or ideational, it seems, is incapable of being hubbed. These claims and visions are clearly being made by those who have influence in political and economic affairs. They are reiterated in international political contexts, as when, during an Indian Ocean Conference at the German Foreign Office in Berlin on 9 June 2015, Jean-Claude de l'Estrac, the Mauritian Secrétaire Générale de la COI, proclaimed Mauritius to be 'at the cross-roads, at the heart of the globalized world.' More modestly, it transpires from the statements and facts assembled in this section that Mauritius wants to be or become a *regional* hub, that is, a hub catering especially for the southwest Indian Ocean, in particular its island world of Madagascar, the Mascarenes, the Comoros and the Seychelles, as well as for countries on the East African littoral, like Mozambique, Tanzania, and even as far south or north as South Africa and Kenya respectively.

Furthermore, in many statements on why Mauritius is or could be an ideal hub, its favourable geostrategic location is combined with the claim that it possesses a relatively crisis-free and well-diversified economy, as well as a stable and reliable politico-jural framework for investors and clients. One also finds repeated hints regarding the island's advantageous sociocultural characteristics and its historical path. Mauritius is said to have a long history of hospitality: the diversity of its population, with ancestral languages such as Hindi, Chinese, Arabic or French, is praised, and in addition all these languages are spoken against the background of English as the national language and the language of higher education. Mauritius's work force, in a nutshell, has 'globality'; it is cosmopolitan. This human factor is presented as a decisive asset that allows the island to be an important player in global streams of finance, information, knowledge, men, plants, animals, ideas and things.

PRESENT-DAY 'PILLARS' OF THE MAURITIAN HUB ECONOMY

These Mauritian voices, advocating and even celebrating the island's capacity to act as a modern-day service hub, reflect the diversified nature of the Mauritian economy today, highlighting its areas of greatest success and assumed potential. Apart from the sugar industry's history of profit, two of the major 'pillars' of the island's extraordinary 'economic miracle'[34] since the 1970s have been the textile and tourism industries. Furthermore, since the advent of the new millennium, Mauritius has also made headway in international financial services (IFS) and international communication technology (ICT). All these branches of the economy have important hub dimensions of various kinds, which are important to look at more closely.

Since the establishment of an 'Export Processing Zone' (EPZ) in the 1970s, textiles have become one of the island's main exports. Up to 90,000 jobs were created by this industry, leading in the 1990s to a low unemployment rate in Mauritius of just under 3 per cent. Significantly in many respects, around 70 per cent of the workers are women. This industry has continued to thrive despite a crisis in the early years of this millennium, and even though wage levels have risen so continuously that for investors Mauritius no longer represents a very attractive low-wage economy.[35] As Mauritius does not raise sheep or grow cotton, the materials for producing designer clothing and fine textiles have to be brought to the island from elsewhere. Moreover, the fashion and designs are European or American in origin, while large amounts of capital and of managerial and technical expertise have come from East Asian 'tigers'. In particular, businessmen from the former British crown colony of Hong Kong were looking for safe havens in which to invest their capital and relocate their companies after the return of Hong Kong to China in 1997.[36] It goes without saying, for an industry producing in *export*-processing zones, that the Mauritian 'textile hub' produces goods not for its own market, but for foreign ones, especially the luxury sectors of European and American consumers. Hence, in its material, manufacturing and consumer dimensions, textiles do not have their home in Mauritius. The material may start in Australia, and it is then processed into cloth in Calcutta or Bangladesh before being finished in Mauritius. The finished products go to the West, where American and European consumers may soon get tired of their purchases and hand them over to the second-hand market and charities that export some of their goods to Africa. For the inner working of that hub, the Mauritian state provides a political and legal framework that offers tax and customs advantages and relatively favourable manufacturing conditions in the EPZ; the Sino-Mauritian community plays a vital role in establishing links for this business across the Indian Ocean into the South China Sea; Franco-Mauritians use former sugar fields to build factories and invest in making this hub workable and profitable; while the Indo-Mauritian and Creole parts of the Mauritian population, especially females, provide the qualified, but relatively low-cost workforce that transforms cloth into valuable designer clothes.[37]

Tourism, the second of the modern Mauritian economic pillars mentioned above, was initially introduced to Mauritius quite literally 'by the way' because, in the early pre-jet era of commercial air traffic, planes could not travel the long distances that an A380 or Boing 747 can cover today. In its search for intermediate stops on the long journey between Europe and South Africa on the one hand and Australia on the other, Qantas Airways discovered Mauritius as a convenient stopover, strategically well located and politically safe, turning flights to and from 'Down Under' into two-stop flights only.[38] On 1 September 1953 regular plane services were started, with Mauritius as an airport hub. While this date could be seen as the beginning of the Mauritian tourism industry, in those days passengers did not come to enjoy the beauties of the island and relax on its beaches but stopped over for a day or two only in hotels in Curepipe, a town in the cooler upland plateau of the island, to wait for an ongoing connection. Nowadays tourists stay longer, ten days on the average. And they certainly do not come to Mauritius as travellers merely passing through. Mauritius has become a major tourist destination attracting more than one million tourists a year. These tourists arrive pale and stressed, though after a time enjoying the three great tourist attractions of sun, sand and sea, they usually depart from this 'paradise island' tanned (or sunburned), and in better shape. Since the mid-1980s, therefore, tourism has provided a substantial income for the island's hotels and associated enterprises, such as catering or tour operators. With over one hundred hotels and 27,000 employees (in 2010), tourism has developed into a major taxpayer for the state and a large job-provider for the Mauritian population, at times even surpassing the sugar and textile industries in these two regards. This potential seems not yet to have been exhausted, as the oft-mentioned target figure of two million tourists a year makes clear.[39]

From roughly 2000 onward, the Mauritian economy has diversified and strengthened furthered, due to the great success of services in the offshore banking and communication technology sectors. These pillars of the Mauritian economy have catapulted Mauritius right into the centre of the present-day global economy. As far as international financial services are concerned, it is especially Indian capital going to and coming from Africa that is routed through and administered in the Mauritian financial hub, which employs roughly 15,000 people. As mentioned above, services in international communication technology have only become possible relatively recently, since Mauritius connected itself to the optical fibre cables of LION 1 and 2. As Mauritius has managed to become a node in these lines of communication, it has become an explicit target for the island's politicians and the over 300 ICT companies with their more than 12,000 employees to become a 'cyber island', 'data hub', or 'Hub 2.0'. Indeed, this branch of the economy is growing faster than the rest. Since the beginning of the millennium, Mauritius has emphasized its aspiration to position itself as a major ICT-hub by

Figure 6.2: Cyber City

inaugurating a constantly growing 'Cyber City' near the inland area of Ébene and the University of Mauritius, tellingly on the site of former sugar fields.[40]

EXTENSIONS AND TRANSLATIONS

So far I have argued that Mauritius was 'born to be a hub' and that its hubbing activities were maritime in origin and essence. Furthermore, I have shown that the island's first and most basic function as a hub was as a naval hub, aiding ships and their crews *en route* to move on elsewhere. This function soon required a more permanent population on the island and in its port, with a small settlement of soldiers, administrators as well as both free and enslaved labourers. When this settlement stabilized, growing in size and functions, it gradually acquired other hubbing functions as well. These were still maritime in character, but they entailed a number of extensions of and refinements to the island's original status and function of a naval hub. Not only were passing ships and their crews hubbed, but ships arriving at and departing from Port Louis also brought and took away with them commodities which in different ways realized a surplus for the merchants and other inhabitants of the island, turning it into a mercantile and information hub. However, no matter whether these commodities were basic or luxury, whether they consisted of sugar, pirate prizes, or merchandise, none of them were of Mauritian origin, and none of them were meant to stay there.

The fact that what reached Mauritius was mostly in transit was noted by Jean Houbert when he wrote: 'Mauritius as an entity then, through its very genesis, was doubly dependent on the outside world: for all its export, and almost all its imports' (1981: 77). However, what to Houbert looks like dependency, and hence like a deficiency, can be regarded as an asset seen from the perspective of a theory of hubs. Maybe initially the island's situation was indeed characterized by its heavy reliance on outside forces, but since then Mauritius has made the best of this seemingly negative situation and even turned it to its advantage by realizing and enforcing its hub potential in all domains. In fact, the situation was never one of dependency but from the start a quality. What is certain, however, is that if we want to understand fully the development of this small island and, arguably, of other 'Small Island Developing States' (SIDS) as well, one has to question received theories of dependency, which so often find application when it comes to analysing the economic plight of colonial and postcolonial countries. Instead, at least in the case of Mauritius, it transpires that the island's success in the economic domain does not lie in it having an abundance of natural resources, nor is it based on its productive capacities, not even in the cases of sugar and textiles, both industries with their very own cut-and-trim activities. Instead, Mauritius has been successful because throughout its history it has realized and developed its own qualities in distributing and circulating things. In short, the Mauritian 'miracle' is based on its expertise in providing the varying and historically changing qualities and services of a hub.

While the original maritime functions of the island as a hub were gradually extended into non-maritime spheres, the island's activities and expertises a maritime hub continued to provide the basis and rationale for these new, non-maritime activities. These maritime foundations and logics live on, albeit in new guises. One of the most striking illustrations of this can be seen in the Mauritian expertise in helping the sick recuperate on the island. This service was first developed when a 500-bed hospital was constructed as one of the earliest permanent buildings on the French island, allowing sick sailors or travellers to recover. It lives on today in the hospital(ity) industry of tourism, which can be said to have reinvented and adapted many of the old skills necessary for servicing sailors and maritime travellers.[41] In a similar transformed continuation of services that were first offered to ships, sailors and maritime cargoes, the island is now offering services in areas such as finance, textiles and communication technology. What has changed in these instances is the fact that things and ideas are no longer arriving on the ocean surface alone, but also underwater in cables at the ocean's bottom, as well as over the water in planes or as information travelling in cyber space.

In stressing the island's transport and transit function, it has been pointed out that one must inevitably acknowledge that during stop-over periods – whether long, medium, or short – certain inner transmutations and transformations occur. No matter whether old and maritime or new and cyber in character, all these human, material and ideational goods that were and are serviced on the island do not merely stop over before being transported further on: they are also acted upon and thereby transformed into different kinds of things, often with added or enhanced value.

In the realm of material things, these transformations include the following:

- from run-down ships to repaired ones;
- from goods with a use value only to commodities with an added exchange value;
- from commodities in the storehouse to commodities sold with a surplus value;
- from sugarcane to refined sugar and its derivatives (like rum and, these days, even bioenergy);
- from fish to frozen seafood, waiting to be canned;
- from cotton, wool and rough cloth to designer clothes;
- from information and communication to knowledge and financial transactions;
- from basic knowledge to botanical, agricultural, horticultural, nautical and geographical knowledge and engineering;
- from investment to profit.

In the realm of human beings, these transformations include the following:

- from sick and exhausted sailors, soldiers and travellers to healthy and strong ones;
- from pale and overworked tourists to tanned, relaxed and recuperated persons ready to go back to work;
- from pirates, adventurers, or explorers to settlers;
- from French pauvres to Mauritian *petits blancs*;
- from individual businessman to plantocratic family head;
- from slave to 'freedman';
- from indentured labourer to 'Computer Indian'.

This rather sketchy list of transformations may nonetheless suffice to stress the point made at the beginning of this chapter, namely that hubs have energy and are agentive not only in matters of external circulation but also in changing things that stay within them, if only for a while.

CONCLUSIONS: 'DEAD AS A DODO'?

By including common French settlers, pirates, sugar barons, African slaves and Indian immigrants in the second list above, it becomes clear that any discussion of Mauritius as a hub and any attempt to develop a more subtle theory of hubs and hub societies will sooner or later have to include not only the human beings who passed by, but also those who stayed. The line distinguishing the two is certainly fluid. Some initially wanted to move along, but then stayed and even founded families; others wanted to stay but soon passed (away). Notwithstanding this fuzziness, studying hubs cannot proceed without taking account of the human beings who live and work on the island and who die there. In this context, it is necessary to look more closely not only at how these people did the work of a hub, but also at how the activities of a hub formed and changed the islanders' mentality. Did these activities turn them into persons who were more cosmopolitan and even 'fluid' in their identities than people in other parts of the world, including metropolitan cities?[42] And did this happen not *although* they were living on a small island, but exactly *because* they were? Some such focus would certainly add an awareness of and insights into the specific socio-cultural aspects of a hub society to the politico-economic perspective which has been to the fore in the analysis presented here. In addition, it would add a new perspective to diaspora and migration studies, which have often pointed out that certain diasporas and migrants, in forming 'middlemen economies', are winners in the global economy on account of their greater mobility, flexibility and better networks across long distances.[43]

This plea to include human actors in any investigation of the Mauritian hub is not meant to imply that valuable studies in this field do not already exist. On the contrary, students entering the field of Mauritian studies will quickly find themselves confronted with a great number of excellent works by scholars from Mauritius and overseas. It certainly is one of the best-studied small islands worldwide.[44] However, while these studies provide an abundance of excellent information on the island's history and present, they do so mostly against the background of the rather unquestioned assumption, held implicitly or explicitly, that Mauritius is – or at least was – in essence

Figure 6.3: The Dodo as Tourist Souvenir

a 'plantation society'. While this claim is not totally unfounded, what is suggested here is that it needs to be relativized and even critiqued. What is necessary for a new perspective on the abundant data we already have, as for the discovery of new data, is to acknowledge the fact that Mauritius in essence was, is and will continue to be a 'hub society'.

If Mauritian society can only be understood fully by acknowledging its hub character, as argued here, what about the dodo? Anyone visiting the island these days will sooner or later encounter representations of this clumsy but enchanting creature, not only in the form of tourist souvenirs or products of popular art, but also depicted on such official documents such as immigration forms, stamps or the twenty-five-rupee note. In a publication of the National Heritage Fund on the occasion of the 'International Day for Monuments and Sights' in 2011, the dodo is even celebrated as 'A Mauritian Heritage'. How does this extinct bird, which was endemic to the island, but could not fly and therefore was quickly killed and eaten by the early colonizers, corroborate the picture of a hub society? How could such an immobile animal, which in the well-known expression 'dead as a dodo' synecdochically stand for all *faits perdus*, have achieved the status of a totem-like national symbol of a society which in essence has ever been a transient and mobile hub? Tragically the dodo did not hub and was not hubbed. In a sense, it is a world-famous example of failed hubbing.[45]

It thus seems paradoxical that this immobile bird has become something like the emblematic representative of this small island nation, second only to the rainbow. Seeking for an explanation for this enigma, it quickly becomes apparent that the image of the friendly, but pitiful dodo stands for authenticity and indigeneity on an island where everyone seems to come from elsewhere.[46] However, to understand fully why such a creature as the dodo might become the icon of a 'hub society', one needs to briefly recall some basic insights from economic anthropology. To make things circulate, we learn,[47] always requires one or two very special things that quite definitely do not circulate, being 'inalienable possessions' (Weiner). In this sense of what Weiner also aptly calls the 'the paradox of keeping-while-giving', and one could add here of 'staying-while-moving', the flightless dodo is the perfect creature to represent the ever-wheeling Mauritian hub. During a discussion at the University of Mauritius in February 2016, one participant even went so far as to characterize those who were born and are living on the island as 'the human dodos of Mauritius'. By contrast to the drones of old, these 'human' avatars of a bird are, however, very much alive and mobile, even when they stay put.

NOTES

1. Parts of this chapter were published in Schnepel (2018); they are here reprinted with the kind permission of SNCSC.
2. On hubs, see also here Chapter 1, 'Conclusions'. Furthermore, in accordance with Hodder, I am using the word 'thing' very generally 'to refer to human-made objects, but . . . just as well to naturally occurring objects, animals, plants, and humans . . . in which humans have an interest' (2011: 155).
3. When placing emphasis on the transport of things, these are best termed and understood as 'cargoes'. See Schnepel (2022).
4. Again, the most insightful studies into the early maritime history of Mauritius, which I have made good use of here, are those of Toussaint (1966, 1973, 2013 [1936]).
5. Before Mauritius, the *Compagnie* had already founded trading posts in Pondicherry and Chandernagor on India's east coast in 1674 and 1690 respectively.
6. For these points, see Toussaint (1966: 9–16).
7. In addition, timber, especially the valuable ebony, had been severely depleted by the Dutch, at least at those places on the island where it could still be reached from the coast without too much effort and danger. See Toussaint (1966).
8. See Allen (1999: 17–19).
9. On Mauritius's relations with La Réunion during these early years of Mascarene colonization, see also Toussaint (1966: 21–2).
10. On these points, see especially Toussaint (1966). In addition to these islands, French ships from the Mascarenes also traded with several islands along the Swahili coast such as Kilwa, Mozambique and Zanzibar.
11. See Allen (1999), Storey (1997),Teelock (1998).
12. See Piat (2010: 168–79).
13. See Carter (2009).

14. On Mauritian corsairs in the second half of the eighteenth century, in a way the legitimate successors of the pirates discussed above in Chapter 3, see Toussaint (1966: 17–23), Allen (1999: 11–13), Piat (2010: 168–79), Carter (2009).
15. Remember that the United States of America had declared independence from France's arch-rival England just one year before.
16. See Toussaint (1966: 17–23), Allen (1999: 11–13).
17. See Teelock (1998: 34–40), Allen (1999: 14), Vaughan (2005: 75–81).
18. See Piat (2010: 64–5, 92–7).
19. On Poivre, see Grove (1996: 168–263),Osterhammel (1997), Piat (2010: 81–97), and Poivre (1997).
20. On Saint-Pierre's time in Mauritius, where he worked from 1768 to 1771 as engineer under Poivre, see Grove (1996: 244–54).
21. On other scholars and travellers visiting Mauritius during the Age of Enlightenment (and thereafter), such as Philibert Commerson, Nicholas Baudin, Matthew Flinders, Charles Darwin, and Mark Twain, see Grove (1996: 216–23, 237–43), Vaughan (2005: chap. 2), and Piat (2010: 141–52).
22. *L'Express*, 20 February 2012.
23. See http://www.dboffshore.com (last accessed 18 March 2013).
24. *L'Express*, 13 February 2014. On this issue, see also *Le Mauricien*, 29 July 2013; and *L'Express*, 20 February 2014.
25. See *Le Mauricien*, 1 January 2006; 11 and 22 February 2006; 2 March 2006. On Mauritian ambitions to extend the island's role as a 'seafood hub', see also Sellström (2015: 252).
26. Reference is made to the pre-coronavirus period.
27. http://www.petredec.com/storage.shtml (last accessed 18 March 2014).
28. http://en.indian-ocean-times.com/Mauritius-wants-to-export-liquefied-petroleum-gas (last accessed 26 July 2013).
29. *Le Mauricien*, 5 April 2012. See also 12 July 2012; and 20 December 2012.
30. For the development of modern forms of communication and of Mauritius's role in them, the history of submarine telegraph cables is important. In 1893, Mauritius and the Seychelles were linked to each other and to Zanzibar by telegraph. These links were extended to South Africa and Rodrigues in 1901, and linked Mauritius and Réunion in 1906. See Sellström (2015: 18).
31. http://ministry-education.gov.mu/English/Documents/knowledgehub.pdf.
32. See Sellström (2015: 45–6), Wagner (2013).
33. For the program of the COI since 1994, see *Le Mauricien*, 1 July 2015.

34. The Mauritian economy is often regarded as a 'miracle', not only on account of positive figures in all financial and economic fields, but also against the background of the pessimistic prognosis of a Nobel prize-winning economist made in 1961. See Meade et al. (1961). On the 'economic miracle', see among others Houbert (1981: 88–95) and Sellström (2015: 241–5).
35. Capital in this branch is slowly but surely being transferred to places like Madagascar or back to locations in South and Southeast Asia, where labour is cheaper and controls over working conditions are less strict, if they exist at all.
36. Unlike most export-processing zones elsewhere in the world, Mauritian textile factories are not located in one especially demarcated enclave but are scattered all over the island in around 600 locations.
37. On the Mauritian textile industry, see Meisenhelder (1997: 287–92), Neveling (2012, 2014) and Sellström (2015: 246–7, 251).
38. The second intermediate stop was the Cocos (Keeling) Islands, an Australian archipelago midway between Sri Lanka and Australia.
39. The numbers here refer to facts and expectations in pre-coronavirus times. Quite a number of critical voices have been raised by those who fear the 'Costa Bravaization' of the island, whose tourism industry so far has, by and large, been operating in the luxury sector of five-star hotels. For more on Mauritian tourism, including its socio-cultural dimensions, see below, Chapter 7.
40. See also Sellström (2015: 249–50).
41. As also noted by Falola, Parrot, and Sanchez (2019: 20).
42. In this context, one remembers how often, in statements discussed above, the population of Mauritius itself was praised to potential international investors as a highly qualified, linguistically varied and hardworking cornerstone of the Mauritian hub.
43. See Cohen (1997) and Srebrnik (1999).
44. See, among numerous others, Boswell (2006); Carter (1995, 1996); Eisenlohr (2006); Eriksen (1998); the contributors to Hookoomsing, Ludwig, and Schnepel (eds. 2009); and Vaughan (2005).
45. On works from within the field of 'dodology', see especially Grihault (2005) and Richon (2008).
46. On this capacity of the dodo to convey a sense of authenticity and indigeneity, see Vaughan (2005: 3–4, 278).
47. See especially the critical re-appraisals by Weiner (1992) and Godelier (1996) of Malinowski's *Argonauts of the Western Pacific* (1961 [1922]) and Mauss's *The Gift* (1976 [1950]).

REFERENCES

Agha, S., and E. Kolsky (eds.). 2009. *Fringes of Empire.* New Delhi: Oxford University Press.

Allen, R.B. 1999. *Slaves, Freedmen and Indentured Laborers in Colonial Mauritius.* Cambridge: Cambridge University Press.

Boswell, R. 2006. *Le Malaise Créole: Ethnic Identity in Mauritius.* Oxford: Berghahn Books.

Carter, M. 1995. *Servants, Sirdars and Settlers: Indians in Mauritius 1834–1874.* Delhi: Oxford University Press.

——, 1996. *Voices from Indenture: Experiences of Indian Migrants in the British Empire.* Leicester: Leicester University Press.

——, 2009. 'Pirates and Settlers: Economic Interactions on the Margins of Empire'. In Agha and Kolsky (eds.) 2009: 45–68.

Cohen, R. 1997. *Global Diasporas: An Introduction.* Seattle: University of Washington Press.

Eisenlohr, P. 2006. *Little India: Diaspora, Time and Ethnolinguistic Belonging in Hindu Mauritius.* Berkeley: University of California Press.

Eriksen, T.H. 1998. *Common Denominators: Ethnicity, Nation-Building and Compromise in Mauritius.* Oxford: Berg.

Falola, T., R.J. Parrott, and D.P. Sanchez. 2019. 'Introduction: Arbiters and Witnesses of Change. Contextualizing Conversations on African Islands'. In Falola, Parrott, and Sanchez (eds.) 2019: 1–35.

Falola, T., R.J. Parrott, and D.P. Sanchez (eds.). 2019. *African Islands. Leading Edges of Empire and Globalization.* Rochester: University of Rochester Press.

Godelier, M. 1996. *L'énigme du don.* Paris: Librairie Arthème Fayard.

Grihault, A. 2005. *Dodo. The Bird Behind the Legend.* Mauritius: Imprimerie Commerciale.

Grove, R.H. 1996. *Green Imperialism: Colonial Expansion, Tropical Island Edens and the Origins of Environmentalism, 1600–1860.* Cambridge: Cambridge University Press.

Hodder, I. 2011. 'Human-thing Entanglement: Towards an Integrated Archaeological Perspective'. *Journal of the Royal Anthropological Institute* 17: 154–77.

Hookoomsing, V.Y., R. Ludwig, and B. Schnepel (eds.). 2009. *Multiple Identities in Action: Mauritius and Some Antillean Parallelisms.* Frankfurt: Peter Lang.

Houbert, J. 1981. 'Mauritius: Independence and Dependence'. *The Journal of Modern African Studies* 19: 75–105.

Meade, J.E. et al. 1961. *The Social and Economic Structure of Mauritius.* London: Her Majesty's Stationery Office.

Meisenhelder, T. 1997. 'The Developmental State in Mauritius'. *The Journal of Modern African Studies* 35: 279–97.

Osterhammel, J. 1997. 'Einleitung'. In Poivre (1997): 7–41.

Malinowski, B. 1961 [1922]. *Argonauts of the Western Pacific.* New York: E.P. Dutton.

Mauss, M. 1976 [1950]. *The Gift.* New York: Norton.

Neveling, P. 2012. *Manifestationen der Globalisierung. Kapital, Staat und Arbeit in Mauritius, 1825–2005.* Halle: Martin Luther University Halle-Wittenberg (PhD thesis).

——, 2014. 'Three Shades of Embeddedness, State Capitalism as the Informal Economy, Emic Notions of the Anti-Market, and Counterfeit Garments in the Mauritian Export Processing Zone'. *Research in Economic Anthropology* 34: 65–95.

Piat, D. 2010. *Mauritius: On the Spice Route.* Singapore: Editions Didier Millet.

Poivre, P. 1997. *Reisen eines Philosophen.* Translated and edited by Jürgen Osterhammel. Sigmaringen: Thorbeke Verlag.

Richon, E. 2008. *Le Reveil du Dodo.* Mauritius: Editions de L'Ocean Indien.

Schnepel, B. 2018. 'The Making of a Hub Society: Mauritius' Path from Port of Call to Cyber Island'. In Schnepel und Alpers (eds.) 2018: 231–57.

——, 2022. 'Cargoes in the Indian Ocean World: A Thematic and Methodological Introduction'. In Schnepel and Verne (eds.) 2022: 1–23.

Schnepel, B., and E.A. Alpers (eds.). 2018. *Connectivity in Motion. Island Hubs in the Indian Ocean World.* New York: Palgrave.

Schnepel, B., and J. Verne (eds.). 2022. *Cargoes in Motion: Materiality and Connectivity Across the Indian Ocean.* Athens: Ohio University Press.

Sellström, T. 2015. *Africa in the Indian Ocean. Islands in Ebb and Flow.* Leiden: Brill.

Srebrnik, H. 1999. 'Ethnicity and the Development of a "Middleman" Economy on Mauritius: The Diaspora Factor'. *The Round Table* 350: 297–311.

Storey, W.K. 1997. *Science and Power in Colonial Mauritius.* Rochester: University of Rochester Press.

Teelock, V. 1998. *Bitter Sugar: Sugar and Slavery in 19th Century Mauritius.* Moka, Mauritius: Mahatma Gandhi Institute.

Toussaint, A. 1966. *Harvest of the Sea: The Mauritius Sea Story in Outline.* Port Louis: Mauritius Printing CY. Ltd.

——, 1973. *Port Louis: A Tropical City*. London: Allen and Unwin.

——, 2013 [1936]. *Port Louis: deux siècles d'histoire, 1735–1935*. Port Louis: Editions VIZAVI.

Vaughan, M. 2005. *Creating the Creole Island: Slavery in Eighteenth-Century Mauritius*. Durham, NC: Duke University Press.

Wagner, C. 2013. 'The Indian Ocean Rim Association for Regional Co-operation (IOR-ARC). The Futile Quest for Regionalism?' *Journal of Indian Ocean Research* 9: 6–16.

Weiner, A. 1992. *Inalienable Possessions: The Paradox of Keeping-while-Giving*. Berkeley: University of California Press.

CHAPTER 7

Paradise Island? Tourism and Life on Mauritian Beaches[1]

INTRODUCTION

In this chapter, I examine the socio-cultural life and economic significance of Mauritian beaches. I shall argue that, although the beach is a special kind of place, studying it can provide some important insights into the society and culture of Mauritius in general, that is, beyond the beach. In the sense used here, then, a beach is more than just a geographical fact, as when dictionaries describe this kind of the landscape somewhat humourlessly as a 'sandy stretch of land' or in similar words. Rather, the beach is considered in the increasingly conventional and popular sense of a place which people visit to find some sort of recreation close to the water. And in this sense, one could say with Löfgren that in 'global history some beaches occupy a limited stretch of sand but take up a huge mental space' (1999: 215).

To understand the situation in Mauritius fully, a basic distinction must be introduced, namely that between 'public beaches' and 'hotel beaches'. Although there is an overlap between these two categories, with visitors on either sort of beach encountering each other, public beaches and hotel beaches are marked by important differences in their environments. The most obvious difference is in their respective clienteles, but there are also variations with regard to the trees found on them. Roughly speaking, public beaches have filao trees and are frequented overwhelmingly by Mauritians and others living permanently on the island, whereas hotel beaches are spotted by palm trees and are enjoyed by tourists who have come long distances and stay for short periods of time only. By studying Mauritian beaches, therefore, one is confronted with dimensions of beach life and of socio-cultural life beyond beaches which transcend the local and the national to embrace the global phenomenon of tourism. This industry, one of the world's largest in pre-COVID times, is not only a universal phenomenon, but is itself globalizing in its effects, being one of the strongest, if not the strongest such force in the world today. Tourism globalizes so heavily and sometimes irreversibly because it moves around not only goods, technologies and money, but also people by the million. Tourism thus brings its customers into contact not only with other tourists and with touristic infrastructure (such as hotels and beaches), but also with the local residents of the places they visit. Often, each of these (unequal) parties to the deal has its own ways of acting and interacting, as well as its own habitus, etiquette, moral standards and values. More than in most other 'contact zones' of the world, then, it is within tourism that a global world is created, or rather, that 'the local' and 'the global' meet and clash, sometimes even being merged into new forms of living. And within this touristic field, for more than a century now, beaches have been the favourite sites on which to play and work.[2]

WATERFRONTS

The total coastline of Mauritius measures about 323 kilometres, not all of which are beaches in the emphatic sense being discussed here. Take the following official statistics:[3]

Usage	*Kilometres (km)*	*Percentage (%)*
Public beaches	26.6	8.2
Hotel sites	41.9	13
Bungalow sites	52	16
Building sites	25	7.7
Diverse activities	12.78	3.9
Agricultural	17	5
Grazing	28.7	8.9
Under vegetation	76.24	24.2
Coastal road	16.1	4.9
Cliffs	10.2	3.2
Cliffs/grazing	11.5	3.6
St Antoine Sugar Estate	4.5	1.4
Total	322.5	100

The beach kilometres which concern us here are the first three: public beaches, hotel sites and bungalow sites. Of the total kilometres of coast in Mauritius, 120.5 kilometres or 37.2 per cent consisted of beaches in 1996. In greater detail, 13 per cent of the coastal zone was fronted by hotels and 16 per cent by private bungalows, while only 8.2 per cent was open to the public. In other words, of the beaches available for recreational purposes in Mauritius, in 1996 more than four times as many kilometres (taking bungalows and hotels together) were accessible for private users as there were for the Mauritian public. In the following discussion, I concentrate on the two paradigmatic types of the beach mentioned above, namely hotel beaches and public beaches, where the proportion of beach kilometres used by hotel guests to publicly frequented beaches is roughly two to one.

The total length of Mauritian beaches of both types is not consistent, but has increased, especially in recent decades, and is still growing. Two modes of extension can be considered. To start with, new beaches can be developed by making semi-rough but still suitable coastlines into smoother, socio-culturally usable ones, which are good

Figure 7.1: Dangerous Bathing

enough for picnicking, relaxing and sometimes bathing. At weekends these beaches will be frequented not only by local tourists, but also by ice-cream vans, food vendors and hawkers. If the sea is rough or the currents dangerous, signs warning of dangerous bathing conditions or even forbidding bathing altogether will be put up.

Where it is possible to swim and bathe, floating buoys may mark the area beyond which swimmers should not go. A second way of extending the length of beach is more drastic, labour-intensive and costly, but it generally creates beaches of a higher quality than those just mentioned. For example, to develop beaches for some new luxury hotels in the south, the coastal road, which previously ran immediately parallel to the ocean front, was moved in a semi-circle some five hundred metres inland so it returned to the sea again approximately one kilometre later. The land in the semi-circle between this new road and the sea was first cleared of most plants, bushes, trees, sugarcane and so on, the houses of the local inhabitants were expropriated, and an old sugar factory was dismantled. The ground was then flattened and otherwise prepared to construct bungalows, restaurants and other buildings connected with the new hotels. On the actual beach, the immediate approach to the water was smoothed, and white sand was brought in to supplement the poor-quality local sand, and in some areas to replace pebbles and grass. Palm trees were planted to fill the empty spaces of the beach line and to replace the supposedly less spectacular and less appropriate casuarina (filao) trees that had been growing there before. In such major reconstructions of the coastal zone, changes are made even under the water, with a large underwater vacuum-cleaner clearing the bathing area of stones, rocks, broken pieces of coral, sea urchins, seaweed and ugly seacucumbers, though environmental laws now prevent the seabed from being cleaned as thoroughly as before. In places where the sea is rough or the currents are tricky, barriers such as stone walls or piers have been built out into the sea, as well as jetties to cater for water sports. As is obvious, the first type of extension usually leads to public beaches, the second to hotel beaches.

Where these two ways of increasing beach length have ceased to be possible, there is yet another way to provide new beach kilometres, namely by extending one's own beach at the expense of a neighbouring one. In practice this means, and every so often in Mauritian history has meant, that a hotel beach encroaches on a public beach, which then vanishes or becomes smaller. One variant of this is that some hotels, usually simpler and cheaper ones, come to dominate the second line of hotels near a public beach, from where they send their clients – 'alternative' tourists, European old-age pensioners who spend the whole winter on the island, not-so-well-to-do families with children, local tourists and other less affluent tourists – to the public beach across the road. Some public beaches of this sort then acquire a different character in several ways: (a) visitors will now be more mixed, being both local and foreign in origin; (b) beaches become more crowded, especially at weekends; and (c) certain amenities start to be provided which were not there before and which turn some stretches of the formerly unstructured public beach into a kind of hotel beach, with local vendors starting to provide deckchairs, parasols and/or boats. This mode of encroachment has been the fate of many Mauritian public beaches. Statistically this means that the amount of beach kilometres available to the Mauritian public has been shrinking even further.

This sort of *ex*tensification of beach kilometres will eventually reach a natural limit, or it simply becomes impossible to extend one's beach further for political and legal reasons. However, there are other ways of getting more out of the existing beaches and increasing the yield produced from the same amount of land. Thus, *in*tensification can be achieved by simply increasing the number of hotel beds and improving the occupancy rate. For the corresponding hotel beach, this would mean that the hotel would put out additional deckchairs, parasols or shady palm trees, or else that it increase the size or number of swimming pools as artificial substitutes for the beach. This kind of intensification has its limits in terms of the available space, as well as of the amount of crowding a hotel's guests are willing to accept. Generally, one can say that the less space a guest has to him- or herself, the lower the category of the hotel and the less money it can charge for accommodation and other services. So even if there is still some space in which further amenities for sunbathing and swimming are added, some hotels hesitate to do so lest they lose their reputation and/or guests in the future.

For those hotels that do not wish to make any compromises as far as the quality and carrying capacity of their beaches are concerned, there is another way of increasing the yield of the beaches in front of them: they can increase their profile by improving the quality of their rooms, their service and other facilities, for example, rising from a three-star to a four- or even five-star category. This has happened to many hotels in Mauritius which started as simple bungalows and today are luxury hotels. The tendency to improve hotels and charge more for the higher standard is in line with the island's declared policy, which is not to attract mass tourism, but to compete on the world market for the upper and more affluent sectors of the business. In this sense, the same stretch of beach still caters to the same number of people but is more profitable.

Figures confirm the ever-increasing demand from hotels in Mauritius for beach space.[4] In 1968, the year of independence, the number of tourists visiting Mauritius was 16,000. In 1970, the tourist sector, which up to then had been almost completely controlled by the Mauritian company *New Mauritius Hotels*, was opened to foreign investors at the instigation of Gaetan Duval, the then minister of tourism. As a result of this policy and of the worldwide expansion of tourism that was taking place at that time, the number of tourists visiting Mauritius more than quadrupled within six years, to 72,000 in 1974. Since then, the number of tourist arrivals has constantly increased, from around 150,000 in 1985 to 200,000 in 1987, 536,000 in 1997, 680,000 in 2002, 702,000 in 2003, and 719,000 in 2004. As far as the numbers of hotels, hotel rooms and hotel beds are concerned, in 1985 there were 55 hotels in Mauritius, while eleven years later, in 1996, there were already 90 hotels with 6,668 rooms. In 2004 there were 103 hotels on the island with 10,640 rooms and 21,335 beds. From 1985 to 2004, therefore, to take these two decades as our frame of reference, the number of hotels almost doubled, while the number of rooms and beds probably more than doubled. This increase in hotel capacity has also been accompanied by a rise in the amount of money that tourists spend on the island. According to figures provided by the Bank of Mauritius, tourist expenditure increased from 845 million Mauritian rupees in 1985 to 11.5 billion in 1998 and 23.5 billion in 2004. This means that in 1985 each tourist spent around 5,650 rupees, while in 1998 the average tourist spent about 28,530 rupees; in 2004 this increased to 32,638 rupees per tourist. In other words, from 1985 to 2004, not only has the number of tourists multiplied almost five times, the money that the average tourist spends has also risen almost six times. While these increases certainly reflect exchange-rate fluctuations and the increasing cost of living on Mauritius, they also reflect the intensification of the tourist business, and especially the fact that not only more, but also better (and more expensive) hotels have been built and filled in recent decades. Consequently, beaches had become the third-largest source of income in Mauritius by 2004, immediately after sugar and textiles.

PUBLIC BEACHES AND HOTEL BEACHES

Strictly speaking – that is, from the legal point of view – the distinction between publich beaches and hotel beaches is not entirely valid. In Mauritius there are no private beaches in the usual sense of the term, for according to the law all beaches are open to the public up to their 'high-water mark'. Since this is the farthest point to which the water may reach at high tide, there is usually a narrow strip of sandy or pebbly beach where anyone may picnic, bathe, walk, run or simply pass by at any time. As regards property relations and ownership patterns in the hinterland, all stretches of land from the high-water mark up to 81.21 metres inland, known as the *Pas Geometriques*, belong by law to the government, which, however, can lease it to private individuals or hotels for periods of up to thirty years. The cost of these leases has been low, and they can be and are renewed easily and cheaply. It will be remembered that of the total of 120 kilometres of beaches in Mauritius, approximately 42 kilometres (more precisely, the *Pas Geometriques* behind these beaches) were leased out to hotels in 1996, a figure that has been increasing ever since through new beaches being built or hotel beaches being extended at the expense of public beaches and bungalows. With all beaches being open to the public, one might then well stroll along the beach of, let us say, the six-star Dina Robin Hotel, and even get a glimpse of Zinedine Zidane by the swimming pool or of some other celebrity in a deckchair. However, this is only possible from a distance and under the eyes of the hotel's watchmen, and if anyone tries to take the path ten to twenty metres inland, or indeed tries to enter the hotel premises, one will be sent back in a friendly but firm manner to the public part of the beach. Hence, although the beach up to the high-water mark is by law open to the general public, leases of the *Pas Geometrique* land immediately behind it decisively influence what happens on the beach in front. In other words, *de jure* all beaches are open to the public, but *de facto* this is the case only with so many restrictions and obstacles that most members of the public will not dare or bother to visit, let alone use, the public part of a hotel beach.

One further qualification must be introduced here. So far we have spoken of 'public beaches' in the colloquial sense of beaches that are open to the public or accessible to all. But there is another, more official meaning to the term. According to the Beach Authority Act of 2002, a 'public beach means a space along the coast which, by notice published in the Gazette, has been declared to be a public beach by the Minister responsible for the subject of housing and lands' (*Beach Authority Act* 2002, Part 1, Section 2a). Thus, in this sense a public beach is specified land owned and controlled by the state, which must take care of it, ensure law and order as well as security, provide certain amenities on it and, in the most general terms, allow users to 'derive maximum enjoyment' (ibid.) from it. Hence, according to law all beaches in Mauritius are (open to the) public, but not all are 'public beaches' in the meaning of this Act.[5]

There are certain basic differences between public beaches and hotel beaches. Even if a visitor does not look at the hinterland of a particular beach – let us imagine, for the time being, that s/he has arrived by boat from the sea and sees the immediate coastline only – s/he will note a number of differences, which at second glance also conform to the distinction between hotel beaches and public beaches used here. Generally, public beaches are rougher: there are more pebbles, and even if there is white sand, it is thinner and coarser, being mixed with broken pieces of coral or stones and with dark sand. The direct approach to and from the water is often a little steep because of a broken shelf, sometimes a metre or more high, where the water has washed away the earth and uncovered tree roots during a storm or flood. Furthermore, in the picnic and parking areas of public beaches one usually finds filao or casuarina trees, as well as sometimes baobab and pine trees. Public beaches and their hinterland, though they are generally well maintained by the Beach Authority, tend to be messier than hotel beaches, especially at the end of a long and sunny public holiday or weekend. Furthermore, on public beaches you find dogs constantly searching for food and playmates. Hotel beaches in Mauritius, by contrast, generally conform to the worldwide image of beaches on tropical 'paradise islands'. The sand is white and smooth, the water sparkling clear, and one can see the nicely maintained underwater floor when walking into or swimming in the sea. This sea is smooth and 'civilized' because the currents and the waves, as well as the sharks and other large and potentially disturbing fish, are kept well away by the coral reefs that lie some hundred metres offshore. At the high-water mark, the beach gradually slopes upwards to the first stretch of firm land, usually a patch of grass that belongs to the hotel and is not open to the public. At this boundary line, one might find signposts saying 'private property' or posts restricting and forbidding access in other ways. Just on the other side of this line, one usually finds a row of deckchairs, which in the higher category of hotels are often arranged in groups of two or three around parasols and at some distance from the next such group. On hotel beaches, the trees providing additional shade and flair are palm trees planted in equal rows and at equal distances. Usually, at both ends of the hotel beach, we find boat houses, bars or even restaurants; in the middle is usually the hotel's main restaurant and the swimming pool, which, seen from the inside, looks as if its water stretched without interruption out into the green-blue-turquoise sea beyond ('infinity pools'). Dogs are totally absent from these beaches, and if any do appear, they are immediately and aggressively chased away by the hotel guards.

The differences between public and hotel beaches pointed out so far are basically environmental and infrastructural in character, even 'natural'. However, those beaches that might be considered the remains of a so far undiluted paradise – sandy beaches with slightly drooping palm trees and clear water – are actually the more artificial or less natural ones. This is not to devalue their beauty – on the contrary, by many standards these are beaches that have been significantly beautified, as well as made more secure, convenient and

Figure 7.2: Two Beaches

pleasurable. In this context, it should also be remembered that the island was only populated relatively late, hardly at all before the middle of the eighteenth century. Since then, however, the environment has been altered and cultivated continuously and radically in order to make human habitation and exploitation of its resources possible, so much so that not only all the human population, but also most of the plants and animals to be found on the island today (sugar and deer being prime examples) are foreign and have been imported, while many indigenous animals and plants (such as the famous dodo and most of the high-quality timber) have vanished. Or, in other words, *both* the filao trees on the public beach *and* the palm trees on the hotel beaches are imports, the former from Australia, the latter from Madagascar and East Africa.

'SUR LES PLAGES': SOCIAL, ETHNIC AND NATIONAL COMPOSITIONS

When it comes to identifying the social, ethnic and national background of life on Mauritian beaches, one of the first and most obvious differences to be observed is that of the skin colour of their respective users. While on public beaches this tends to be dark or brown, on hotel beaches most users are white to red in skin colour. The reason is obvious: public beaches are frequented to a high degree by Mauritians, hotel beaches by tourists. But let us look more closely and comparatively at the actual composition of these two beach populations.

As far as hotel beaches are concerned, a good overall indicator of the social composition of those who use them can be found by examining the countries of origin of the tourists who arrived at the airport in 2004. All in all, 66.4 per cent or 477,041 of a total of 719,000 came from European countries, 24.4 per cent or 175,649 from African countries, 6.3 per cent or 45,325 from Asia, 12,068 from Oceania, and 8,409 from America. From within Europe, the largest group, namely 210,411 (or 44.1 per cent of the European category and 29.3 per cent of total tourist arrivals), was of French nationality. The next largest group came from the United Kingdom (92,652), followed by Germany (53,277) and Italy (41,277), with Switzerland, Austria and Spain accounting for between 16,000 and 8,000 visitors each. The African category is somewhat misleading, because most African tourists come from the neighbouring islands and from South Africa only. Réunion led this category with 96,510 visitors,[6] followed by visitors from South Africa (52,609) and the Malagasy Republic (8,256). Of the Asian contingent, Indians made up the majority with 24,716, followed by the Chinese (6,127). The label 'Oceania' refers overwhelmingly to people from Australia (11,373), while the category 'America' basically means citizens of the United States (4,305) and Canada (2,341).[7]

Some amendments have to be made when transferring these figures to the beach. The label 'tourist', as officially used by the government, does not just refer to holidaymakers. Only 91 per cent of tourists arriving in Mauritius in 2004 were tourists in this strict sense of term. The rest were visitors who had come to Mauritius for conferences, business reasons, social visits, sport events, or were in transit. These people seldom go to hotels with beaches, but stay in business hotels or with friends, family members or business partners. For a variety of social, historical and economic reasons, one may well assume that most of the tourists from Réunion and Madagascar, as well as many from India and China and a considerable number of French and South African visitors, belong in this category. Hence, only a small overall proportion of these will be found on the hotel beaches. Furthermore, many proper tourists – that is, those who belong to the remaining 91 per cent who come to Mauritius as holidaymakers and thus primarily for the beaches – do not stay in hotels with beaches either. Rather, they rent rooms, apartments or bungalows in the informal sector of the 'second row', or else stay in the grey market of adjacent towns like Flic en Flac, Grand Baie, Trou d'Eau Douce, or La Gaulette. It is estimated that about 25 per cent of tourists do not stay in hotels.[8] All in all, therefore, on hotel beaches we basically find Europeans, with French tourists still forming the majority, followed in number by British, German, Italian and Swiss. This group of Europeans using hotel beaches is substantially completed by overwhelmingly white South Africans and increasingly, since the Bali bombings of 2002 and again in 2005, as well as since the Tsunami disaster on Southeast Asian coasts in 2004, Australians. Moreover, as a reflection of the greater wealth and new spending patterns that have developed in their countries in the last decade, there are more and more Indian, Chinese and Russian tourists.[9]

In order to obtain an approximation of the social and ethnic composition of the users of the public beaches, let us first briefly remind ourselves of the composition of the Mauritian population and its particularities, as discussed in greater detail in Chapter 5 above. One way of classifying the island population is to state that, of the nation's 1.2 million citizens, 68 per cent are of Indian origin, 27 per cent are Creoles, 3 per cent Chinese and 2 per cent French. However, certain other criteria were used in the last official government census, carried out in 1982, where the Mauritian population is given as consisting of 52 per cent Hindus, 16 per cent Muslims and 3 per cent Sino-Mauritians, with 29 per cent belonging to the category of General Population.[10] All these 'identities' or better criteria for 'making and unmaking differences'[11] play an important role, not only in the census, but also for the actors themselves in their socio-cultural, political, economic or religious lives. However, here the question of which identity comes to the fore, and when, depends on situational dynamics and relativity, i.e. who is speaking to or dealing with whom, in what situation, for what purpose, etc.[12] How do these figures translate on to the beach? Do more Hindus frequent beaches in Mauritius and do they do so more often or stay longer than, say, Muslims? Do Sino-Mauritians like the beach better than the Creole descendants of African slaves? On a given beach at a given time, how many come from this or that group? How many are men or women, young or old, twice-born or low-caste, rich or poor, educated or uneducated?

To our knowledge, there have been neither quantitative nor qualitative investigations into these questions, and so one cannot say with any scientific certainty to what degree the census figures given above are reflected on the beach. But what can be said quite confidently from observations and interviews is that there are no striking imbalances or even absences. In other words, all ethnic and/or religious groups, all generations, all genders, poor as well as rich Mauritians, use public beaches, and they do so in significant numbers, reflecting to a certain degree their numerical proportions away from the beach. This result could not have been taken for granted, nor is it as obvious as it might seem; as a matter of fact, it should surprise us, because some Mauritian groups have the reputation as well as a self-image of being more oriented in their ethics towards work and discipline (namely the Hindus), while others (namely the Creoles) are regarded and often regard themselves as being more focused on enjoying life. Alternatively, it might have been expected that Muslim communities, especially Muslim women, could not be found at all or at least in fewer numbers on the beach on account of the stricter morals and restrictions on exposing the female body in Islam. But on the public beaches of Mauritius there are Creoles and Coloureds as much as Indo-Mauritians and Sino-Mauritians; or, to reshuffle the criteria, Hindus as well as Christians and Muslims, men as well as women, old as well as young, rich as well as poor, low caste as well as high caste. Only Franco-Mauritians seem to be rare visitors, even taking into account the fact that they make up just 2 per cent of the population. As they represent the strata of the population which has the highest income and wealth, they are more likely to be found in much larger proportions and even to dominate the beaches in front of private bungalows. But this does not mean that 'white' skins are totally absent from public beaches. We must remember that not all tourists end up in hotels with beaches. Even though the desire of members of this group to go to the beach may be weaker than in the case of more prototypical holidaymakers, it is likely that many of these will eventually appear on public beaches, and they may even start to dominate some of them where the 'hinterland' has been filled up with second-row hotels, private apartments and bungalows for rent.

Up to this point we have looked at the social, ethnic and national composition of the users of public and hotel beaches from an overall perspective. Looking more closely at who is actually to be found on the beaches and where exactly people take up their abode, it seemed to us that existing public beaches are *not* divided up between the island's population according to ethnic or religious belonging or to other criteria such as class, caste, gender or age. Generally, all groups can be found on all public beaches, or in other words, and remarkably: on Mauritian public beaches, there are no implicit or explicit rules of distribution such that, for example, Sino-Mauritians go to one beach while young people go to another, Christians yet another one, and so on. On hotel beaches too, one can also find a good mixture of all the nations we have identified above. Of course, hotels are largely filled by the tour operators with whom they have contracts, which are usually organized nationally. However, there are very few if any mono-national or bi-national hotels. Users of a given hotel beach, then, usually come from many nations; and, especially in the large hotels, they will be found roughly in the national proportions indicated above with regard to tourist arrivals.

The hotel beach is frequented by small groups: prototypically we find couples, some of them honeymooning, or families with one or two children, a unit which in some cases is supplemented by accompanying grandparents, who may also have volunteered to pay the substantial bills. Only occasionally does one find larger groups of friends or relatives who have booked a holiday together. If one finds larger groups at all, these are not formed by family connections, but consist of company employees having been sent on a holiday together by their employers in appreciation of their good work in the past or as an incentive aiming at lifting the team's spirit in the future. Alternatively, such groups may consist of people united by common interests, such as participating in golf or fishing competitions. Groups on public beaches tend to be larger than those on hotel beaches. One prototypical 'peer group' on public beaches, seldom found on hotel beaches, consists of extended families, such as when brothers or cousins join up with their respective families, or when families unite for a picnic. These groups tend to huddle close to the car, van, pick-up truck or even bus that has brought them there. Sometimes the cars are arranged in groups, forming a sheltering and somewhat inward-looking semi-circle within which the group gathers. Within a typical group of this sort of anything from five to twenty individuals, there may be some internal dividing lines, not necessarily between nuclear families, but according to criteria of sex or age. Elderly men sit under one tree to play cards and drink, while women, girls and small children make themselves at home on a carpet on the other side of the tree, where they chat, play or relax in other ways. Similarly, young unmarried men like to get away for a while, to play soccer on an open space elsewhere, go down to the beach or just stroll about to see whether friends or anyone interesting can be seen. But the effects of these centrifugal tendencies are always countered by phases of reunification, especially when it comes to having a barbecue together or going for a bathe.

BEACH LIFE IN COMPARISON

Up to this point, we have described some of the characteristic features of socio-cultural life on the beach in general terms. We shall now look in greater detail at how people actually fill the Mauritian beaches with life. What are the more typical patterns of behaviour and etiquette on each of the two types of beach?

To start with, it is necessary to consider the temporal dimension of it all. When are beaches frequented the most? When do they tend to be full, and when empty? One obvious answer, which applies to both kinds of beach equally, is that when the sun is shining and the temperature is warm or even hot, then beaches tend to fill up. However, other common features are less striking and even lacking. Public beaches, in being used mostly by Mauritians, are visited more densely at weekends and on public holidays. An increase in numbers can also be found in the late afternoon and early evenings of fine days during the week. Hotel beaches, by contrast, are filled equally and continuously throughout the week, provided, again, that the weather is fine. This is hardly surprising, because the life of a holidaymaker is not determined by his or her working routine. All days are there for the tourist to enjoy. Differences in the numbers of those using hotel beaches depend rather on external factors, such as whether it is the season for travelling in Europe, or whether tourism is experiencing a boom or a crisis. By and large, then, and seen within the temporal framework of a single week, public beaches experience greater fluctuations in use than hotel beaches. During normal weekdays they are filled, if at all, only sparsely by tourists from the informal sector or by Mauritians enjoying a day off, whereas at weekends they sometimes become crowded to bursting point. Hotel beaches tend to be emptier and more even in use, being crowded only at peak seasons such as Christmas and New Year.

As far as the distinction between night and day is concerned, both hotel beaches and public beaches tend to empty once the sun has gone down. But life in the area immediately behind the high-water mark, in the *Pas Geometriques*, goes on, albeit in different ways. Public beaches tend to empty completely in this hinterland, though at weekends, on warm summer nights and on the more popular public beaches, some groups of people stay into the night and even overnight. Some sleep out in the open, while others rest in their cars or under makeshift plastic sheeting, and yet others bring tents. Just as on the public beaches, on hotel beaches the direct sandy waterfronts and the areas with deckchairs and parasols tend to empty after dark. Certainly, in the early evening some people still use the swimming pool or even the sea for a last refreshing swim; and in some hotels, on certain days of the week, a professional Séga group offers a short 'Séga typique' performance on the beach to the delight of some of the guests. The occasional person alone or couple strolling leisurely along the beach or lying dreamily on deckchairs during moon-lit or fine starry nights can also be found. However, in the evening the centre of social and cultural activities shifts just behind the sandy and grassy line of the beach proper. Hotel bars and restaurants are usually near the waterfront, so that tourists can take a cocktail while viewing the sea and, if on the west coast, with a view of the sun setting beautifully into the sea. From around 7.30 o'clock onwards there is dinner, with the hotel buffets often sporting a theme on particular days of the week: e.g., a Creole night on Wednesday, an Indian night on Thursday, a Chinese night on Friday. Later during the evening, there will be a music show, further within in the hotel's open-air entertainment area, which sometimes continues the theme of the dinner, so that, in the example used here, on Wednesday hotel guests will be able to enjoy a show of 'Séga modern'. Ironically, tourists will be told that the Séga, as they are seeing it within their all-inclusive shelter, is exactly what they would see on the public beaches if they were ever to go there. In fact, those who do stay overnight on the public beach will witness no such thing. There may be a cassette player blasting out the latest song by Cassiya and Gangsta Beach, or more often the latest MTV hits by Madonna, James Blunt, Shakira, or the like. There will be the occasional young Creole or Hindu with a guitar interpreting a Séga song by, say, Serge Lebrasse or Fan Fan. But, more often than Séga, one will hear songs from the worldwide outdoor musical repertoire, from *No Woman, No Cry* by Bob Marley to *Leaving on a Jet-plane* by Jefferson Airplane. In general, however, unplugged manifestations of musical talent on public beaches are rare, and the kind of Séga dancing and singing that tourists, safe behind their own stretches of beach, believe to be the authentic, contemporary Mauritian folklore are almost never found on public beaches.

Returning now to the daytime as the main time-space of comparison here, we will point out some of the most common forms of behaviour then and there. Users of hotel beaches spend much of the day lying on deckchairs sunbathing and tanning. This leisurely activity, which entails some careful timing in turning one's body so as to achieve an even bronze colour on all parts of it, can be combined with other activities, such as sleeping or day-dreaming, massaging one's own and others' bodies with sun lotion, exchanging caresses, or trying to take a secret (sometimes critical, sometimes appreciative) glance at the bodies of others, comparing their tans and other physical features with one's own. Hence, much of the time is spent creating and displaying 'the properly relaxed beach body' (Löfgren 1999: 214). When this becomes boring, many people take up reading, albeit of light stuff.

Moving to the public beach, one finds a somewhat different situation. While lying in the sun is not completely unknown among the users of public beaches, this activity does not figure as prominently as someone might expect who comes from a culture in which achieving a tan has acquired a cult status, the 'cult of *bronzage*', as Löfgren (ibid.: 223) calls it. Prototypically, a public beach user sits rather than lies, and chats with others rather than daydreaming or reading a book. Sometimes plastic chairs and even sofas are brought along in the van or pick-up, but more often people sit on mats and carpets. Most set up their picnic areas a little inland, just across the high-water mark. The reason for this difference in attitude compared with behaviour on the hotel beach lies in a combination of a lower interest in sunbathing and tanning and in the fact that on public beaches there are no parasols or other permanent artificial structures to provide shelter from the sun. Hence, in order to find shade and a cool place, one has to move into the *Pas Geometrique* area, with its filao and pine trees. What happens there is best described as 'car camping': people sit next to their cars, and occasionally some plastic sheeting is put up

Figure 7.3: Car Camping

between cars or trees to act as a sunroof or to allow an undisturbed change of clothes. In these little enclaves, people have barbecues, or spread out the tupperware they have brought from home containing spicy food.

Instead of the water bottle (a must for the European tourist on the hotel beach), we find more coke and other sweet drinks for the women and children, or Phoenix beer and even stronger stuff for the adult men. And instead of the seaside restaurants and bars of the hotel beaches, we find stalls selling samosas, *dholpuris*, coconuts, pineapples, sweet drinks and various other refreshments. One can also buy ice cream from one of the ever-increasing number of vans, called 'Baby neige', which can easily be spotted on account of the loud jingles they repeatedly play, drowning out everything else. There are other noises too: the sounds of ghetto blasters, the yelling of hawkers, the screaming of kids, the shouting of men and the laughing of women, all mixed up together. In general, then, the scene on public beaches on a lively weekend is more crowded, noisy, active, lively and filled with the smells of different foods than life on the hotel beaches, which rather displays a certain serenity, an atmosphere of contemplation and meditation, of dreaming the day away, filled with the smell of sun lotion.

Hotel beaches are, of course, not devoid of all bodily movement. People tend to move along the well-kept little lanes between their apartments on the one hand and the bar, reception, souvenir shops, spa and invariably the beach on the other. This moving between places within the microcosm of the hotel provides an opportunity to try to walk and ultimately show how to walk slowly and in a relaxed way, forgetting the hustle and bustle of life back home. One can find many activities and even a degree of exuberance going on at and in the nearby swimming pool, the favourite playground for families with little children, as well as for those who like the pool bar a lot. On the beach, peddlers (licensed and let in by the hotel management) have to be kept at bay or, if one is in the mood, one might start negotiations with them about the quality and prices of what they are offering.

Out on the sea, others are trying to stay upright on water skis, only a few showing some expertise in doing so. Yet others, usually groups of teenagers, let themselves be towed behind speedboats while clinging to small rubber boats and trying not to fall into the water when there is a sharp turn or a big wave. These speedboats create the loudest noise on the hotel beaches, noise of a kind that is usually absent from the public beaches. Yet other people take a more relaxed excursion in a glass-bottomed boat to the nearby coral reefs to admire the wonders of the sea while remaining in the dry. More sporty hotel guests go snorkelling or even diving to get closer to the reefs. Most hotel beach users, however, restrict their activities to the occasional plunge into the water just in front of their beach. Some do so just to get some refreshment and to put salty water on their skin so that the tanning process can be continued in somewhat cooler circumstances and with the enhancing effects of the salt. Others swim leisurely around, gliding, floating, paddling or diving, or simply crawl and get some distance behind them. In the late afternoon, just before sunset, there are other activities such as strolling along the beach, finding some nice corals or stones, and maybe even venturing beyond the hotel beach to see 'authentic native' life on the nearby public beach. Others, at this time of the day, use the hotel's sports and spa facilities, playing tennis or golf or enjoying a massage. Yet other guests prefer a sundowner at the bar. Watching the sun set and taking photographs of it, preferably with a loved one in front, is yet another of the favourite activities to be observed on hotel beaches.

Users of hotel beaches, should they walk towards and along a neighbouring public beach, will be struck by a difference there: while on hotel beaches people tend to swim alone or as couples, public beaches are characterized by some sort of communal bathing, reflecting the communal patterns found on the beach itself. One seldom goes into the water alone, preferring to do so in the company of family members and friends. It is possible to see groups of anything between five and fifteen people of all generations in the sea together. They seldom go far into the water but keep close to the shore so as to be able to feel the ground beneath their feet. The most common activity is to linger leisurely with the body up to the waist or shoulders under water, sometimes chatting the time away. Teenagers and young men may fool around, splash water in their faces, try to push one another under and even swim a little, though never straying too far from the group. Women and young children stay closest to the coast and to each other, forming a sort of inner group surrounded by the more daring and active men and teenagers. While this kind of behaviour may mirror the strong feeling of belonging within picnic and barbecue groups, it also seems to express a certain need for security. In the absence of lifeguards or other safety measures, and on account of the sometimes rather dangerous bathing conditions off the public beaches, there is a practical side to this. The sea may be rough, the waves and the current strong, there may be some shells and animals, like sea urchins, that one wants to avoid stepping on, and not all family members are able to swim, at least not well. Some bathers may still be made cautious in their activities by the traditional Hindu view of the ocean as *kala pani* or 'black water'. Hence, these communal expressions of bathing also offer psychological and emotional shelter, creating a feeling of *social* security which may reflect, and be reflected back upon, what is happening out of the water.

Figure 7.4: Beach Wear

Finally, dress codes on the two types of beach differ to some degree. Certainly, the same kind of globally worn beachwear can be found in both cases, consisting of shorts or trunks for men and bathing suits or bikinis for women. But the actual interpretation of this global code may differ, especially regarding women. On hotel beaches, women often wear very slim bikinis and even tangas, not a few of them tanning and swimming without a top. On public beaches, Mauritian women are more conservative in their dress, wearing bathing suits rather than bikinis. In addition, they often wear *pareos* and T-shirts; some bath in *salvakamis* or even saris. Occasionally, Muslim women can be seen totally clad in black, with only their eyes showing.

FROM ONE BEACH TO THE OTHER

So far we have discussed the two major kinds of Mauritian beach as if they were completely separate from each other. But in fact there are certain zones of transition and points of contact where they overlap and where their two respective clienteles see and meet each other. To start with, and as already mentioned, by law all Mauritian beaches are accessible to the public. Nonetheless, hotels are able to offer their users some sort of privacy and shelter from intruders: members of the public may walk along hotel beaches, but they are not allowed to cross the boundary beyond the high-water mark. Moreover, even as far as moving from one beach to another is concerned, there are some means and devices which discourage too many people on nearby public beaches from moving over to a hotel beach. Certainly there are no fences or other solid constructions physically restricting or hindering access. What one can find, however, are walls separating the *Pas Geometrique* area leased to the hotel from the adjacent land, though these invariably stop at the high-water mark and do not go all the way down to the water. In addition, boats and other equipment are sometimes placed close to this wall to reduce still further the gap between the wall and the sea, so that, especially at high tide, there is only a narrow stretch of beach left for one to move along. Sometimes there are physical obstacles like a big rock or the roots of a tree, which have been left standing at these points of transition, or else there is a creek which is difficult to cross. Finally, at both ends of a hotel's land, there are invariably small houses or huts where some of the hotel watchmen are stationed. Day and night one or two of these, nicely dressed in uniforms and with caps, can be seen monitoring everyone entering and leaving the hotel beach. They do not prevent people from moving around, and contact with the users of the public beach is generally friendly, as the latter may also be the watchmen's neighbours from a nearby town or village. But it is their duty, especially at the better hotels, to report anyone suspicious to their colleagues stationed further down the beach by walkie-talkie, in particular whether anyone is walking there with the attention of trying to cross the magic line on to the hotel premises. Hence, the borders between public and hotel beaches, where they are adjacent to each other, are marked, if only subtly or invisibly. And by and large the great masses on the public beaches are kept out, or rather they stay away of their own free will. Not being allowed to cross the high-water mark of the hotel beaches also means that it is not possible to find any shade and picnic grounds there. In any case one would have to move some distance from the car, carrying all one's things and possibly one's children too.

In most cases, the transition from one beach to another is an entirely straightforward affair. One moment you are standing on the public beach among filao trees and Mauritians, the next alongside European tourists lying on their deckchairs between the palm trees. There are, however, some interesting exceptions where there is some overlap and where one can find certain 'grey' areas which are *neither* hotel *nor* public, or alternatively *both* hotel *and* public. An example is the crowded public beach at Trou-aux-Biches, which adopted the character of a hotel beach on account of its being frequented by a relatively large number of European tourists from second-row apartments and bungalows. On busy days, this public beach tends to be extended up to 50 metres on to the adjacent hotel beach, with quite a number of public-beach users putting their towels along the trees of the hotel beach up to the high-water mark. Technically these people are still on the right side of the law, but they have somehow broken the unwritten law not to lie down for too long on a beach in front of a hotel. What is remarkable here is that those who have encroached upon the hotel beach are overwhelmingly second-row Europeans, not Mauritians. A similarly opaque situation can be observed on the border between Belle Mare public beach and the Hotel Residence on the east coast. There is a geophysical reason for this, for exactly at the point where the public beach ends and the boat house of the Hotel Residence marks the beginning of its land, the waterfront makes a slight curve away from the hotel into the water, resulting in a little sandy peninsular. Hence, though technically one has left the public beach and stepped on to the hotel beach, in following the waterfront directly, one is still as far away from the hotel proper as one was before. The sandy dunes that break up the otherwise straight line of the coast along this stretch of waterfront have become a favourite space for recreational activities such as playing soccer and volleyball, with teams of hotel guests and staff filling their ranks with youths from the neighbouring public beach. When it comes to lying down and relaxing, this 'no man's land' is filled neither by the hotel guests nor by the Mauritian families occupying the public beach nearby. Rather, groups of 'alternative' Italian, French, Spanish and German tourists can be seen here, who have taken cheaper accommodation in the adjacent town. Just as in Trou-aux-Biches, the social background of these groups tends to reflect the liminal status of the land they occupy: they do not belong to the Mauritian public, nor to the usual four- or five-star hotel clientele. These groups are strangers to both sides, their attitude and behaviour often objectionable to both, as when they bring their own beer and food (which hotel guests would not do) *and* lie bare-breasted in the sun (which Mauritians on the public beach would not do). They are often also misfits in terms of their skin colour. Many of them stay in Mauritius for weeks and even months at an end because their vacation is cheaper, and they belong to the drop-out scene anyway. Thus, they have a much darker tan than most of the usual tourists, though not as dark as most Mauritians. The geophysical betwixt-and-between character of the stretch of this particular beach is therefore matched by the ambiguous and liminal social status of its users and their skin colour.

LIFE IS A BEACH

Coming back to the clearer distinction of beaches and their users that has informed this chapter so far, we have to ask how these two beach populations actually meet and interact. As already indicated, occasionally users of both beaches may stroll along the coast and thus along the 'other beach', where they can see what people on these other beaches look like, how they spend their time, how they bathe, etc. While there may be an occasional exchange of greetings and even brief conversations, these kinds of contact are mostly ocular in character, a matter of seeing and being seen, though what is being observed and noticed may, of course, have repercussions, leading to comparisons, evaluations or judgements. Sometimes the reaction may be sharp and adverse, while in other cases one may feel inspired, consciously or unconsciously, by what is happening on the other side and try to imitate it.

Some of the Mauritians who stroll along hotel beaches are there to make money, namely peddlers of various goods and services, such as *pareos*, corals, shell necklaces, local handicrafts, pineapples or boat excursions. The contacts between these Mauritian peddlers and hotel guests are only sporadic and hardly lead to any mutual socio-cultural influences, though it seems strange that negotiations between sellers and buyers often take place between scantily clad, sometimes even topless European women on the one hand and men from quite conservative Indo-Mauritian and even Indo-Muslim backgrounds on the other. Many contacts on hotel beaches are, of course, between hotel staff and guests. In general, in the hotels there is a rough division of labour according to skin colour and 'race'. The upper management is dominated by Europeans and Franco-Mauritians, the middle level by *gens de couleurs*; Indo-Mauritians work in the restaurants and bars, while Creoles, especially young men from nearby fishing communities, predominate in the area of leisure, especially when it comes to water sports. Among these groups, contact between waiters and guests ordering a drink or food is frequent, but limited in scope and intensity. The closest and most intensive contact is between the so-called 'beach boys' and hotel guests. Due to the nature of the activities that link these two groups, these interactions often take place in a relaxed, friendly and open spirit, and there is some physical contact. Occasionally friendships and flirtation develop, especially between hotel teenagers and beach boys, who, on account of their being sporty, cool and trendy in their outfits and behaviour (Rasta look, etc.), sometimes impress and even attract certain younger visitors.

If life on Mauritian beaches has anything to tell us about Mauritian society and 'the world' at large, as has been argued here, it is nonetheless true that beach life does not reflect the wider society and culture directly or as in a mirror. It may certainly do so in some respects or with regard to some socio-cultural aspects. In others, however, patterns and styles of life on the beach rather distort, invert and camouflage what is common and valued on the streets of everyday life. Furthermore, and vice versa, not only does wider socio-cultural life find some resonance on the beach, but certain beach activities, styles of behaviour and etiquette can be observed finding their way into, and shaping life in, the streets, homes and even offices of Mauritius and beyond. Influences thus go in both directions, with the beach sometimes representing a sort of testing ground for new forms of behaviour and morals, which might well be transported back inland by those who are willing and daring enough to claim that 'life is a beach'. With Geertz (1973), one may therefore argue that the beach is not only a model *of*, but also a model *for*, the usual lived-in world.

The beach itself is a 'betwixt-and-between' space. It connects land and water, and, from a structuralist point of view, it even mediates between nature and culture.[13] However, does the beach's transitory nature mean that it is 'liminal' in a social sense as well, liminal as suggested by Victor Turner (1969) in his theory of the rite of passage? In other words, are Mauritian beaches spaces dominated by anti-structure and *communitas*? In order to answer this question, we must again remind ourselves of the multi-ethnic and poly-religious nature of Mauritian society, and of the fact that in 'real' life the dividing lines and conflicts of interest between the nation's various subgroups are sometimes strong. Against this background, it is remarkable that (a) all Mauritian subgroups go to the beach; (b) all go to all beaches; and (c) only mild forms of clustering can be observed on any particular beach. And once you are on it, the beach (just like the night[14]) represents a space which allows one to be different, or to do things differently, from what you are and do in your everyday working life. On the beach one can escape the strictures and burdens of life further inland.[15] But ultimately this does not mean that we find a sort of democratic *communitas* on Mauritian beaches. Beaches are less mirror images of reality than utopian versions of it. Hence, the mise-en-scène of the beach presents the *ideal* of an egalitarian 'unity in diversity', which becomes a playful reality only on the liminal space of the beach and for a limited period on a sunny afternoon.[16]

The ever-increasing space taken up by hotel beaches, often but not always at the expense of public beaches, has started to alarm and frustrate Mauritian citizens, who see their beaches dwindling in size and number. Some are voicing their complaints in newspapers or in other ways, others are organizing communal protests, as in a movement called 'Pas tous nu la plaze' ('Don't touch our beaches'), and yet others are even resorting to illegal means, as when some of those opposed to the Croix du Sud Hotel near Mahébourg committed arson. The heightened sensitivity of the Mauritian public in realizing that the beach is a limited, but highly sought after and therefore contested good has also been taken more and more seriously by vote-seeking politicians, who have introduced stricter environmental laws and other obstacles to make it more difficult (and expensive) for investors to build new hotels and absorb more beaches. Thus, for example, one group of investors has failed in its attempts to build a 'Blue Bay Maritime Park' near Mahébourg, while another has been refused permission to develop the Île aux Benitiers opposite La Gaulette into a luxury bungalow resort, and yet another has faced great difficulties in building a tourist resort at the foot of Le Morne. In the latter two cases, opposition has been voiced by the local fishermen, who see more and more of the natural resources on which they rely for their livelihood dwindling, and not all of them want to become beach boys, watchmen or gardeners for the new hotels.[17] Nonetheless there are also examples, like the hotel compounds on the newly developed south coast, where local people have welcomed or at least not objected to their waterfronts being converted into hotel beaches because they have been promised jobs and infrastructural improvements – promises which, however, in their eyes have not (yet?) been as fully realized as promised or hoped for.

GLOBALIZING MAURITIAN BEACHES

In discussing hotel beaches, we have reached the point at which Europeans, and in fact the 'world', enters the picture. We have argued so far that two distinct, though not completely different beach cultures can be found on the two kinds of the beach in question, each reflecting to a certain degree the wider cultures of their respective 'populations of origin'. But the two beaches and their respective visitors also show commonalities in that they are only local adaptations and interpretations of the 'global beach' – largely based on the Polynesian model of Waikiki Beach, Honolulu – which visitors to both beaches undoubtedly have some common knowledge and experience of. Furthermore, we have seen that the two kinds of beach often overlap at their margins, and that there are various points or even zones of contact. It was argued that, as far as mutual influences are concerned, these are strongest when Mauritians and Europeans encounter each other on the public beaches.

This latter contact has led, at several places, to some significant changes in Mauritian public-beach culture, changes which can be observed well in Flic en Flac, one of the most crowded and mixed public beaches in Mauritius. On the first part of this beach, one will no longer find the typical socio-cultural environment of public beaches as characterized above, but instead a preponderance of cool, hip and trendy Mauritians, sprinkled with young Europeans. Hence, on this stretch of the beach there are fewer families or groups of adjacent families, and one no longer finds several generations on the beach or bathing together. Instead, there are young couples or groups of friends, often of diverse ethnic and national origins, no longer in saris and swimsuits, but in bikinis, some of them quite daring and chic. All in all, even though things are still not like it is on Mediterranean beaches or those in Rio, a decidedly trendy and sexy subculture has established a kind of a stronghold here, with the characteristics of a 'global beach' emerging more and more. Only gradually, the further one walks along this public beach, does the scene become familiar again, with groups of families camping in front of their cars and bathing communally.

This development could be described as Mauritian public beaches starting to go global. This involves processes of imitation and learning which clearly go in one direction only, namely from the European tourists, who by and large know how to be global better, especially on the beach, to the local Mauritian visitor to the public beach. In other words, as far as the establishment of a global beach culture is concerned, the learning and adaptation processes are hegemonic and uni-directional. And Mauritians have to be quick: within a decade or two, it seems that they are having to go through and absorb processes that in Europe and America took almost a century. It is not just the outward appearance, not just the overt exhibitions of resting, bathing, moving and behaving, which have to be imitated and possibly made into one's own. Rather, all these things go together with a change of habitus in a deeper sense, that is, by changing bodily routines and even shaping new bodies, and last but not least by questioning one's old sexual morals and adopting new, generally looser ones, for the beach is also becoming a playground for trying out new and more daring gender roles.

Mauritians are well aware of the dangers involved in these processes, and some are full of apprehension. In general, there is in Mauritian society a feeling that might be called the 'Grand Baie Angst', because all these dangers seem to be epitomized and most strongly exhibited in this, the oldest and most advanced holiday resort in the north. Apart from the very real dangers of crime, drugs and prostitution, this anxiety also involves the more amorphous fear of what is seen as a loosening of sexual morals. However, it would be misleading, naive and even patronizing to say that tourism is a bad thing for the island. Especially for those Mauritians who make a living out of it, tourism has proved a blessing, providing the means to build oneself a house, send one's children to school and not only to make a living, but lead a better life. And it is not only the material side of tourism which Mauritians see as beneficial: for many, judging from their own explicit statements, tourism has also brought improvements in a socio-cultural sense. One cook from La Pirogue Hotel, who had been working there for two decades now and whose children had started to do so as well, looked back at the times when people in his village not only lived in miserable conditions, but also, in his own words, wore dirty clothes, lacked hygiene and did not know how to eat properly. This is a point of view which many Mauritians expressed in similar ways, and which is thus an important respect in which they view themselves.

Globalization, then, is a more complex and more local process than many grand theories tend to acknowledge. Actually, it can be doubted whether there actually exists, a priori, an independent 'world system' or 'global society' somewhere out there. Rather, one could see the global as the ephemeral, ever-appearing, ever-changing but also ever-disappearing secondary result of all the millions and millions of encounters of people at one place with the goods, ideas, technologies, cultures and, last but not least, people from other parts of the world. Moreover, even if globalization in general, and the making of a global beach culture in particular, are hegemonic in character, the simple model of the west conquering the rest does not always apply.[18] In many parts of the world, including Mauritian beach culture, people exhibit an astonishing capacity to select from 'the global' only those things which they feel to be important to them. And when they have exhibited such agency and selected certain things, ideas, technologies, ideals, etc. (while ignoring or rejecting others), they often use these in ways that are at first unintended, but often quite original.

The process of globalization may move in unusual circles and unforeseen directions. One final example: a waiter of Indo-Mauritian background, who works in a five-star hotel in Le Morne, talked about a new kind of tourist who has arrived in Mauritian hotels: the tourist who comes from India. During the last two decades, this country has produced not only a rich upper middle class with the means to travel to relatively expensive places like Mauritius, it also has changed its spending patterns and mentality. In India tourism is no longer regarded as an unnecessary waste of money but has become legitimate and even prestigious. Now, the waiter complained, Indian tourists do not know how to eat with forks and knives, and Indian women go into the swimming pool fully clothed. To this waiter, these and other practices are expressions of a lack of civilization and are inappropriate for a five-star hotel. This Indo-Mauritian, whose ancestors came from the lowest strata of Indian society more than a century ago, was worried about the embarrassing socio-cultural impact of the newly arrived upper-middle-class tourists from India. How, in the coming decades, Indian tourists in Mauritius, Mauritian hotel staff an European tourists meet and possibly confront one another in the hotels and on the beaches of Mauritius is another matter for investigation.

NOTES

1. This article was first published in Schnepel (2009) and is reprinted here with kind permission of the publisher. Other publications on Mauritian beaches, namely Schnepel and Schnepel (2008, 2009), have partly been integrated into this chapter.
2. The study of beaches and life on beaches has been relatively neglected in anthropology, history, sociology, anthropogeography and cultural studies. Among the few studies to deal with the topic, Löfgren in particular (1999: 213–39) provides many insights into what he calls the 'Global Beach'. Other studies to be mentioned here are Dening (1980); Enloe (1990); Edgerton (1979); Lenèek and Bosker (1998); Urbain (1994).
3. Ministry of Land, Housing and Town Planning (1996);also www.intnet.mu/iels/coastal_mau.htm.
4. The following data are taken from the publications of the Ministry of Tourism and Leisure (2000, 2001, 2004, and 2005), a critical discussion of which can be found in Carlsen and Jaufeerally (2003) and Jaufeerally (2000). The socio-cultural impact of tourism in Mauritius is also discussed in Jahangeer-Chojoo (1998).
5. In the discussion that follows, I shall use the term 'public beach' in this more official sense. The most important public beaches in this understanding of the term are in Péreybère and Mont Choisy in the northwest of the island, Flic en Flac in the west, Tamarin ('La Preneuse') and Le Morne in the southwest, and Blue Bay and Belle Mare in the southeast and east respectively.
6. As far as their official nationality is concerned, citizens from Réunion should properly be included under the rubric 'French', as Réunion is a '*Department d'Outre Mer*' of France.
7. See the brochure published by the Ministry of Tourism and Leisure in 2004.
8. See Jaufeerally (2000). On the basis of the fact that one quarter of tourist arrivals in Mauritius do not stay in hotels, Jaufeerally argues that the Mauritian government should establish and maintain new public beaches, not only for the sake of the pleasure of its own citizens, but also with a view to strengthening the tourist industry (see ibid.: 7).
9. From the statistically less well-informed but nevertheless significant point of view of hotel staff, the French and the British form the two largest groups, with the Germans and the Italians clearly taking the next places, in equal numbers.

10. On census questions in Mauritius, see Christopher (1992), Dinan (2003), and Lutz (1994).
11. See Rottenburg, Schnepel and Shimada (eds. 2006).
12. See Schnepel (2005).
13. See Urbain (1994).
14. On the anthropology of the night, see Schnepel and Ben-Ari (2005), Schnepel (2006).
15. In this regard, beaches are also 'heterotopias' as discussed by Foucault (2005).
16. The capacity of the beach to level out, to some extent, social and class distinctions has been observed regarding British seaside resorts in the nineteenth and early twentieth centuries by Walton (1983).
17. The case of Île aux Benitiers is extensively discussed in Schnepel and Schnepel (2008).
18. At least the role model of the global beach comes from Polynesia, not America (as with most other globalizing matters, 'from the west to the rest'), though it was during the Second World War, when American soldiers (among them Elvis Presley) were stationed in Honolulu, that the Polynesian beach started to become global.

REFERENCES

Carlsen, J., and K. Jaufeerally. 2003. 'An Analysis of Tourism Trends in Mauritius'. In Ghosh and Siddique (eds.) 2003: 128–39.

Carter, M. (ed.). 1998. *Consolidating the Rainbow: Independent Mauritius, 1968–1998*. Port Louis: Centre for Research on Indian Ocean Societies.

Christopher, A.J. 1992. 'Ethnicity, Community and the Census in Mauritius, 1830–1990'. *Geographical Journal* 158: 57–64.

Dening, G. 1980. *Islands and Beaches: Discourse on a Silent Land, Marquesas 1774–1880*. Chicago: Dorsey Press.

Dinan, M. 2003. *Mauritius in the Making: Across the Censuses 1846–2000*. Port Louis: Nelson Mandela Centre for African Culture.

Edgerton, R.B. 1979. *Alone Together: Social Order on an Urban Beach*. Berkeley: University of California Press.

Enloe, C. 1990. *Bananas, Beaches and Bases*. Berkeley: University of California Press.

Foucault, M. 2005. *Die Heterotopien*. Frankfurt: Suhrkamp.

Geertz, C. 1973. *The Interpretation of Cultures*. London: Fontana Press.

Ghosh, D., and M.A.B. Siddique (eds.). 2003. *Tourism and Economic Development: Case Studies from the Indian Ocean Region.* Aldershot: Ashgate.

Gottowik, V., H. Jebens, and E. Platte (eds.). 2009. *Zwischen Aneignung und Verfremdung. Ethnologische Gratwanderungen.* Frankfurt: Campus Verlag.

Hookoomsing, V.Y., R. Ludwig, and B. Schnepel (eds.). 2009. *Multiple Identities in Action: Mauritius and Some Antillean Parallelism.* Berlin: Peter Lang.

Jahangeer-Chojoo, A. 1998. 'Le tourisme à l'Île Maurice'. In Carter (ed.) 1998: 51–62.

Jaufeerally, K. 2000. An Analysis of Tourist Arrivals, Spending and Other Trends in the Tourism Industry of Mauritius'. Institute for Environmental and Legal Studies, www.intnet.mu/iels/tap 1_99.htm.

Lange, K., and K. Geisenhainer (eds.). 2005. *Bewegliche Horizonte: Festschrift für Bernhard Streck.* Leipzig: Leipziger Universitätsverlag.

Lenèek, L., and G. Bosker. 1998. *The Beach: The History of Paradise on Earth.* Harmondsworth: Penguin Books.

Löfgren, O. 1999. *On Holiday: A History of Vacationing.* Berkeley: University of California Press.

Lutz, W. 1994. *Population, Development and Environment: Understanding their Interactions in Mauritius.* Berlin: Springer Verlag.

Ministry of Tourism and Leisure. 2000. *Handbook of Statistical Data on Tourism.* Mauritius: Ministry of Tourism and Leisure.

——, 2001. *Survey of Outgoing Tourists 2000.* Mauritius: Ministry of Tourism and Leisure.

——, 2004. *Tourism Statistics 2003.* Mauritius: Ministry of Tourism and Leisure.

——, 2005. *International Travel & Tourism: Year 2004.* Mauritius: Ministry of Tourism and Leisure.

Rottenburg, R., B. Schnepel, and S. Shimada (eds.). 2006. *The Making and Unmaking of Differences.* Münster: Transcript Verlag.

Schnepel, B. 2005. 'Inder auf Reisen'. In Lange and Geisenhainer (eds.) 2005: 165–84.

——, 2006. 'Strangers in the Night: The Making and Unmaking of Differences from a Perspective of the Anthropology of the Night'. In Rottenburg, Schnepel, and Shimada (eds.) 2006: 123–44.

——, 2009. 'Two Beaches: The Globalization of Mauritian Waterfronts'. In Hookoomsing, Ludwig, and Schnepel (eds.) 2009: 287–317.

Schnepel, B., and E. Ben-Ari. 2005. 'Introduction. When Darkness Comes . . . Steps toward an Anthropology of the Night'. *Paideuma* 51: 153–64.

Schnepel, B., and C. Schnepel. 2006. 'Bilder vom Séga'. In *Performance im medialen Wandel*, edited by Petra Meyer, 463–97. München: Wilhelm Fink Verlag.

——, 2008.'"Finger weg von unserem Strand": Tourismus auf einer multikulturellen "Paradiesinsel" (Mauritius) im Indischen Ozean'. *Arbeitspapiere zur Sozialanthropologie* (www.oeaw.ac.at/sozant). Wien: Österreichische Akademie der Wissenschaften.

——, 2009.'Die Globalisierung des Strandes: Das Beispiel Mauritius'. In Gottowik, Jebens, and Platte (eds.) 2009: 489–509.

Turner, V. 1969. *The Ritual Process.* Harmondsworth: Penguin Books.

Urbain, J.-D. 1994. *Sur la plage: mœurs et coutumes balnéaires.* Paris: Payot.

Walton, J.K. 1983. *The English Seaside Resort: A Social History, 1750–1914.* New York: St. Martin's Press.

CHAPTER 8

'Something New in the Present' The Politics of Cultural Heritage in Postcolonial Mauritius

INTRODUCTION

For quite some time now, 'heritage' has been used as a slogan all over the world. A great number of diverse and even heterogeneous actors have been putting their energies into preserving what they consider their heritage. Or else they have started to identify and define what pasts may be available to them that can be turned into heritage, that can be 'heritage-ized'. Notwithstanding UNESCO's dominance in setting the tone and defining what heritage ultimately is, for these persons – we shall call them 'remembrancers', in line with Peter Burke's rediscovery of this early modern term (Burke 1989) – the process of reconsidering their pasts and turning them into heritage has acquired a plethora of meanings. To have heritage or to strive to make a certain part of one's past into heritage can be evoked for a considerable variety of purposes, whether political, economic, religious, or socio-cultural in kind. Globally, then, heritage has become a kind of bubble filled with innumerable contents by all kinds of actors for all kinds of purposes.

In view of the worldwide attention that heritage has received in recent decades – and one could start by asking why it has become such a 'cult' (Lowenthal 1998) – researchers from a wide range of disciplines, not only historical ones, but also those concerned with contemporary issues, have begun to investigate this phenomenon in both breadth and depth. In addition to the empirical concerns with this topic, they have asked themselves how heritage discourses and activities are connected with other issues, such as the construction of local or national identities or the realization of economic benefits from possessing heritage, as in tourism or entertainment, for example. Consequently, more and more publications have appeared on these themes that have thrown light on different aspects of what could be called heritage politics.[1]

Against the background of, and informed by, what has come to be called 'Critical Heritage Studies',[2] this chapter discusses the multicultural, dynamically developing and at times hotly contested 'heritage scape' (di Giovine 2009) of Mauritius today. While it starts, in Section 2, with some more theoretical observations concerning heritage politics and concomitant processes of heritagization, in Sections 3 and 4 I discuss the Mauritian Séga, first in the past and then in contemporary manifestations of this performative genre. Thereafter, in Section 5 this chapter provides an overview of the diverse manifestations of heritage in the Mauritian heritage arena as a whole. In Section 6, entitled 'Travelling Pasts', I again take up some of the heritage considerations raised at the start by extending and deepening them into a discussion of the particularities of heritage that is not only distant in time but also in space. This chapter concludes with an assessment of the role heritage plays in contemporary Mauritian politics and its contestations concerning identity, status, prestige and power both on the island and beyond.

HERITAGE POLITICS[3]

There is a consensus among those engaged in heritage studies that heritage is not just out there waiting to be identified and preserved, but that it is something which is produced or constructed, not simply given. This social construction of heritage out of a great reservoir of possible historical events, processes, persons, and material remnants is not a straightforward matter. The heritagization of things past is often prone to contestations and negotiations between a number of remembrancers, who have different, if not diametrically opposed interests and aims. What is ultimately at stake, then, is not heritage as such but the politics of (cultural) heritage and heritagization.

The fact that heritage discourses and practices are entrenched in and strongly influenced by power relations and struggles has been acknowledged by quite a number of heritage studies, both implicitly and explicitly. Certainly, there can be different interpretations or foci concerning what these politics are. Some take the term in the widest sense of what could be called a Foucauldian approach, subsuming under politics not just the deeds and decrees of great men, but also all the minutest and even hidden strategies that are used in the everyday enhancement of status, in the creation of opportunities and the (re-)allocation of resources, or simply in struggles for power. This all-embracing concept of politics is sharpened when scholars concern themselves with institutions, practitioners and sponsors of heritage, such as UNESCO, the World Bank, the European Union or the Aga Khan Foundation, as well as with the innumerable state and regional institutions and actors which promote and manage heritage around the world.[4] Yet others go into international politics, looking at 'heritage diplomacy' used by a nation state as a 'mechanism for advancing its foreign policy and soft power strategy' (Winter 2016: 2). Most pertinent, maybe, is what could be called identity politics, that is, that dimension of politics which is concerned with creating solidarity and social cohesion within a given community and marking it off from others. The heritagization of the past, or better of certain elements of the past, and the concomitant politics of the forgetting and even erasing of other elements play a vital role in these processes and strategies of identification, providing legitimacy and meaning to the present, as well as direction and goals for the future. Furthermore, the newly emerging neoliberal heritage industry, often in close collaboration with the tourism industry, plays a crucial part in the branding and commercialization of culture, ethnicity and identity. Thus, it has a significant role in the socio-cultural and politico-economic processes that affect and alter the internal composition and dynamics of those groups that seek to establish themselves as the rightful owners of these new kinds of cultural and historical commodities.[5]

One thought-provoking approach to heritage has been formulated by Barbara Kirshenblatt-Gimblett, when she writes: 'Despite a discourse of conservation, preservation, restoration, reclamation, recovery, recuperation, revitalization, and regeneration, heritage produces something new in the present that has recourse to the past' (1995: 369–70). There are various ways in which this statement can be deepened or pursued in other directions. Basically, Kirshenblatt-Gimblett is arguing here for the need to go beyond (but not necessarily against) the official and dominant discourse of heritage as simply something which needs to be preserved. To be sure, a concern with preservation, which is very much at the forefront of the minds of many remembrancers when they investigate and deal with monumental and natural heritage, is both legitimate and worthy. It is also a leading motive for many social anthropologists, linguists, musicologists, folklorists and others when they deal with 'culture' or, as one would say now, 'intangible heritage' that is seen to be in danger and in need of being rescued from damnation and oblivion. However, any conservation concerns, valuable as they are, ultimately need to be appraised critically. Preservation discourses tend to forget or neglect what those things that seem to need preserving mean to whom and what they do for whom. This is where Kirshenblatt-Gimblett's dictum that heritage is 'something new in the present', is significant, especially if it is seen in close alliance with the last sub-clause of the statement cited above, namely that this 'something new' has 'recourse to the past'. These last words are crucial, as they invite fruitful cooperation between those scholars who are critically concerned with heritage and heritage politics today and those who deal with the past. And this 'recourse to the past' opens up two further intricately interwoven fields of inquiry: first, the vexed question of what precisely constitutes 'the past' and how it can be reconstructed; and secondly, the issues of who exactly has recourse to the past and what are their motives.

As far as the first question regarding the epistemological status of 'the past' (and the methodological intricacies of finding and reconstructing it) is concerned, there is, of course, the age-old Ranke-ian quest of historiography, that is, the historians' desire to reconstruct and describe the actual past objectively and in neutral ways in a 'wie es eigentlich gewesen sei' mode. Certainly, some such a positivist view of 'how it actually has been' has by and large come under criticism, most radically in the postmodern historiographical approach propagated by Hayden White and others.[6] In line with the dissolution of facts and the deconstruction of supposed truths, which has also taken place in other disciplines, such as social anthropology, since the 1970s, some historians of this school of thought began to doubt the facticity and historicity of their sources. They started to distrust the assumption that there are pure facts and, even more, that behind the signs there is *only one* historical reality waiting to be discerned. In this view, any attempt to find out 'how it really was' looks futile and leads in the wrong direction. There are, or so it is thought, only *res fictae*, not *res factae*. The past is not out there waiting to be found and *re*constructed; it is constructed through those, including professional historians, who have recourse to it, emerging only in the process of doing so. Furthermore, and consequently, in this postmodern view nothing is to be seen in the singular any longer: there is no reality, only realities; no identity, only identities; no culture, only cultures; no history, only histories. And all these pluralized and deconstructed entities, including 'the state', 'society' or, coming back to the issue at hand, 'the past', are inextricably linked with adjectives like 'contested', 'entangled', 'connected', 'negotiated' and the like. Thus, we have, for examples, pairs like 'contested identities', 'entangled histories', 'imagined communities', 'invented traditions', 'unfinished pasts' and 'ambiguous pasts', as well as 'contested cultural heritage' or 'dissonant heritage'.[7]

It is useful, I think, to reconnect the *pre*-postmodern Ranke-ian concern with matters of fact and the ideal of finding out 'how it really was' to the postmodern emphasis on plurality, ambiguity and constructivism. In developing such a view, which one might call '*post*-postmodern', it is misleading to suppose that Ranke or any of his followers were or are naive: we must not assume that their concern was (or is) a 'wie es eigentlich gewesen *ist*,' but a 'wie es eigentlich gewesen *sei*' – that is, not how it actually was, but how it might have been. It is also obvious that the difference between *res fictae* and *res factae* cannot be an absolute one, but is one that makes itself felt in degrees and shades. What is fact and what is 'fake' (to use a currently popular expression), or better, what is seen to be the one or the other, is dependent on the situational relativity and dynamics in which an event or process in the past has happened and is assessed in the present. Consequently, in any attempt to reconstruct certain pasts, the clues that may lead us there are more opaque, ambiguous and contradictory than many historians in pre-postmodern times will have assumed. This skepticism also applies to assessing sources. Most of these are quite decisively to be seen not as primary sources, but as the secondary results and products of past negotiations, hegemonies, agencies and power. The pasts, then, are multiple, not only because their remembrancers in the present have multiple interests and forms of patronage, but also because life in the pasts was not a clear-cut, homogeneous and undisputed matter, but featured many diverse actors with contesting claims, potencies and world views.[8]

This leads us to the second issue raised by our discussion of Kirshenblatt-Gimblett above, namely the question of who has recourse to the pasts and why? What are the aims of persons, groups and institutions that have recourse to the pasts? And finally, how do those who have recourse to the pasts make use of them? This is where Friedrich Nietzsche comes in usefully. In his essay 'On the use and abuse of history for life', written in 1874 (Nietzsche 2009), he identified three major types of remembering: the 'monumental', the 'antiquarian' and the 'critical'. Nietzsche had something positive to say about all three, but in the end he condemned them all as being potentially counter-productive and even harmful. They are not for life but against life if they are used in what Nietzsche calls 'hypertrophic' ways. In other words, it is too much history or, better, too much remembering that worries Nietzsche, since this 'hyper' hinders the individual, nation or *Cultur* to live forcefully in the here and now, and to move forward according to his, her or its free will and requirements. Consequently, Nietzsche also argues in favour of forgetting, not as something which is due to any mental deficiency, but as the social and political capacity and the will not to remember. For Nietzsche, as one could expand on this thought, there was not just a politics of remembering, but also a politics of forgetting.[9] The main question for Nietzsche was not whether anyone uses or abuses history – for him, all ways of taking recourse to the past are either uses or abuses, or rather both uses and abuses. It was not his business to distinguish between them or to evaluate them as good or bad. In this context it may be pointed out that the title of his essay in German is '*Vom Nutzen und Nachtheil der Historie*'. Strictly translated, then, it is definitely not 'use and abuse' – words that even a revised translation of 2010 retains – but the 'advantage' (*Nutzen*) and 'disadvantage' (*Nachtheil*) of *Historie* for life that is at issue. The question that arises out of this, then, is not whether some people today have recourse to the past as it really was or whether they misrepresent, distort or even abuse it for some dubious intentions. Rather, one needs to identify what different actors in the heritage-scape, including professional historians, do with their version of history 'for life' both at present and in/for the future.

But it is time to look at these issues more empirically and turn our attention to heritage in the small island that is the focus of this book.

SÉGA IN THE PAST[10]

Trying to pin down the Mauritian Séga, both empirically and by way of defining it, proves to be difficult. The name is applied to quite a variety of manifestations of this performative genre, there also being different kinds of Séga on the neighbouring islands of Rodrigues, Réunion, Madagascar and the Seychelles. In Mauritius itself, people distinguish, among others, between 'Séga typique', 'Séga authentique' and 'Séga ravanne', on the one hand, and 'Séga modern', 'Séga hotel' and 'Séga touristique' on the other. The latter three are seen as being less pure or authentic. There are also variants such as 'Seggae', a mixture of Reggae and Séga, 'Séga salon', enjoyed at home, and 'Séga engagée', a politically minded form of the genre. As for the participants in the dance, a first, major division emerges between the actual practitioners – musicians, dancers, singers, song-writers – and the consumers, who delight in the dance and songs, among them tourists from all over the world. Special mention must also be made of those who sponsor the dance and have more than just an aesthetic or leisure interest in it. These include radio and TV stations, politicians, entertainment agencies, Air Mauritius, hotel groups, city mayors and tourist agencies. To all these interested parties, Séga can mean different things.[11]

To determine with whom the dance is associated most or, in the context of heritage, who claims to own it, the answer clearly points to the Creole section of Mauritian society. Members of this group assert that Séga was originally part of their cultural heritage, since it was their ancestors who created and developed the dance on the island as slaves. This claim is not disputed by the other ethnic groups in Mauritius. However, to claim exclusive Creole roots for Séga is a simplification of the matter, as this performative genre shows traces of many influences. The multi-layered, multi-facetted, polysemic and hybrid genre it has become today developed out of different sources of inspiration. This hybridity is not only the result of diverse African traditions having come together, with Madagascar and Mozambique counting as the most likely African sources; there are also influences of West and South Asian musical and dance traditions, as exemplified by the ravanne drum that may have Middle Eastern ancestors, or by the Séga ladies' dancing dresses that are roughly the length of an Indian sari. Even traces of French Cancan could be asserted. Nonetheless, in the context of a discussion of heritage politics, it is important to note that the dance is associated chiefly with just one group, the Creoles.

While today Séga is proudly and almost unanimously regarded by the island's population and by outside admirers as an all-Mauritian cultural symbol, this has not always been the case. For a long time, in fact up until the 1960s, the dance and its Creole practitioners were viewed negatively by most, except its practitioners. In the period of slavery, to start by looking at some of the stepping stones and passages in Séga's troubled history, the dance could not be practiced openly and was even expressly forbidden, though the desire to dance and make music seems to have been strong enough for the slaves to transgress this prohibition whenever an opportunity arose. One observer who wrote with some sympathy for the difficult lot of the Mauritian slaves was Bernardin de Saint-Pierre, who stayed on the island in the late 1760s. Writing in his *Journey to Mauritius*, he notes:

> By temperament, Negroes are naturally playful, but after some time as slaves they turn melancholic. Only love seems to still conjure away their sorrows. (. . .) Sometimes they arrange to meet in the middle of the night and dance behind some boulders to the sad music of a gourd filled with dried peas. But if they spy a white or hear a dog bark, they scatter immediately. (2002 [1773]: 129)

The last statement especially requires some explanation. In Article 12 of the *Code Noir*, an eighteenth-century French legal treatise devised for the penal treatment of the slaves, it is stated: 'We equally prohibit slaves belonging to different masters to gather by day or night under the pretext of marriage celebrations or otherwise, either at the premises of one of their masters or elsewhere, and even less on the highways or more distant places'.[12] Such gatherings were to be punished by whipping or even death. In an amendment to the Code of 1759 (originally issued in 1721), whites were also condemned for attending such meetings. Hence, what made the dance subversive to the slave-owning hegemonic class was not only that it provided their slaves with some relief and a sense of commonality, thereby potentially inciting rebellious behaviour, but that some whites participated at the gatherings and thus made porous what from the slavers' point of view was ideally a watertight boundary between the slaves and their owners.[13]

Even after emancipation, the colonial attitude towards the dance did not alter substantially. However, negative assessments of it now referred less to its devotees gathering and enjoying it than to what de Saint-Pierre had indicated in his use of the word 'love'. The dance, with all its erotic movements and its hedonistic undertones, was now considered an insult to the sensibilities of all 'good' and 'decent' citizens, who saw in it an example of what the *Code Noir* had already condemned as 'practices in contradiction to the standards of good conduct'.[14] This is precisely the impression that also emerges from the following statements by a visitor to the island, a certain Milbert, in 1810: 'Negro dance as such is very significant, they make the most lascivious gestures, which leave one in no doubt. Their favorite dances are the most libertarian. Their passion for women is extreme'.[15] Similar statements can be found in a report written by a colonial officer named Beaton in 1859, hence some twenty-five years after the ending of slavery:

> (The) slave population and their descendants retain their original taste for dancing and music. Evening reunions for dancing, though not so frequent as immediately after the emancipation of the slaves, are still highly popular (. . .) These assemblages are highly objectionable in many respects, and the Roman Catholic priests have very properly set their faces against them.[16]

Therefore, even after the abolition of slavery, with its prohibition on dancing, one can find the ex-slaves' supposedly inborn love of dance, music and sex being condemned. The only difference is that at this point in the post-emancipation period, Séga's opponents were no longer slavers with dogs, but Christians who thought of themselves as standing on a higher level of morals and civilization than the Ségatiers, whom they considered primitive and obscene.

Another reaction to the dance was to deride it and regard it as a minor art form, if indeed it was art in the first place. Such sentiments are clearly discernible in a 1937 report by a missionary called Dussercle:

> On the dancing ground one or more fire-places of coco-palm leaves are spluttering, these will be used to heat the ravannes so that they sound better. Once the skins of the drums have been carefully tested for the power of the resonance, the drummers get to work: *dum, dum-dum, dumdumdum, dum-dum,* first with a fairly slow rhythm, on the scales of the notes of the songs which they are beginning to 'run', to 'grumble': this is the preparation for the dance. Then, with a more accelerated rhythm, at the same time as the voices are getting louder, to the point where they are 'yelling' – this can sometimes go to the point of frenzy. This is the moment for the dance to begin.
>
> A man steps forward, raises his hat, and bows before a woman with a gesture of invitation, she will be his lady. There will be several of these. Then, in the middle of the grass, each drumming the sand with the *dum, dumdum* rhythm, slowed down or accelerated, the partners still keeping a distance of four or five feet from each other, without any contact between them. The woman has lifted the hem of her skirts with her hands, and sometimes waddles, with a disdainful air in the way of encouragement and pleasure with the man's attentions who, arms waving and shaking, mimes appeal to her in a rather silly fashion. (cited from Police 2000: 64)

The choice of verbs such as 'grumble' and 'yell' to describe the musical qualities of Séga, the dismissal of the dancers' movements as 'waddling' and the writer's conclusion that the entire dance is performed 'in a rather silly fashion' leave no doubt as to the negative and racist evaluations of Séga during the colonial era.[17]

Mauritian Ségatiers are keenly aware of this historical burden. Their historical imagination, expressed in songs, interviews and other performances, is replete with references to a tragic and tormented past of slavery, though their songs also address more contemporary issues of poverty and maltreatment, as well as of individual turmoil and troubles. Take the following statements from an interview with (the late) Serge Lebrasse, conducted in 2005:

The slaves worked during the week and had no time off. The only free time they had was Saturday evening. (. . .) On that evening they left their plantations. Families and friends gathered somewhere far away from the master's house. They brought food and drink along and prepared a special drink . . . called 'baca', a very strong rum made from sugar cane. And it was there that they enjoyed themselves. At that time Séga was a family affair. (. . .) And it was there that they found a way to let themselves go. They would sit together thinking of their homeland, about the way they had left their homelands. (. . .) Someone would be singing and slowly instruments would accompany (. . .) him. He would describe his feelings, perhaps of sorrow, because he was thinking of his parents, his homeland, the hard work he had to do, the blows he suffered. But there were also songs about love (. . .), and there were also songs about quarrels. With a quarrel, one person would sing first and another one would reply, and in between there was a pause. And this is when the whole group would join in with the words 'ti la-eh, ti la-la' (. . .) This 'ti la-eh, ti la-la' was a symbolic participation of the group who shared in the joy or sorrow of the singer. Finally, everyone stopped, they drank, they ate, they drank some more, the arguments continued, they stopped again, they drank more and so forth. This would continue until everybody was drunk. By two or three in the morning the discussions would sometimes turn to fights. These gatherings could last until seven or eight o'clock in the morning.

SÉGA TODAY

The contemporary history and eventually positive reception of Séga started in the wake of independence, that is, at a time when more and more Mauritians were becoming aware of shared cultural forms that distinguished them from the rest of the world. Séga became one of these cultural markers of a small island in a large ocean. 'La nuit du Séga', a music contest held on 30 October 1964, illustrates this change in reception and this new more encompassing status of the dance. The winner of this contest was Alphonse Ravaton, alias Ti Frère, a musician with Malagasy roots, hailing from Quartier Militaire in the centre of Mauritius. In the decades following his success, Ti Frère became the renowned and cherished 'Father of Séga typique'. Performances of Séga were now no longer confined to private homes, the courtyards of estate houses ('Séga lakur') or family beach parties but increasingly could also be found at public events such as weddings, civic or business events or national festivals. It became fashionable and respectable, not only among poor Creoles, but also among upper-class *gens de couleur* as well as among members of other ethnic communities and socio-cultural groups.

This quality of Séga to transcend social boundaries manifests itself most strikingly when Mauritians meet each other and others outside the island. Numerous Mauritians living abroad in steadily increasing diasporas in Europe, South Africa, Australia or the USA cherish and practice Séga salon. This fact clearly transpires in Le Breton's novel *Emmenez-moi à l'Île Maurice* (1986), which features a Franco-Mauritian living in Paris who seeks to convey his memories of Mauritius to his French friends by describing a nocturnal Séga dance, lighted by a bonfire on a palm-studded beach. In Jacques K. Lee's insightful study of the Séga, the first of its kind (Lee 1990), we also find descriptions of how, at parties and festivities this time celebrated by Mauritians in London, ethnic, religious and class boundaries (which may be felt strongly when back home) are forgotten and substituted by a common longing for an island that is now missed.[18] This fact of transgressing social boundaries and producing shared sentiments through Séga is also conveyed by the statements of a Mauritian Muslim telling Thomas H. Eriksen about his stay in England as an assistant nurse: 'And every Friday night, we'd have a huge *séga* party at somebody's place, where we'd drink some rum – even I had a few glasses sometimes . . . Man, there were so many Mauritians there – Creoles, Hindus, you know; it's so nice to meet fellow Mauritians when you're far away from home' (1998: 160–1). In the imagination of diasporic Mauritians, then, Séga tends to become a *lieu de mémoire*, lying at a distance not only in time, but in space as well.

Similar images of a place where it is warm and life is easy are of course also at the heart of tourist imaginations, constituting important assets to the tourism industry worldwide and to warm-water islands such as Mauritius especially. In this context it is noteworthy that the Séga competition mentioned above, which Ti Frère won, was organized and sponsored by a group of businessmen associated with tourism. However, it is not the Séga typique of the kind performed

Figure 8.1: Séga Dancer

by Ti Frère and Fan Fan, in which the ravanne, the maravanne (a rattlebox), a metal triangle and the human voice predominate, that eventually became a commercial and cultural success within tourism, but the so-called Séga modern, played with modern electric instruments in a much more vibrant style. Proponents of this style, like Serge Lebrasse, were successful in hotels and in other performance venues throughout Mauritius itself. Some of them even travelled around the world to Europe, Australia and India as cultural ambassadors on occasions staged and sponsored by the Mauritian government and Air Mauritius.

This interest of the outside world in Séga comes to the fore most clearly in the performances of Séga artists in Mauritian hotels, i.e., in performances referred to as Séga hotel. In pre-coronavirus times, there were about two dozen separate groups of twelve to fifteen members – singers, musicians and dancers – catering to the entertainment needs of the island's booming tourist sector. Luxury hotels offered their guests at least one Séga night a week, with a first performance, about an hour in length, during sunset on the hotel beaches, and a second one later at night after dinner in the hotel itself. Although we know of no official agenda, master script or regulations, all the twenty to twenty-five post-dinner performances we observed in Mauritian hotels between 2002 and 2018 were similarly structured. Dressed in colourful costumes, which were supposed to date from slavery but are clearly also designed to please contemporary tourist tastes and imaginations, the Ségatiers usually start their repertoire with three or four songs in the style of Séga typique. After this there is a semi-ceremonial presentation of three what the Ségatiers call 'traditional' Séga instruments: the ravanne, the maravanne and the triangle. All this is done with some explanations of how the instruments are made and with demonstrations of how they are played and what they sound like. The presentations of the traditional Séga instruments are in English and French, and the instruments themselves are shown to the tourists with the words: 'Ladies and gentlemen. This is the maravanne (respectively ravanne, triangle)!' Then the instrument is shown to the spectators in all directions and is briefly played alone. This sequence, which ends with the tourists somehow applauding the instruments as much as their musicians, marks the end of Séga typique after about fifteen to twenty minutes. The rest of the evening of approximately an hour and a half consists of Séga modern. At the very end of these evenings, the tourists themselves are invited 'to share our Mauritian culture' (as it is often called) by first taking a short course in the art of Séga dancing, and then dancing in the company of the professionals to the tunes of yet another and final piece of Séga modern.[19]

THE MAURITIAN HERITAGE ARENA

Séga is just one element in the multifaceted and contested heritage scape of Mauritius. To acquire an initial idea of the diversity and variations in Mauritius's heritage arena, one may well start with a stroll along the Caudan Waterfront, in particular along the 'Basdeo Bissoondoyal Esplanade' at Port Louis's old harbour. Bissoondoyal himself is embodied there by a statue showing him 'in traditional dress, with his arms raised in guru style' (Hookoomsing 2009: 19), being remembered 'for his contribution in the 1940s to the cultural and spiritual upliftment of the Hindu masses' (ibid.). Most striking and central on this esplanade, however, are two other bronze statues, dedicated respectively to the French governor Mahé de Labourdonnais (1699–1753) and to Seewoosagur Ramgoolam (1900–85), the independent nation's first prime minister. Both larger-than-life statues are prominently displayed on the promenade, but in their more particular forms of representation they reveal some significant differences, as again observed by Vinesh Y. Hookoomsing:

> . . . Sir Seewoosagur Ramgoolam, the Father of the Nation, cast in a bronze statue, with his back to the sea, triumphantly brandishing a book signifying education or the constitution of independent Mauritius, or both, at the face of Mahé de La Bourdonnais, founder of Port Louis, the capital of the Isle de France, that is of French Mauritius. La Bourdonnais proudly looks towards the sea, ostentatiously holding a document meant to symbolize the development plan of the capital. (2009: 19)

Figure 8.2: Labourdonnais

Figure 8.3: Ramgoolam

If the visitor turns away from the sea and, with Ramgoolam, looks inland, he or she will see the former 'Place d'Armes', now renamed 'Place Sookdeo Bissondoyal', after a brother of Basdeo's, who is also honoured with a statue. At the end of the avenue, lined with palm trees and leading up to Government House, is a statue of Queen Victoria. Not far away we find a statue of Sir John Pope Hennessy, governor of Mauritius from 1883 to 1889. Hence, within a space of some three to four hundred metres, we find – 'in perfect alignment between the sea and the national assembly' (ibid.: 20) – statues remembering eighteenth-century French, nineteenth-century British and twentieth-century Mauritian historical figures. The roads and avenues leading to or departing from this core area of Mauritian reminiscences have partly been rechristened to erase French colonial pasts. Besides the Place d'Armes, the busy Desforges Street was renamed into Sir Seewoosagur Ramgoolam Street; others have retained their names, thus still remembering a British past (e.g., Duke of Edinburgh Avenue; Queen Elizabeth Avenue); or they refer to some postcolonial politicians of international renown, such as President Kennedy Street.

In this area between Caudan Waterfront and the Place d'Armes (and its immediate vicinity, including the nearby 'Jardin de la Compagnie') one can find numerous other statues and busts. In the overwhelming majority, these are dedicated to Indo-Mauritians or more specifically Hindu-Mauritians. Among this group one finds busts of Renganaden Seeneevassen (1910–58, politician, bust unveiled in 1987); Dazzi Rama Pandi Sahadeo (1899–1987, Marathi priest, unveiled in 1999); Sir Satcam Boolell (1920–2006; politician, in 2008); and Sir Veerasamy Ringadoo (1920–2000; Tamil politician, in 2004). One Moghul-style miniature gate (and hence not a depiction of a person) is dedicated to Sir Abdul Razack Mohamed (1906–78; Indo-Muslim politician, in 2006). A next major group represented by busts and statues are the Franco-Mauritians, among whom, it must be assumed, there are also *gens de couleurs*. Apart from their common French roots, this is quite a heterogeneous group. There is, for example, a bust of Dr Maurice Curé (1886–1977, unveiled in 1988), founder of the Labour Party in 1936 and a staunch fighter for the rights of workers, and another bust (unveiled in 1916) remembering Remy Ollier (1816–45), a journalist and dedicated fighter for the rights of the coloured population. But overtowering these busts, right in the middle of the Company Garden, we find a larger-than-life statue of Adrien d'Epinay (1794–1839). While this statue may be meant to honour a man of letters and the founder of the 'Royal Society of Arts and Science of Mauritius', d'Epinay actually became famous, or better infamous, as a slave-holder. He also was one of the fiercest opponents of British plans to abolish slavery on the island and claiming compensation when that fight was lost. With the statues of Labourdonnais and d'Epinay we thus find two monuments representing Franco-Mauritian slave-traders and slave-holders. Astonishingly, both statues were inaugurated during the British colonial period respectively in 1853 and 1939, making one wonder which sponsors and supporters these statues had and why the colonial government, which prided itself on having abolished slavery, assented.

This list of busts and statues, incomplete though it is, allows one to detect a first pattern in Mauritian politics of heritage and heritagization. To start with a simple observation, all the personifications mentioned so far, with the notable exception of Queen Victoria, are men. Furthermore, all are politicians who either had posts in government or were heavily engaged in politics as lawyers, journalists, and priests. The numerical superiority of Hindu-Mauritians in the island's demography today is clearly reflected in the number of busts and statues dedicated to men from this spectrum of Mauritian society. That is, most busts in Port Louis are dedicated to 'great men', especially 'great Hindu men'.

In recent decades the assemblage of busts and statues has become more diversified. Some monuments or *lieux de mémoire* remember poets, not politicians, such as the 'Parcours Culturel Malcolm de Chazal', a Franco-Mauritian poet and painter, in the centre of Port Louis, set up in 2002; and a statue for Leoville L'Homme, a Franco-Mauritian poet, in the Jardin de la Compagnie, erected in 1881. In addition, a bust of Bernardin de Saint-Pierre (1737–1814) of *Paul-et-Virginie* fame was erected in the Botanical Gardens in 1944. But there are further variations in and additions to the dominant Hindu-scape of heritage in Port Louis. In a more recent addition to the Company Garden, for example, one can find a statue unveiled in 2000 representing Alphonse Ravaton (1900–92), better known as Ti Frére, playing the ravanne. In this part of the garden, there also is a stone monument with a small marble face on it depicting Soeur Marie Barthelémy, a Franco-Mauritian Catholic nun noted for her dedicated care of the sick and the poor. This rare monument for a woman was inaugurated in 2015. Furthermore, near the Supreme Court one can see a statue representing and remembering a Tamil lady, Anjalay Cooper, a pregnant woman who was shot at the so-called Belle Vue Harel massacre of 1837. She thus stands for the working-class movement and anti-colonial rebellion of that time. In this particular field of remembrance, she stands alongside Dr Maurice Curé, though, by contrast to him, she is not an upper-class male politician but a working-class woman – not a 'great man' but a 'little woman', if you will. Significantly, remembrance celebrations at her statue do not take place on 1st May, International Labour Day, but on 8th March, International Women's Day. In connection with syndicalist personalities and working-class movements, one should also not forget a huge stone head of Lenin located next to the dockyards, i.e., at a place where strikes and uprisings in Mauritius have always found fertile ground. All in all, visitors to Port Louis's city centre and its harbour region can find such an abundance of statues, busts, plaques and historic buildings as to make the city a serious candidate to win any global contest of how many manifestations of heritage can be accommodated in one square mile.[20]

In trying to draw a more complete picture of the heritage scape of Mauritius, one now must add museums to the portfolio and, of course, also go beyond the port city's border. The island hosts various museums, many of which can be found, again, in the vicinity of the Caudan Waterfront: the Blue Penny Museum; the Postal Museum; the Windmill Museum and, near the Jardin de Compagnie, the Natural History Museum. On the island's east coast, in the bay where the Dutch made their first landing in 1598, we find the Frederik Hendrik Museum and archaeological remains of the first Dutch fort. Some twenty kilometres away from Port Louis is a museum dedicated to the history of sugar plantations and production ('L'Aventure du sucre'), located on the premises of an old, now defunct sugar factory; and close-by, in Pamplemousses, one finds the open-air museum of the Botanical Garden, now also connected with the name of Ramgoolam. The National History Museum is situated in Mahébourg, where it was opened in 1884, while the Robert Edward Hart Memorial Museum, a coral-made house called 'Le Nef' where this Anglo-Mauritian poet (1891–1954) lived and died, is likewise to be found in the south of the island, near Souillac. The 'good old' times of sugar plantations and colonial grandeur can be re-imagined and re-lived by visiting several colonial and Creole-style mansions, among them La Mansion Eureka near Moka, built in 1830 and made into a museum in 1986; the Chateau de Labourdonnais, erected for the Wiehe family in Mapou in 1859 and now a museum with a restaurant and souvenir shop attached; and the Chateau Bel Ombre, belonging to the Telfair family, who arrived on the island soon after the British take-over. The latter mansion and its splendid garden (part of it being a golf course celebrated for its beauty) belongs to a five-star hotel complex owned by a group called 'Heritage Hotels'. And, indeed, many of the grander hotels on Mauritius have devised their buildings in a nostalgic re-imagination and re-fashioning of the so-called Creole style, which apparently attracts tourist to the island a lot.

Several sites in Mauritius are more maritime in character, for we find several statues, busts and monuments dedicated to mariners and explorers who stopped on the island for longer or shorter spells. On the Caudan Waterfront is a bust dedicated to Nicolas Baudin, the French explorer of the sea route to Australia, who tragically died in Port Louis on his way back home in 1803. Another bust in the south of the island reminds us of Captain Matthew Flinders (1774–1814), the British explorer and cartographer of Australia, who also stopped on the island in 1803 and was detained there (albeit under comfortable conditions) for six years because the French, at that time caught up in Napoleon's final struggle with the British, feared that he could convey secrets about the island to 'Perfide Albion'. This 'travelling dimension' of the Mauritian past, remembering a time when famous voyagers made a temporary or sometimes permanent halt at the island, is also evoked in yet another memorial site in the new part of the Company Garden. Here we find a so-called 'Traveller's lane' which is dedicated to some of the most famous travellers in world history, like Ibn Battuta or Marco Polo, even though they did not visit Mauritius. A stone monument erected in Baie du Cap, remembering a shipwreck, with only a few survivors, of the S.S. Trevassa in 1923, acts as a warning of the most dangerous aspect of sea journeys. Another monument near Mahébourg is dedicated to the remembrance of the French and British sailors who were killed during a sea battle off the Île de la Passe in 1810. The shipwreck of the Saint Géran near the island's northern tip, wrecked in August 1744, is remembered not only in one of the most luxurious hotels on the island is named after this ship, but also in the Paul-et-Virginie monument (Virginie in that novel being one of the deplorable persons who drowned at that incident) near Poudre d'Or in the north.

All these *lieux de mémoire* point to certain events, achievements or processes in the island's past that are considered significant (by some, for various reasons) and were made into heritage. In having done that, it would of course be significant to determine exactly who the remembrancers in each case were and with what ideational and/or material motives they acted. Without being able to pursue this matter at greater depth here, it is obvious that these persons must have been individuals or groups possessing power and money. There is also a striking temporal pattern: while the statues of Labourdonnais, Queen Victoria and a few others were erected in the mid-nineteenth century, most of the other *lieux de mémoire* to be found on Mauritius were only inaugurated, erected, unveiled or opened (as the case may be) in the first decade of this millennium. This decade, then, was an extraordinarily busy one for the politics of cultural heritage and for processes of heritagization in Mauritius. Asking why this was so, more comparative research would probably reveal that this valorisation of things, persons and events of the past was a global, and not just an insular phenomenon. One factor that certainly brought a new dynamics to Mauritius's heritage were the activities of a 'National Commission', which was established on Mauritius by UNESCO and which, in cooperation with the National Heritage Fund, assisted very much in instigating and implementing heritage initiatives on the island.

SMALL ISLAND HERITAGE WITH OUTSTANDING UNIVERSAL VALUE

For some decades now, heritage discourses and practices, whether local, regional or insular in character, follow the role model of UNESCO's extremely successful World Heritage program, which began with the rescue of Egypt's Abu Simbel temple in 1979. Even when heritage politics is quite decidedly limited to a locality or to a specifically defined group, remembrancers feel motivated and guided by what they see is happening and is being propounded in the UNESCO arena of world heritage. Furthermore, not a few local heritage sites, as well as local or regional manifestations of 'intangible heritage', have actively been seeking an upgrade, so to speak, wishing to become world heritage as well. So far, around 1,200 sites quite different in kind – from cathedrals, old cities and temples to routes, forests and mountains – have been successful in being inscribed in the UNESCO list as 'Patrimoine Mondial'. Furthermore, on the 'Representative List of the Intangible Cultural Heritage of Humanity' (which was started almost twenty years after than the material one), as of 2022 one can find more than 120 awards, among them Durga Puja in Kolkota, transhumance in the Alps, tango in Argentina, finding truffles in Italy and, maybe soon, German bread and *Wurst.* To be successful in their endeavours, applicants need good arguments that their sites or practices have *universal* human value. To prepare the laborious nomination dossiers they also need a financially well-equipped infrastructure, a dedicated group of remembrancers, endurance, and political support. Not a few of the applications submitted to UNESCO for consideration have been prepared by professional remembrancers who can be hired or otherwise enticed globally and who have no direct personal interest in what they are promoting. Despite the large numbers of sites, monuments, practices, traditions, and routes, etc. that have already been awarded the title of World Heritage, competition among the world's nations to have many, if not most sites (with China on the verge of outdoing Italy as world leader) is still hard. Many nations see in gaining world heritage, in both its material and intangible manifestations, an important arena in which 'soft power' can be won and asserted. It is noteworthy that applications can only be submitted by nation states. However, competition is not only strong *between* nations, but *within* nations as well, a fact which is enhanced by the rule that a given nation can only submit one application per year, which usually entails waiting for some.

The first decade of the new millennium was an extremely successful year for Mauritian heritage aspirations at the level of *world* heritage. Indeed, Mauritius already prides itself on hosting two material manifestations of world heritage. One, the so-called Aapravasi Ghat, is the site where indentured labourers arrived on the island after their journeys from India. This *lieu de mémoire*, some five hundred metres away from the Caudan Waterfront in an offshoot of Port Louis harbour, was inscribed into UNESCO's World Cultural and Natural Heritage List in 2006. At the actual site, visitors will find the coolies' archaeologically well restored living quarters, where they stayed before they were taken to the sugar plantations allocated to them, and a few other dockside buildings formerly used to register them and for health-care purposes. Symbolically highly charged are the so-called 'Steps of the Aapravasi Ghat', about which we read: 'When the immigrants arrived in Mauritius, they climbed up the steps to start a new life in the colony'. In addition to these buildings and steps, the site prominently features a newly built, air-conditioned museum dedicated to the history of indentured labour in Mauritius. In line with UNESCO's guidelines that world heritage sites need to have 'outstanding universal value', the official inscription states that the Aapravasi Ghat is 'among the earliest explicit manifestations of what was to become a global economic system and one of the greatest migrations in history'.

The second world heritage site in Mauritius is listed as 'Le Morne Cultural Landscape', inscribed in 2008, two years after Aapravasi Ghat. This site consists of Le Morne Brabant in the southwest of the island, with the buffer zone of this mountain site extending to the foothills and coast. It is dedicated to reminding visitors of the runaway slaves who took shelter on the rugged mountain top and even formed maroon communities up there. Some of them, oral tradition has it, even jumped to their deaths off the mountain's cliffs to escape approaching policemen and thus being enslaved again. The official UNESCO inscription for this heritage site emphasizes its more global significance: 'The oral traditions associated with the maroons have made Le Morne a symbol of the slaves' fight for freedom, their suffering, and their sacrifice, all of which have relevance to the countries from which the slaves came – the African mainland, Madagascar, India, and South-east Asia.' At the foot of this mountain, in a sort of memorial garden opposite Le Morne Public Beach known as the 'Slave Route Monument', half a dozen stone sculptures, made by artists from various African and Caribbean countries, remind the visitor of slavery and maroonage, symbolizing the slaves' fight for freedom worldwide. Besides being open to individuals and groups throughout the year, especially to tourists, this place hosts official festivities on 'Abolition Day', a public holiday in Mauritius on 1 February. This site is also the venue of commemorative events connected with UNESCO's 'International Day for the Remembrance of the Slave Trade', which takes place each year on 23 August.

As far as the 'Representative List of Intangible Cultural Heritage of Humanity' is concerned, Mauritius has managed to have three specimens inscribed, all belonging to the category of music and dance.

The first, entitled 'Traditional Mauritian Sega' was inscribed in 2014.[21] Hence, not all manifestations or derivations of the overall Séga genre discussed above are subsumed under the rubric of world heritage, but only those that are considered traditional. Furthermore, the inscription emphasizes the dance's capacity to transcend social boundaries by stating that 'representing the multiculturalism of Mauritian society, Sega breaks down cultural and class barriers, creates opportunities for intercultural encounters, and unifies various groups around a shared Mauritian heritage.' In view of the privileges (and resources) that accrue to those performers who presumably adhere most stringently to the UNESCO ideal of preserving something 'traditional', there have been arguments within the community of Ségatiers as to which are the dance's most authentic and time-honoured elements. In particular, the materiality of the ravanne and the question of how to play it in a traditional way have generated internal discussion and even conflict. The second specimen of cultural heritage that made it onto the Representative List of UNESCO's intangible heritage in 2016 was 'Bhojpuri folk songs in Mauritius, Geet Gawai', i.e., songs sometimes performed at the weddings of Indo-Mauritians. Note that this time the 'Indian' application to world heritage status succeeded only two years after the 'African' one. A final inscription, so far, was made in 2017, when 'Séga tambour of Rodrigues Island' entered the list, adding another Séga variation to the world's heritage.[22]

TRAVELLING PASTS

All these manifestations of heritage have their own historicity, as well as their own distinctive values in the present. However, heritage is not just about restoration, preservation, and the like. It needs to be reiterated that heritage also, and most importantly, 'produces something new in the present that has recourse to the past' (ibid.). As for the reasons for this looking back while moving forward into the future, one can follow Jan Assmann, who, in his path-breaking book *Das kulturelle Gedächtnis* (1992), argued that each culture must develop a 'connective structure' so as to establish and experience meaningful communality. For Assmann, this connective structure has two closely interdependent dimensions. One of these, the 'social dimension', binds together individuals into a moral community to which it gives identity through common norms and values in the here and now. The other, the 'temporal dimension', goes back in time, connecting yesterday to today. This temporal dimension, to continue with Assmann, supports, or better, complements the social dimension of the connective structure in its quasi-Durkheimian work of creating solidarity. Having recourse to common and now valorized pasts contributes decisively to creating social cohesion and to constructing an identifiable identity for individuals, groups, and nations in the present.[23]

We shall come back to Assmann's two-dimensional proposition in a little while. However, before we do so, the obvious needs to be stated, namely that in the maritime region of the Indian Ocean as a whole, any politics of heritage is necessarily *postcolonial* in kind. Hence, what it is in their pasts that people have recourse to either belongs to *colonial* pasts, or – transcending this period, but keeping to the yardstick of colonialism – to *precolonial* pasts. What is identified and claimed as heritage is the result of the translations and transformations of precolonial and colonial pasts into the present for current and future purposes. Especially when it comes to heritagizing one's pasts at the UNESCO level, colonial pasts can turn out to be a challenge and even an embarrassment for many of the young independent nation states that have emerged since World War II into a seemingly postcolonial Indian Ocean world. There are various reasons for this dilemma. To start with, when having recourse to their pasts for reasons of nation-building, empowerment, and gaining recognition, these postcolonial states have to play the globally accepted 'heritage game' (Hervitz 2012: 3) according to rules and values that, by and large, are colonial in origin and that continue to be so. It is also not without irony that the status of a '*world* heritage' can only be applied for, as mentioned above, by states. The early-modern ideal of the state as a *nation* state, then, lingers on in this postcolonial heritage game. However, this role model now appears less as a 'one-nation, one-language, one-culture' ideal than as a matter of 'unity in diversity', which many multi-ethnic and poly-religious states of the post-colonial Indian Ocean world have adopted as their official motto. Hence, while world heritage is national in its politico-legal and administrative implications, once one looks at heritage on the ground, it is seen to be embedded in a multifaceted and even heterogeneous arena of competing heritages.

Furthermore, many postcolonial states in the Indian Ocean world cannot avoid having recourse to pasts which were not their own in an emphatic sense, but which were decisively shaped by the erstwhile European colonial powers that entered and changed their worlds from the early sixteenth century onwards. For example, we find Portuguese heritage made into world heritage in Mozambique, Kenya, India, Malaysia, and China. To deal with these and other colonial pasts, and even to praise them for their beauty, etc., creates ambiguities and discrepancies for ex-colonies that are now independent states, at least politically. For it often transpires during these projects of constructing heritage out of colonial pasts that the 'postcolony' is not as 'post' as nation-builders and nationalists might wish it to be, but rather 'late' or even 'neo'. There are still many ongoing influences from, and new dependencies on, the erstwhile colonizers. Just think, among other instances that could be mentioned, of the western tourists whose expenditures form an important economic resource for many regions of the Indian Ocean world. Apart from sun, sand and sea, these tourists often also see the consumption of seemingly authentic local culture as an essential part of their all-inclusive packages.[24]

Local and seemingly authentic culture often manifests itself to tourists as the material and immaterial remains of a *colonial* past. For remembrancers in the postcolonies, however, it is exactly because of colonialism that the more indigenous and genuine pasts that existed before the colonial period were deprecated and interrupted in their march through history up to the present.[25] In their attempts to re-evaluate and/or remake such devalued and even dispossessed precolonial pasts as present-day heritage, it is tempting for nationalist heritage-makers in a postcolonial world to leapfrog over their colonial pasts, giving 'precedence to their putatively *precolonial* past: that part of the past which predates the colonizer's entry' (Herwitz 2012: 10, original emphasis). This is an understandable strategy. However, the Roman imperial *damnatio memoriae* strategy that sought to downgrade and even erase the memory of rebellious, subaltern and subjugated groups also lurks behind anti-imperial recourses to the pasts by postcolonial states and their elites. This is because their politics of cultural heritage does not just erase the European colonial pasts, which, like it or not, have made their way into the present. Postcolonial heritage politics – jumping in time over colonial pasts – are also bound to minimize and ignore the histories of the many minorities of both colonial and precolonial times, many of whom are still minorities today that find it hard to promote 'their' heritage. One could think here of Malaysia's contemporary heritage politics, which seeks to go back to Malayan times and achievements, thereby ignoring not only Portuguese, Dutch and British historical influences, but also those brought to the peninsula by Persian, Chinese and Indian immigrants from roughly the thirteenth century onwards.

The Indian Ocean world, to push the argument one step further, has a long and intensive history of movements across the sea – in longer and shorter, single or repeated, flowing and hopping modes. The colonial period was especially intensive and extensive in this regard, and present-day matters in all domains still bear the imprint of these movements and migrations. It is therefore hardly surprising that not only have human beings, animals, cargoes, languages and religions travelled, but so have varying pasts as well. Now, when they move *spatially*, like these other things the various 'configurations of remembered pasts'[26] are transformed as well. These transformations and alterations already start while travelling at sea, but they become even more pronounced at their destinations, i.e., when settling down in new environments. In these instances, then, remembrancers have recourse to pasts which, after their journeys, are distant not only in time but also in space. The politics of cultural heritage in a mobile world therefore connects those who remember now at one place to a place where oneself or one's ancestors once lived before, and where others belonging to the same community of remembrance might still be present. In brief, the heritagization of what can be called 'travelling pasts' (Schnepel and Sen, eds. 2019) also has recourse to a spatially and not only temporally distant past and, occasionally, to those who are still in that faraway space. The politics of cultural heritage in a mobile world therefore connects in one dimension more than the two dimensions (social and temporal) pointed out by

Assmann. There is a third dimension of connectivity in motion, which connects those who remember now at one place to a place where oneself or one's ancestors lived before, and where others belonging to the same community of remembrance might still be present. What takes place in this specific way of having recourse to the past are temporal and at the same time spatial translations of the 'then and there' into a 'now and here'.

This travelling dimension brings with it several other particularities. The new locations in which some such politics of cultural heritage takes place are usually multi-ethnic, poly-religious and socio-culturally heterogeneous postcolonial states. The emerging heritagized pasts that have travelled are therefore bound to encounter other pasts of other communities living in the same place that also have a history before migration and of it. Yet other pasts in that encounter of heritages are indigenous to the heritage arena. We then find a situation in which several travelling pasts and the one or other dwelling past compete with each other for hegemony and validity. Sometimes other pasts are found to be equally legitimate as well, while at other times they are downgraded in comparison to one's own. Sometimes other pasts are 'othered', but at other times, by contrast, they are shared and even 'nostrified', i.e., made into one's own. Every now and then two or more pasts even align with each other and merge into one, creating new conglomerate pasts on an equal footing, or else submerging the weaker side of these agglomerations.

INTO THE FUTURE

Mauritian heritage politics, to which we now return more directly, can be assessed against the background of three propositions that have been put forward so far: (1) heritage is a reflection onto the past of the various Mauritian remembrancers' contemporary socio-cultural, religious and political disputes over identity, prestige, status, resources and power; (2) heritage politics in Mauritius have a strong colonial imprint, with no precolonial past that could be jumped back to; and (3) manifestations of heritage in this island hub reflect a history of travel and thus have recourse not only to distant times but also to faraway places.

Concerning the first proposition, in view of the multi-ethnic and poly-religious character of Mauritian society, it is not surprising that the Mauritian heritage arena is as manifold and diversified as are the backgrounds of the island's remembrancers. While its historic buildings mostly recall its Franco-Mauritian past, the plethora of statues, busts, plaques and the like signify the dominance of a narrative of great (Hindu) men. Only recently has the portfolio become richer and more varied by including women and downtrodden social groups such as slaves, indentured labourers, or exploited labourers in the post-indenture period. As for the internal struggles and disputes to have one's own past recognized as heritage, this is best exemplified by looking first at Séga. The performative genre of Séga clearly belongs to the island's Creole community. As such it plays an important part in the identity politics of a group that was maltreated then and is still underprivileged now. It is striking to see that the dance, as heritage, developed from the clandestine possession of one group only, first forbidden and later detested by the island's non-Blacks, only to become an all-Mauritian symbol later, respected and even cherished by most. This widening of the scale of appreciation did not come about on the island itself, but rather in a shift that took Séga from a local and sectional heritage to an international tourist attraction and piece of world heritage, and only then to an all-encompassing Mauritian heritage. It seems that the non-Creole sections of Mauritius's population came to see the aesthetic, ideational and material worth of the dance *only after* it was appreciated by the tourism industry and inscribed on UNESCO's list of intangible world heritage. Séga's first and primary heritage politics, then, despite world heritage status, is not in the global heritage arena, but concerns the local, sectional and insular identity politics of one part of Mauritian society that still feels disadvantaged in many dimensions of contemporary life and that is struggling to overcome these setbacks.

As far as Aapravasi Ghat is concerned, various inner-island disputes mostly between Hindu remembrancers on the one hand and Creole remembrancers on the other led to a crisis reaching into the island's uppermost political echelons. In 2005, the Aapravasi Ghat dossier, after three years of hard work by the committee appointed to review it, was ready for submission, while there still were some negotiations to be done for the Le Morne dossier. At that time Mauritius had a dual premiership consisting of the left-wing Franco-Mauritian Paul Berenger and the Indo-Mauritian Pravind Jugnauth. For some time Berenger was suspected of failing to submit the dossier for the Aapravasi Ghat nomination. After some pressure from Hindu groups threatening to withdraw their support, Jugnauth sent it while Berenger was abroad on a state visit to China. What really happened is not all that clear, but it transpires that the UNESCO rule of just one dossier per country, only recently introduced, had not been known to either prime minister and that it was this lack of information that created confusion and delays, rather than Berenger's opposition.[27]

Regarding the second proposition concerning the colonial impact of heritage politics, it should be emphasized that the island does not have a precolonial past. As a result, Mauritius cannot but remember its colonial legacy, as well as more recent events concerned with the building of an independent nation. Certain manifestations of this past, such as some of the impressive Creole-style mansions, appear as grand; others signify respect and admiration, such as the busts and their plaques, which speak of the determination and feats of certain maritime explorers. Yet other elements of the colonial past are dark pasts, especially slavery and indentured labour, with all their dimensions of cruelty and injustice. In a global comparison of processes of heritagization, the fact that Mauritius has put a lot of energy into remembering these bleaker sides of its colonial past, seeking to turn reminiscences of difficult and, for many, horrible times into something more positive, can only command great respect. Aapravasi Ghat is indeed the only world heritage site globally that remembers the indentured labour system. In this context, both world heritage sites, Aapravasi Ghat as well as Le Morne, exemplify how the heritagizations of a colonial past can be turned into a claim that one has successfully managed to steer one's way out of colonial servitude and dependency towards the life of an independent, economically successful nation with a free and self-determined population enjoying equal rights and (presumably) opportunities.

Referring to the third proposition made above, it is hardly surprising that most of the configurations of remembrance found on the island today refer to events, processes, persons, ideas or cultural elements that have their origins overseas. They are 'travelling pasts' with all the transformations, adaptations and conglomerations that their journeys and their new homes away from home have brought forth. This predominance of the overseas character of Mauritian heritage could hardly have been otherwise, since none of the humans who live on the island today are indigenous to it. Even most specimens of the flora and fauna that dominate the natural environment of contemporary Mauritius were brought there from elsewhere at some point in the island's settlement history. Of all the plants or animals of old, only the dodo, dead though it may be, is still alive, albeit only in the island's *kulturelles Gedächtnis* and material representations thereof.

If one considers the travelling dimension of Mauritian heritage more concretely, first with reference to Séga, it is of course undeniable that this performative genre has its roots in Africa, especially in Mozambique and Madagascar. Here one can follow Alpers when he writes: 'Studies of the African diaspora in the *Atlantic* world show that wherever Africans were forcibly relocated they carried their music and dance with them; indeed, these have become integrated – sometimes centrally – into the culture of different host societies' (2019: 90, my emphasis). This general observation will probably hold true not only for transatlantic slavery, but for slavery in the Indian Ocean world as well. However, if we focus less on the question of 'how it actually may have been' than on the heritage question, i.e., on the question of what, how and why certain remembrancers recall and re-perform elements out of their pasts, it transpires that Ségatiers remember their times as slaves, but do not recollect their prior times and places in Africa to any extent. Again, in Alper's words: 'Like the blues, traditional séga lyrics are mainly concerned with the everyday affairs of ordinary people – work, family, community, and love – and do not hark back to places of origin' (ibid.: 9).[28] In this sense, the Ségatiers' past is not a *travelling* past; Séga does not have the third dimension, mentioned above, of remembering a distant place. Rather, Séga is regarded as something which had its origin on the island. It is Creole in the original sense of 'island born', and in this respect it is comparable to Mauritian Créole (the language), and again the dodo. Consequently, when we look at the similarities between musical traditions on Réunion, Rodrigues, the Seychelles and Mauritius, we find they point less to common African roots than to *diasporic* exchanges and transfers, including new adaptations from other parts of Africa and Asia, probably with Mauritius as the *chef lieu* and hub in the centre of these circulations of music and dance.

Looking at the travelling dimension in the case of Aapravasi Ghat, the link to a place of origin is obvious. This *lieu de mémoire* undoubtedly points to India as the place from which the indentured labourers came. The recollections connected with Aapravasi Ghat, then, are bilateral and connect Mauritius with a subcontinent which is seen as homogeneous, no matter how large and diversified this country of origin actually is. Some Hindus in Mauritius even hold that the sacred lake called Ganga Taloo in the island's upland, which is the central place of the grand Shivaratri festival in March, is connected to the Ganges by an underwater stream. It is only on account of UNESCO's insistence that sites of world heritage need to be of universal human value that one could acknowledge other places of coolitude in the world as well, from Fiji to Trinidad, though in all cases the dominant link to India remains. Finally, with regard to the travelling dimension of heritage, Le Morne is the *lieu de mémoire* at which African slavery is remembered and condemned. While the actual Mauritian place of remembrance recalls maroon communities living and dying on this mountain, the historical link clearly refers to African roots (even though some 10 per cent of Mauritian slaves were from India and Southeast Asia). In this respect Le Morne differs from Séga, which tends to stick to what happened on the island. Regarding their respective 'roots and routes', therefore, Séga, Aapravasi Ghat and Le Morne as travelling pasts show similarities, as well as some striking differences.[29]

Seen in this light, the politics of cultural heritage in the postcolonial Indian Ocean world is very often more about discontinuities, ruptures and turning points than about unbroken tradition and continuity; it is invariably also about getting one's own (history) back and forgetting or erasing the alien part of it; it is about innovation and revolution rather than continuation and evolution; it is about travelling and dwelling, in as much as it is about dwelling and travelling; and it is about moving forward in time. One could, then, well agree with Arnold Esch (1994: 7) when he argues, with reference to the Danish philosopher Sören Kierkegaard, that we live our lives forwards, but understand them backwards. This chapter has sought to push this insight one step further by arguing that it is not enough to qualify this looking backwards merely as an intellectual attempt to *understand.* Rather, in an almost Nietzsche'ian drive, remembrancers seek to profit from having recourse to their pasts, even inventing them, when moving forward into new futures.

NOTES

1. See, among others, Ashworth, Graham and Turnbridge (2007); Bendix, Eggert and Peselmann (eds. 2012); Brumann and Berliner (eds. 2016); Meskell (ed. 2015); and Smith (2006).
2. See Harrison (2013).
3. For a more extended discussion of the issues raised in this section, see also Schnepel (2019).
4. See, for examples, Breglia (2006), Brumann (2014), Harrison and Hitchcock (eds. 2005).
5. See Comaroff and Comaroff (2009), Bruner (2005).
6. See White (1973, 1978), as well as the authors assembled in Veeser (ed. 1989), and Conrad and Kessel (eds. 1994).
7. See, among others, Silverman (2010), Turnbridge and Ashworth (1996), Worden (2019).
8. That history is made not only by 'great men' has come to be a historiographical commonplace and is well acknowledged, among others, in so-called 'subaltern studies'.
9. On forms of forgetting, see also Assmann (2016).
10. My wife Cornelia and I have published on Séga before and I have made use of these earlier publications, revising and rewriting them in parts, in this and the following section. See Schnepel and Schnepel (2006, 2009, and 2011).
11. For studies of Séga, which we consulted for this chapter in addition to our own observations and interviews, see Alpers (2019), Ballgobin and Antoine (2003), Boswell (2006: 61–8), Didier (1987), Lee (1990), Police (2000, 2001).
12. Quoted in Police (2000: 61).
13. On the Code Noir, see also Police (2001: 83–8).
14. Quoted in Police (2000: 61).
15. Quoted in Police (2000: 63).

16. Quoted in Ballgobin and Antoine (2003: 77). Milbert's stance is discussed in greater detail in Police (2001: 86–93).
17. Further historical sources that would by and large corroborate the picture reached so far are discussed in greater depth by Police (2001) and Alpers (2019).
18. Significantly, Lee's book on Séga, the first of its kind, is that of an expatriate Mauritian living in London in the 1980s; it is especially meant by the author to transfer knowledge of the dance to the children of the (at this time) more than 100,000 overseas Mauritians.
19. For a more detailed account of the various stages in a Séga hotel performance, see Schnepel and Schnepel (2006).
20. Not discussed here are the roughly six dozen historical buildings in Port Louis that are considered by the National Heritage Fund as being of historic value, among them the Line Barracks, Government House, the Citadel Fort and the Municipal Theatre, whose origins in most cases go back to the early decades when Mauritius was known as l'Isle de France.
21. In preparing a nomination dossier and in *scribing* Séga, an important shift was made, namely adding scriptural and bureaucratic dimensions to the hitherto predominantly performative and oral expressions of Creole identity. The Mauritian Creoles' political struggle for recognition and support is best studied in Boswell (2005, 2006, and 2008). See also Miles (1999).
22. Here one should also add Réunion's or, more correctly, France's Maloya, which was awarded world heritage status as early as 2009; and recently, inscribed in 2021, the Seychelles' Moutya, again a performative genre of the Séga type. See also Wergin (2010).
23. See Assmann (1992: especially 16–17).
24. See Schnepel, Girke and Knoll (eds. 2013), Schnepel (2013).
25. For the seminal role of heritage practices and beliefs in nation-building processes, see especially Herwitz (2012: 3–15).
26. This is how one could translate Jan Assmann's concept of *Erinnerungsfiguren* (1992: 52).
27. Information on these events can be found in various newspapers of that time. Cornelia and I have also profited from informal discussions with Vijaya Teelock on this matter and from her unpublished paper given at a conference at the Max Planck Institute for Social Anthropology in Halle in 2017.
28. More detailed presentations and interpretations of Séga lyrics than could be provided here can be found in Police (2000), and Schnepel and Schnepel (2006).

29. While working on the final version of this chapter (Winter 2022), Mauritian politicians have at long last decided, after almost two decades of deliberations, that Port Louis will host a 'Musée Intercontinental de l'Esclavage' within the historic premises of the old military hospital.

REFERENCES

Alpers, E.A. 2019. 'When Diasporas Meet: The Musical Legacies of Slavery and Indentured Labor in the Mascarene Islands'. In Alpers, Karghoo, and Teelock (eds.) 2019: 89–110.

Alpers, E.A., S. Karghoo, and V. Teelock (eds.). 2019. *History, Memory and Identity. Comparative Perspectives*, vol. 2. Mauritius: Nelson Mandela Centre for African Culture Trust Fund.

Ashworth, G.J., B. Graham, and J.E. Turnbridge. 2007. *Pluralising Pasts: Heritage, Identity and Place in Multicultural Societies*. London: Pluto Press.

Assmann, A. 2016. *Formen des Vergessens*. Göttingen: Wallstein Verlag.

Assmann, J. 1992. *Das kulturelle Gedächtnis: Schrift, Erinnerung und politische Identität in frühen Hochkulturen*. Munich: C.H. Beck.

Ballgobin, D.V., and M. Antoine. 2003. 'Traditional Musical Instruments from Oral Tradition: Folk Music in Mauritius'. *Revi Kiltir Kreol* 3: 69–82.

Bendix, R.F., A. Eggert, and A. Peselmann (eds.). 2012. *Heritage Regimes and the State*. Göttingen: Universitätsverlag Göttingen.

Boswell, R. 2005. 'Heritage Tourism and Identity in the Mauritian Villages of Chamarel and Le Morne'. *Journal of Southern African Studies* 31: 283–95.

——, 2006. *Le malaise créole: Ethnic Identity in Mauritius*. Oxford: Berghahn.

——, 2008. *Challenges to Identifying and Managing Intangible Cultural Heritage in Mauritius, Zanzibar and Seychelles*. Dakar: Imprimerie Graphiplus.

Breglia, L. 2006. *Monumental Ambivalence: The Politics of Heritage*. Austin: University of Texas Press.

Brumann, C. 2014. 'Shifting Tides of World-making in the UNESCO World Heritage Convention: Cosmopolitanisms Colliding'. *Ethnic and Racial Studies* 37: 2176–92.

Brumann, C., and O. Berliner (eds.). 2016. *World Heritage on the Ground: Ethnographic Perspectives*. Oxford, New York: Berghahn.

Bruner, E.M. 2005. *Culture on Tour*. Chicago: The University of Chicago Press.

Burke, P. 1989. 'History as Social Memory'. In Butler (ed.) 1989: 97–113.

Butler, T. (ed.). 1989. *Memory: History, Culture and the Mind.* Oxford: Blackwell.

Comaroff, J.L., and J. Comaroff. 2009. *Ethnicity Inc.* Chicago: The University of Chicago Press.

Conrad, C., and M. Kessel (eds.). 1994. *Geschichteschreiben in der Postmoderne: Beiträge zur aktuellen Diskussion.* Leipzig: Reclam.

de Saint-Pierre, J.H. Bernardin. 2002 [1773]. *Journey to Mauritius.* Oxford: Signal Books.

Didier, M. 1987. *Pages africaines de l'Île Maurice.* Mauritus: Centre Culturel Africain.

di Giovine, M.A. 2009. *The Heritage-scape: UNESCO, World Heritage and Tourism.* Lanham: Lexington Books.

Eriksen, T.H. 1998. *Common Denominators: Ethnicity, Nation-building and Compromise in Mauritius.* Oxford: Berg.

Esch, A. 1994. *Zeitalter und Menschenalter. Der Historiker und die Erfahrung vergangener Gegenwart.* München: C.H. Beck.

Harrison, R. 2013. *Heritage: Critical Approaches.* London: Routledge.

Harrison, O., and M. Hitchcock (eds.). 2005. *The Politics of World Heritage: Negotiating Tourism and Conservation.* Clevedon: Channel View Publications.

Hervitz, D. 2012. *Heritage, Culture, and Politics in the Postcolony.* New York: Columbia University Press.

Hookoomsing, V.Y. 2009. 'Mauritius: Creole and/or Multicultural?' In Hookoomsing, Ludwig, and Schnepel (eds.) 2009: 19–28.

Hookoomsing, V.Y., R. Ludwig, and B. Schnepel (eds.). 2009. *Multiple Identities in Action: Mauritius and Some Antillean Parallelisms.* Berlin: Peter Lang.

Kirshenblatt-Gimblett, B. 1995. 'Theorizing Heritage'. *Ethnomusicology* 39: 367–80.

Lee, J.K. 1990. *Sega. The Mauritian Folk Dance.* London: Nautilus Publishing.

Lowenthal, D. 1998. *The Heritage Crusade and the Spoils of History.* Cambridge: Cambridge University Press.

Meskell, L. (ed.). 2015. *Global Heritage: A Reader.* Chichester: Wiley Blackwell.

Meyer, P.M. (ed.). 2006. *Performance im medialen Wandel.* Munich: Wilhelm Fink.

Miles, W.F.S. 1999. 'The Creole Malaise in Mauritius'. *African Affairs* 98: 211–28.

Nietzsche, F. 2009 [1874]. *Vom Nutzen und Nachtheil der Historie für das Leben.* Stuttgart: Reclam.

Police, D. 2000. 'Mauritian Sega: The Trace of the Slave's Emancipatory Voice'. *The Indian Ocean Review. Cultural Studies and New Writing* 6: 57–69.

——, 2001. 'Les pratiques musicales de la population servile puis affranchie de Maurice dans les écrits francophones des XVIIIè et XIXè siècles'. In Teelock and Alpers (eds.) 2001: 81–110.

Schnepel, B. 2013. 'Kulturerbe im Zeitalter des Massentourismus. Eine programmatische Einführung'. In Schnepel, Girke, and Knoll (eds.) 2013: 21–44.

——, 2019. 'Travelling Pasts: An Introduction'. In Schnepel and Sen (eds.) 2019: 1–20.

Schnepel, B., and C. Schnepel. 2006. 'Bilder vom Séga: Inszenierungen von Authentizität auf Mauritius'. In Meyer (ed.) 2006: 463–97.

——, 2009. 'The Mauritian *Séga*: Performing Identity in a Multi-cultural Setting'. In Hookoomsing, Ludwig, and Schnepel (eds.) 2009: 275–86.

——, 2011. 'From Slave to Tourist Entertainer. Performative Negotiations of Identity and Difference in Mauritius'. In McCuscer, and Soares (eds.) 2011: 109–26.

Schnepel, B., F. Girke, and E.-M. Knoll (eds.). 2013. *Kultur all inclusive: Identität, Tradition und Kulturerbe im Zeitalter des Massentourismus.* Bielefeld: Transcript Verlag.

Schnepel, B., and E.A. Alpers (eds.). 2018. *Connectivity in Motion: Island Hubs in the Indian Ocean World.* Cham: Palgrave Macmillan.

Schnepel, B., and T. Sen (eds.). 2019. *Travelling Pasts. The Politics of Cultural Heritage in the Indian Ocean World.* Leiden: Brill.

Silverman, H. (ed.). 2010. *Contested Cultural Heritage: Religion, Nationalism, Erasure, and Exclusion in a Global World.* Berlin: Springer Verlag.

Smith, L. 2006. *The Uses of Heritage.* London: Routledge.

Teelock, V., and E.A. Alpers (eds.). 2001. *History, Memory and Identity.* Mauritius: Nelson Mandela Centre for African Culture.

Turnbridge, J.E., and G.J. Ashworth. 1996. *Dissonant Heritage: The Management of the Past as a Resource in Conflict.* Chichester: John Wiley.

Veeser, H.A. (ed.). 1989. *The New Historicism.* New York: Routledge.

Wergin, C. 2010. *Kréol Blouz. Musikalische Inszenierungen von Identität und Kultur.* Cologne: Böhlau Verlag.

White, H. 1973. *Metahistory: The Historical Imagination in Nineteenth Century Europe.* Baltimore: Johns Hopkins University Press.

——, 1978. *Tropics of Discourse: Essays in Cultural Criticism.* Baltimore: Johns Hopkins University Press.

Winter, T. 2016. 'Heritage Diplomacy along the One Belt One Road'. *International Institute for Asian Studies Newsletter* 74: 2–10.

Worden, N. 2019. 'Ambiguous Pasts. The Indian Ocean World in Cape Town's Public History'. In Schnepel and Sen (eds.) 2019: 107–32.

List of First Publications

The following chapters were originally published in the books and journals below. We would like to thank the editors and publishers for their permission to reprint them in this book:

Chapter 3: 'Piracy in the Indian Ocean (ca. 1680–1750)'. *Max Planck Institute for Social Anthropology Working Papers* 160. Halle: Max Planck Institute for Social Anthropology. 2014, pp. 1–26.

Chapter 6: 'The Making of a Hub Society: Mauritius' Path from Port of Call to Cyber Island'. In *Connectivity in Motion: Island Hubs in the Indian Ocean World*, edited by Burkhard Schnepel and Edward A. Alpers. New York: Palgrave. 2018, pp. 231–57.

Chapter 7: 'Two Beaches: The Globalization of Mauritian Waterfronts'. *Multiple Identities in Action: Mauritius and Some Antillean Parallelism*, edited by Vinesh Y. Hookoomsing, Ralph Ludwig, and Burkhard Schnepel. Berlin: Peter Lang. 2009, pp. 287–317.

Picture Credits

Map 1.1: Eric Gaba (Sting - fr:Sting), https://de.wikivoyage.org/wiki/Datei:Mauritius_Island_ map-fr.svg, accessed 21 January 2022, CC BY-SA 4.0 <https://creativecommons.org/licenses/by-sa/4.0>, via Wikimedia Commons.

Map 1.2: Cartography: Jutta Turner, base map: http://www.lib.utexas.edu/maps/world.html, accessed 20 May 2015, © Max Planck Institute for Social Anthropology, Halle/Saale, Germany.

Maps 2.1 and 2.2: Schnepel, B. and E.A. Alpers (eds.) 2018. *Connectivity in Motion: Island Hubs in the Indian Ocean World.* New York: Palgrave.

Figure 5.1: Yang Hai, https://upload.wikimedia.org/wikipedia/commons/b/bb/Republic_of_Mauritius_Flag.jpg, accessed 2 February 2022, CC BY-SA 2.0<https://creativecommons.org/licenses/by-sa/2.0>, via Wikimedia Commons.

Figures 6.1; 6.3; 7.1-7.4 and 8.1-8.3: Cornelia Schnepel.

Figure 6.2: Starts, https://upload.wikimedia.org/wikipedia/commons/7/72/Ebene_at_dusk.jpg, accessed 22 February 2022, CC0, via Wikimedia Commons.